MIDDLE TENNESSEE ON FOOT

Also by Robert Brandt   *Touring the Middle Tennessee Backroads*
Tennessee Hiking Guide

Middle Tennessee On Foot

Hikes in the Woods & Walks on Country Roads

ROBERT BRANDT

John F. Blair, Publisher
Winston-Salem, North Carolina

Design and maps by Liza Langrall
Photographs by the author, unless otherwise noted

Cover photograph:
Fall Creek Falls
(Photo by Murray Lee, courtesy of the
State of Tennessee Photographic Services)

Photo previous page:
Duck River at Old Stone Fort State Archaeological Area
(Photo by Joe H. Allen)

Photo opposite page:
Deciduous magnolia at Virgin Falls,
Virgin Falls Pocket Wilderness State Natural Area
(Photo by Joe H. Allen)

Library of Congress Cataloging-in-Publication Data

Brandt, Robert S., 1941–
Middle Tennessee on foot / Robert Brandt.
p.   cm.
Includes bibliographical references (p.   ) and index.
ISBN 0-89587-212-9 (alk. paper)
1. Hiking—Tennessee, Middle—Guidebooks. 2. Wilderness areas—
Tennessee, Middle—Guidebooks. 3. Parks—Tennesssee, Middle—
Guidebooks. 4. Tennessee, Middle—Guidebooks. I. Title.
GV199.42.T2B73   1998
917.68'50453—dc21   97-52606

To Marshall,

for so many good times on the trail

PHYSIOGRAPHIC REGIONS OF
MIDDLE TENNESSEE

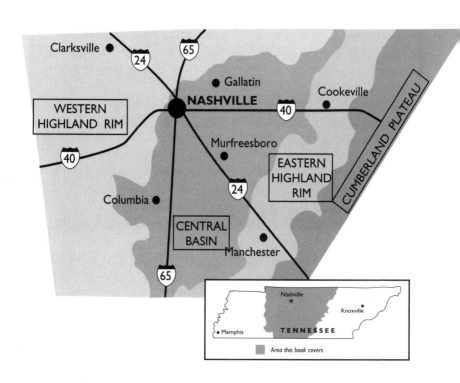

CONTENTS

Part One: Hikes in the Woods

Hikes in the Central Basin

Hikes on the Western Highland Rim

Part Two: Walks on Country Roads

PREFACE

I wanted to write this book for a long time. Not exactly this book, but a hiking guide for the entire state of Tennessee outside the already well-covered Great Smoky Mountains National Park. I got the idea for a step-by-step hiking guide when I wrote *Tennessee Hiking Guide* in the 1980s. That short book is a summary of hiking opportunities. But I wanted to walk every foot of trail in Tennessee, to find out what I could about everything I saw, and to share it with other curious walkers.

Several things conspired to keep me from doing it. Chief among them was the need to earn a living. Then when I finally decided it was time to tackle the project, along came the opportunity to write *Touring the Middle Tennessee Backroads*. That took up the better part of two years.

While I dreamed about my statewide hiking guide, others filled parts of the void. Brenda D. Coleman and Jo Anna Smith walked every trail in the Big South Fork for their detailed and informative *Hiking the Big South Fork*. Russ Manning and Sondra Jamieson did the same for the rest of the Cumberland Plateau in *Tennessee's South Cumberland.* Will Skelton and my East Tennessee Sierra Club friends shared their love of the mountains in *Wilderness Trails of Tennessee's Cherokee National Forest.*

I was tempted to forget it. It looked like all I had was the leftovers. Then I had an idea: I'd write a step-by-step guide just for Middle Tennessee. I've lived in the Midstate most of my life, and I'm an avid hiker. The trails of Middle Tennessee don't get as much attention as those in the mountains of my native East Tennessee. But they are splendid places nevertheless. So I decided to do this book.

Then I had another idea: I'd include some walks on country roads. Many people love to walk, but they're not hikers. They like to stay on pavement. From my work on *Touring the Middle Tennessee Backroads,* I knew some nice country lanes that would be just right for walkers.

Carolyn Sakowski at John F. Blair, Publisher, liked the idea. So I got to work. I took my newly acquired measuring wheel and a small tape recorder and spent much of 1996 and 1997 on trails and country roads. I did research in libraries and at the Tennessee Department of Environment and Conservation (TDEC). I picked the brains of my fellow hikers and the staffs of the managing agencies. And I loved every minute of it.

Just about every Middle Tennessee trail over a mile long is described in this book. But there are a few exceptions, mostly on the Cumberland Plateau. Some of the longer trails I walked—like the two long Cane Creek loops at Fall Creek Falls State Park and some segments of the Sewanee Perimeter Trail—didn't seem worth the effort. At Savage Gulf State Natural Area, I included only the trails accessible from the Middle Tennessee side of the park—those from the Stone Door Ranger Station. And besides, the South Cumberland is already covered in Russ Manning and Sondra Jamieson's book, mentioned above.

There is one discouraging note. I was active in the conservation movement back in the 1970s and 1980s, working with the Department of Conservation, now part of TDEC. *Tennessee Hik-*

ing Guide was a cooperative project with the department. Back then, there was a coordinated, statewide trails program that many believed was one of the finest in the country. I was saddened by what I found when I returned to the department to work on this book. There is no trails program. It's gone. In fact, no one at TDEC seems to know much about trails on a statewide or even a regional basis.

Funds for major maintenance in Tennessee's state parks declined from $4.4 million in 1988 to $2.5 million in 1996. This lack of attention is apparent on the ground. Some trails are maintained and well marked. Others are not. Years of hard work are washing away little by little. Perhaps this book—which concentrates mostly on state-managed areas—will help reinvigorate the state's trails program. Perhaps you'll urge those in authority to pay more attention to trails.

Working on this book was an absolute treat. I returned to places I already knew well—some of my favorite places on earth, in fact—and I also got to know new places. I walked just about every trail from the lowlands along Kentucky Lake to the heights of the Cumberland Plateau.

If you get a fraction of the pleasure out of using this book that I did in working on it, I'll be happy.

ACKNOWLEDGMENTS

The excitement I feel when I'm in Tennessee's outdoors isn't always matched by my knowledge of the living world. So I turned to the experts to teach me enough to write this book.

The sad neglect of our state-managed areas is balanced, thank goodness, by the competence and devotion of so many of the people who work for the Tennessee Department of Environment and Conservation. At the Division of Natural Heritage, Reggie Reeves, Brian Bowen, and Carl Nordman shared their considerable knowledge and directed me to printed sources I was unaware of. Reggie, who heads the division, read my introduction and made some helpful suggestions. At the Division of State Parks, Terry Bonham led me through the files on the areas managed by his division.

The chief photographer for the state of Tennessee, Jed DeKalb, helped me with the photographs, as did up-and-coming Nashville photographer Joe H. Allen. You'll be seeing more of Joe's work.

Deb Beasley of the Warner Parks Nature Center met with me several times to help me understand more about our special part of the world. Tim Netsch with the greenways division of Nashville's parks department enthusiastically introduced me to our newest walking areas, Shelby Bottoms and Beaman Park.

It was a treat to travel back to my hometown of Norris and meet fellow Tennessee Trails Association (TTA) member Judith Bartlow, who shared her knowledge of the TVA areas she manages.

Jim Poteet, another TTA member, patiently read through the entire manuscript to keep me from leading readers astray.

And thanks to the Fairy Godmower for dodging the mole holes.

INTRODUCTION TO MIDDLE TENNESSEE

The Landscape

Think of a target with its bull's-eye and concentric rings. Now, imagine that the target has been crumpled up, spread back out, and pulled out of shape so the bull's-eye and rings are ovals rather than circles. Visualize this and you can visualize Middle Tennessee's landscape. Like the distorted target, Middle Tennessee is made up of distinct sections. It's seldom flat. And no two surfaces feel the same.

The topography ranges from gentle plains to rugged Appalachian uplands, from swampy bottoms to deep mountain gorges. Stately hardwood forests cover much of Middle Tennessee, but in some places, the soil is too shallow and rocky for trees to grow. Rivers and creeks crash off cap rock in some of America's most stunning waterfalls, yet in other places, streams don't travel very far before limestone crevices steal their water.

Some rivers flow unmolested through fertile bottoms below green hills, while others are blocked by dams that create some of the nation's most beautifully situated reservoirs. And wherever you go in this diverse landscape, there is an ever-changing show of wildflowers.

The heartland—the bull's-eye—is the Central Basin. With Murfreesboro at its center and Nashville on its northwestern limit, the basin is a jagged-edged, oval-shaped depression averaging 120 miles in north-south length and 60 miles in east-west width.

The Central Basin is a land of contrasts.

Its inner basin averages 600 feet in elevation and has terrain that is gentle—even flat—in places. The land is crowned with limestone outcrops and dotted with sinks, caves, disappearing streams, and thickets of dark green cedars. You can sample this unique landscape at Cedars of Lebanon and Long Hunter State Parks and at Stones River National Battlefield.

Beyond the inner basin lies an outer basin with an average elevation of 750 feet. This is the quintessential Middle Tennessee heartland of rich bottoms, rolling bluegrass pastures, and wooded hills. Shelby Bottoms Greenway and Bledsoe Creek State Park are in the outer basin. On the fringe of the outer basin, steep green hills—outliers of the Highland Rim—look like mountains as they extend their fingers into the Central Basin, reaching elevations as great as 1,200 feet. Nashville's Warner Parks and Radnor Lake State Natural Area cover parts of these Highland Rim outliers.

The Highland Rim surrounds the Central Basin and consists of two parts: the Eastern Highland Rim and the Western Highland Rim. On the north, the division between the two is the Cumberland River, which flows into Tennessee from Kentucky. On the south, the division is the tiny appendage of the Central Basin protruding into Alabama.

The Western Highland Rim is a land of ups and downs. Its many streams have created rich, steep-sided valleys below broad, forested ridges. The northern part of the Western Rim, however, is a fertile, almost flat plain called the Pennyroyal. The rim is bordered on the west by the narrow valley of the Tennessee River, now impounded as Kentucky Lake. You can hike through the Western Rim's splendid hardwood forests at Montgomery Bell and Mousetail Landing State Parks and at Land Between the Lakes.

Rugged knobs mark the escarpment of the Eastern Highland Rim. Beyond the knobs, the landscape varies. On the south, there is an almost-level, shallow-soil, swampy belt called "the barrens." The rim's interior is different, though. It's not as flat, and the soil is more fertile. To the north, the barrens give way to rolling country. Still farther north, the rim is higher and is dissected by numerous steams that have created near-mountainous terrain.

The Eastern Rim's most dramatic scenery is found where streams rushing toward the Central Basin have carved out gorges featuring many of the Midstate's noted waterfalls. The average elevation on the Eastern Rim is about 1,000 feet. You can hike in the hilly northern part of the Eastern Rim at Standing Stone State Park. Great waterfall walks are at Burgess Falls State Natural Area, Rock Island State Park, and Old Stone Fort State Archaeological Area.

The Cumberland Plateau rises steeply and irregularly above the Eastern Highland Rim. The plateau has an average elevation of 1,800 feet and is part of the geologic province that extends from Pennsylvania to Alabama, the westernmost edge of the Appalachians. The plateau stretches 140 miles diagonally across Tennessee and has an average width of 40 miles.

The plateau includes flat-to-rolling uplands and deep gorges. These gorges—or "gulfs," as they are called in some places—hold magnificent waterfalls, including the tallest east of the Rockies, at Fall Creek Falls State Park. Only the western edge of the Cumberland Plateau is considered part of Middle Tennessee. Most of it is thought of as East Tennessee. Savage Gulf and Grundy Forest (Fiery Gizzard) State Natural Areas and Virgin Falls Pocket Wilderness State Natural Area offer some of America's most scenic hiking.

Travelers can get a feel for Middle Tennessee's varied landscape on the six spokes of interstate highways radiating from Nashville.

I-40 toward Knoxville crosses the nearly flat inner Central Basin around Mount Juliet and Lebanon, then weaves through the outer basin's hills closer to Carthage. It climbs to the Eastern Highland Rim just east of the Center Hill Dam exit, then climbs again to the Cumberland Plateau between Cookeville and Monterey.

I-24 toward Chattanooga stays in the inner basin from the edge of Nashville to the Highland Rim outliers at the Beech Grove exit. After a short, scenic stretch through the outer basin, I-24 rises to the rim and passes through the swampy barrens. It opens onto the rim's rolling interior, then crosses the Cumberland Plateau at Monteagle.

I-65 South stays in the outer basin just about all the way to the Alabama line. Both I-65 toward Louisville and I-24 toward Clarksville climb out of the Central Basin onto the Highland Rim before leaving Nashville-Davidson County.

I-40 toward Memphis rolls through a long stretch of outer basin outliers before climbing to the Highland Rim proper past Kingston Springs. The road then goes up and down over ridges and through valleys to the Tennessee River.

Rivers are an important part of Middle Tennessee's landscape. Except for the Tennessee River, which forms the Midstate's western boundary, the Cumberland is the region's largest and most important river. Given to Tennessee by Kentucky, it twists and turns past Carthage, Gallatin, Nashville, and Clarksville before the Bluegrass State reclaims it on its way to the Ohio River.

The Caney Fork, the Cumberland's longest tributary, cascades off the Cumberland Plateau, crosses the Eastern Highland Rim, and empties into the Cumberland in the Central Basin at Carthage. The Collins River flows off the plateau, too, and gives its waters to the Caney Fork at Rock Island.

The Stones River and the scenic Harpeth River are the Cumberland's main tributaries in the Central Basin. The Stones flows past Murfreesboro and the Harpeth through Franklin and along Nashville's western edge.

Farther south, rivers flow into the Tennessee instead of the Cumberland. The Duck River gets its start around Manchester on the Eastern Highland Rim before falling into the Central Basin and flowing through Shelbyville, Columbia, and Centerville on its way to the Tennessee. The scenic Buffalo River flows into the Duck. Still farther south, the Elk River emerges from a Cumberland Plateau cove and crosses the Highland Rim before flowing through Alabama to the Tennessee River.

The Seasons

Middle Tennessee's climate is like its landscape: diverse and varied. Each season is so beautiful in its own way that it's as if you're in four different places.

Spring is the best time for hiking and walking. The season starts in late February, when the first wildflowers poke their tender green growth above the forest floor. The parade of color then creeps slowly up the hillsides until it reaches the highest elevations on the Cumberland Plateau by the end of May.

Fall is a great time to be outside, too. The air is cool and dry. Fall foliage can be spectacular. The color runs opposite from the spring show, peaking on the Cumberland Plateau around mid-October and a few weeks later in the lowlands. Middle Tennessee's autumns start around the first of October and often extend well into December, though a good Thanksgiving snowfall is not unheard of.

Winter lacks the color of spring and fall but still has its advantages. With the foliage off the trees, you'll see wildlife more often. Winter's wet weather fills the year-round waterfalls and cascades and creates hundreds of seasonal ones. And when the temperature turns really cold, they freeze, making for a true winter wonderland.

Summer arrives by June and brings with it the deep green of Middle Tennessee's hills and pastures. When heavy humidity invades the region, as it often does, most outdoor enthusiasts head for the rivers and lakes or to high country. But the thick air will eventually be broken by spells of cooler, drier weather. The blue sky it brings provides a nice setting for a summer walk.

Average seasonal temperatures don't mean much in Middle Tennessee. The region is situated about midway between the Gulf and Mexico and the Great Lakes, and its weather seldom stays the same for more than a few days. In winter, it can be in the 60s one day and in the teens the next. In summer, it can be in the muggy, hazy 90s and in the clear 80s a few days later. In spring and fall, it's not unusual for temperatures to swing from the 80s to the 30s in a day or two.

The Forests

The gigantic trees of Middle Tennessee—oak, tulip poplar, hickory, black walnut, maple, elm, ash—once measured as much as six or seven feet in diameter. The hunters and explorers who penetrated the Cumberland wilderness in the mid-1700s were overwhelmed by what they found. The ingredients for a rich forest were all here: deep, fertile soil, lots of water, and a long growing season. The forests were made up mostly of deciduous trees, but there were evergreens, too, vast stands of red cedar covering rocky areas with shallow soil.

That old growth is gone now. But Middle Tennessee still has some magnificent forests. In most parks and preserves, trees haven't felt an ax for nearly three quarters of a century, and the woods are returning to their former grandeur. At places along the trails, you'll feel as if you're in virgin timber.

Forests are classified by their dominant species. Oak-hickory forests dominate in the Central Basin and on the Highland Rim. There are places, though, where other trees dominate, like parts the inner basin. There, cedar forests are the norm. Within the cedar forests are areas called "cedar glades"—rocky, thin-soil openings where no trees grow. The cedar-glade ecosystem is unique to Tennessee. In all, there are nearly 30 plants here that are rarely found anywhere else in the world!

The range in elevation, exposure, and soil in the outer Central Basin make for a rich diversity of plants. Moist, north-facing slopes hold stands of tulip poplar and beech and a variety of oak and hickory, all rising above an understory of colorful dogwood and sugar maple. The woods on the drier southern slopes are more like the inner basin's mixed forests of cedar and hardwoods. The dry, shallow-soil ridge crests of the Central Basin's Highland Rim outliers are covered in places with pure stands of chestnut oak and dotted with mountain laurel, giving the crests an appearance much like the Appalachian Mountains.

On the Highland Rim proper, stands of straight, tall tulip poplar and stately beech are mixed with the predominant oak and hickory. Other common trees are sugar maple, black gum, basswood, pine, and, in the moist gorges, hemlock. Mountain laurel is common in places. Redbud and dogwood understories turn the April woods into clouds of pink and white.

The Cumberland Plateau's uplands hold mixed forests of oak-hickory, oak-poplar, oak-pine, and pine. But as you get near the rims of the gorges, the environment changes. Virginia pines flourish in the shallow soil, rising above dense thickets of glossy, green mountain laurel and huckleberry.

The environment is dramatically different in the cool Cumberland Plateau gorges. The forests here are much the same as those found at 4,000 feet in the Great Smoky Mountains, except that the elevation on the plateau is 3,000 feet lower. Directly below the bluffs are nearly pure stands of chestnut oak. Farther down in the gorges, stands of giant hemlock, tulip poplar, oak, birch, beech, and hickory form a canopy above an understory of rhododendron.

Wildflowers are an exciting bonus in Middle Tennessee's woods. You can find some blooming most anywhere between February and November. The variety is enormous—over 300 species. Some are common throughout the region—dwarf larkspur, fire pink, spring beauty, rue anemone, May apple, cut-leaf toothwort, and bluet, to name only a few. Species like rose verbena and Nashville breadroot are found primarily in the cedar glades; Tennessee coneflower is found only in the glades. On the Highland Rim and the Cumberland Plateau, you're likely to find a wider variety of trillium and phlox. And the plateau is the only place you'll find Cumberland rosinweed.

The Wildlife

The richness of Middle Tennessee was not lost on the Indians who came into the uninhabited region to hunt during historic times. The abundant wildlife later attracted long hunters and the settlers who followed them in 1779. Many of the species that sustained Native Americans and early settlers disappeared with shocking swiftness after 1780, due mostly to overhunting and habitat destruction. Look at a map. You'll see the Buffalo, Elk, and Wolf Rivers, Panther and Pigeon Creeks, Raven Point, and too many Bear Creeks to count. Those animals are gone from Middle Tennessee.

As more and more land was cleared, more and more habitat was lost. During the first half of the 19th century, forests on the Western Highland Rim were stripped for the iron industry. In the second half of the century, widespread cut-and-run logging reduced habitat on the Eastern Rim and the Cumberland Plateau. The extensive use of pesticides and other agricultural chemicals contributed to the decline in wildlife, too. The deer, the otter, the beaver, the wild turkey, and the bald eagle just about vanished.

Conservation practices started in the 1930s and regulation begun in the 1970s have reversed the decline in wildlife. Now, it's not timber harvesting and farming that destroy wildlife habitat. It's suburban sprawl. The American Farmland Trust ranks the Central Basin around Nashville as the 12th-most-threatened agricultural region in the nation. And on the Cumberland Plateau, strip mining for coal is a continuing threat.

Nevertheless, Middle Tennessee remains well endowed with

wildlife. Outside the cities, the landscape is a mosaic of crop-land, pasture, grown-up fields, young forests, and old forests. The topography ranges from river bottoms to level plains to sheer mountain bluffs. Rivers, streams, lakes, and ponds abound. This diversity of habitat has produced a diversity of wildlife. Under-standing and observing wildlife will add enormous enjoyment to your walks. Profiles of several species you might encounter are included in the hike narratives.

Most of the 350 or so birds identified in Tennessee can be found in the middle part of the state. These include permanent residents, summer residents, winter residents, migrants, and visi-tors. Some are common, some uncommon, and some rare.

The western edge of Middle Tennessee is in the Mississippi Flyway—the course ducks and geese follow in flying south for the winter. Some stay as winter residents, while others just pass through. The beautiful wood duck nests in Tennessee in late spring and migrates south about the time winter residents start arriving from the North. The Canada goose is now a year-round Middle Tennessee resident.

You can tell spring is approaching when the resident birds start singing in February. Then, beginning in March, you'll hear even more singing as Neotropical migrants start to arrive. These are birds that nest in North America but spend the winter in Mexico, the Caribbean, and Central and South America. Some pass through Tennessee on their way north, while others stay here to nest. During the summer, over half the birds you see and hear may be Neotropical migrants, which include a variety of tanagers, warblers, orioles, thrushes, swallows, and swifts.

Of the 50 or so mammals in Middle Tennessee, you'll surely see squirrels, chipmunks, rabbits, and deer on your hikes and walks. Other mammals are fairly common but elusive. Unless you're purposeful about it, you might never see a raccoon, a bob-cat, a fox, or an opossum. Otters and minks live in lakes and rivers, as do beavers. While you may see evidence of a beaver, it, too, is elusive.

The region is home to more than 70 amphibians and reptiles and countless kinds of fish.

HOW TO USE THIS BOOK

This book is intended for curious walkers—people who enjoy observing, perceiving, understanding, and learning. It includes an abundance of information about Middle Tennessee's topography, forests, wildlife, and history. Rather than being packed into a few pages, this information is spread throughout the book. In the same way, information about a particular place—whether a park, a natural area, or a battlefield—is sprinkled throughout the hike and walk narratives. The narratives should thus provide informative reading even for those who never set foot on a trail or a country road.

Hikes in the Woods

The hikes are arranged by physiographic region: Central Basin, Western Highland Rim, Eastern Highland Rim, and Cumberland Plateau. A chapter is devoted to each place—such as a park, a natural area, or a national battlefield—where there are hikes. Each chapter opens with general information about the place and is followed by details about the hikes. As a rule, walks of less than 1 mile have been left out. A few longer trails have been left out, too, because their rewards didn't seem worth the effort.

Both a summary and a narrative are provided.

The summary gives a quick overview of the hike and important information such as trailhead directions. The directions are designed to get you to the trailhead from a state or federal highway. Practically all the trailheads are marked with signs, but these signs turn up missing from time to time.

Almost all the hikes are configured as loops, which means

you won't have to retrace your steps or run a shuttle. One-way hikes are indicated.

The summaries describe maps not included in the book. The first maps listed are published by the agencies that manage the sites. Some sites have excellent trail maps, while others do not. If all you see listed is a brochure, that means there isn't much of a map. If the word *map* is used, that usually means that there's a decent trail map. The second map listed is the United States Geological Survey (USGS) topographical quadrangle map; some of these maps were actually prepared by the TVA. Be aware that most trails are not shown on the topo maps, and that some maps have not been updated recently. You can get topo maps through the Tennessee Department of Environment and Conservation, Division of Geology, Maps and Publications, 13th Floor, 401 Church Street, Nashville, TN 37243-0045 (615-532-1516). A good map source for any outdoor activity is DeLorme Mapping's *Tennessee Atlas and Gazetteer*, a book of topo maps covering the entire state. Note, though, that elevations are given in meters. A free Tennessee highway map should be all you need to find the trailheads.

Most of the walks in this book are on trails limited to hikers; no horses, mountain bikes, or off-road vehicles are allowed. But there are exceptions. Back-country camping is allowed in some places. If a permit is required, look in the appendix for the pertinent address and telephone number.

A narrative follows the summary of each hike. It describes the hike and gives directions. Most trails are well marked with blazes and/or signs. Distances were obtained by actual measurement, but there is always the possibility of human error. The distances in the narratives are cumulative—that is, they are measured from the trailhead. They are usually rounded off to the nearest tenth of a mile.

You'll notice that there are no difficulty ratings. Just about all the hikes are easy. There are exceptions, though, particularly on the Cumberland Plateau. If a trail is strenuous, it's noted early in the narrative.

Walks on Country Roads

The country-road walks give you an opportunity to sample some distinctive Middle Tennessee scenery. Please remember that these are paved roads used by motor vehicles. There are no sidewalks and in many places no shoulders. Always stay alert.

Within the narratives are details about the location of the walk, the beginning and ending points, the length, and highlights. All distances are one-way, so if you take the whole walk, plan on retracing your steps or running a shuttle.

All these walks are along stretches of road featured in *Touring the Middle Tennessee Backroads*. If you are interested in learning more about the area, you can find it in that book.

CLOTHING AND EQUIPMENT

Middle Tennessee's usually mild weather and mostly gentle terrain don't require much in the way of gear other than sturdy footwear and appropriate outerwear. A good pair of hiking boots will last an adult's lifetime and is definitely worth the investment. The same is true for a good, breathable, waterproof parka, which can serve as a windbreaker and provide protection against rain and snow.

Keep in mind that cotton is a poor insulator when wet. In cold weather, leave the jeans and sweatshirts behind and wear garments made of wool or synthetic fiber. A long-sleeve synthetic undershirt, a wool shirt, and a rain parka are generally about all you'll need except in the coldest weather. In warm weather, wear whatever you like.

For long day-hikes, carry a small pack for water, food, and other items. It's not a bad idea to bring a flashlight, insect repellant, and matches as well.

Backpacking requires its own equipment, such as a sleeping bag, a mattress, a tent, cooking gear, and so forth. If you've never been backpacking, try it with an organized group before you invest in equipment. Rent or borrow equipment for your trial runs.

HEALTH AND SAFETY

There are a few hazards to be aware of in Middle Tennessee's benign environment.

A little common sense is all that's required to avoid weather-related problems. Unlike the mountains of East Tennessee, Middle Tennessee does not have wide variations in altitude that produce wide variations in weather. Temperatures on the Cumberland Plateau are only a few degrees cooler than the rest of the Midstate. But remember that Middle Tennessee's weather seldom stays the same for more than a few days.

The biggest risk is getting both wet and cold. This can lead to a lowering of core body temperature and hypothermia. And it doesn't have to be all that cold. You can easily protect yourself by wearing the right clothing; see the "Clothing and Equipment" section above.

Hot, humid weather invades the Midstate off and on from June through September. Wear cool, loose-fitting clothes and drink lots of water.

Middle Tennessee has its share of thunderstorms, mostly in late spring and summer. If it looks like lightning might strike, seek shelter away from solitary trees, high trees, and open areas such as rock outcrops. Thunderstorms are not good times to walk the country roads.

Streams can flood following heavy rains, and when they do, they're dangerous. Stay out of flooded streams, and never camp where flooding is a possibility.

The beautiful waterfalls of Middle Tennessee present special hazards. The rocks around them are very slick, so *don't climb on them*. Use extreme caution along the bluffs at places like Burgess

Falls, Rock Island, Fall Creek Falls, and Savage Gulf. One careless mistake can result in tragedy.

Animals don't pose much of a threat to walkers. The two most common species of poisonous snake, the copperhead and the timber rattlesnake, shy away from people. You're not likely to ever see one. More people are bitten by messing with snakes than by coming upon them randomly, so if you see one, stay away from it. Watch where you put your hands when you're doing things like sitting down or gathering firewood, and look on the other side of a log before stepping over it.

Insects are more a nuisance than a health risk. Bugs are most common in summer, at which time a good insect repellant can help you enjoy your walk despite the mosquitos and gnats. Ticks present a more serious problem. Insect repellant will help; if you're at a place where ticks are particularly bad, like Land Between the Lakes, you might want to treat your clothes, too. It's a good idea to check yourself now and then and remove any ticks on you. If a tick has attached, pull it off slowly and treat the area with soap and water or a disinfectant such as iodine or alcohol.

Watch out for poison ivy, recognizable by its three-leaf pattern. The vine itself can cause irritation, so even in winter when there are no leaves, stay away from hairy vines running up trees. If you get into poison ivy, washing with soap and water within 30 minutes of exposure usually keeps it from bothering you.

Drinking the water you find along the trail is risky. Some streams flow into parks from outside, and the water may not be fit for consumption. You can carry all the water you will need for day-hiking. When backpacking, treat water you get along the trail by boiling it for one minute or by using one of the new pump-style filters.

Hiking alone in remote places like Virgin Falls and Savage Gulf is not recommended. You may injure yourself on their rocky trails, and it may be awhile before anyone comes along to help you.

Hunting is allowed in parts of Land Between the Lakes and Savage Gulf—and perhaps in other hiking places as well. It's best to inquire ahead and avoid such places during deer season.

Be careful on the country-road walks. They look like they're in tranquil rural areas, but most of them are near sprawling, automobile-dependent suburbs. Drivers are not expecting walkers on the road. Wear bright-colored clothes, especially at dawn and dusk.

Have fun!

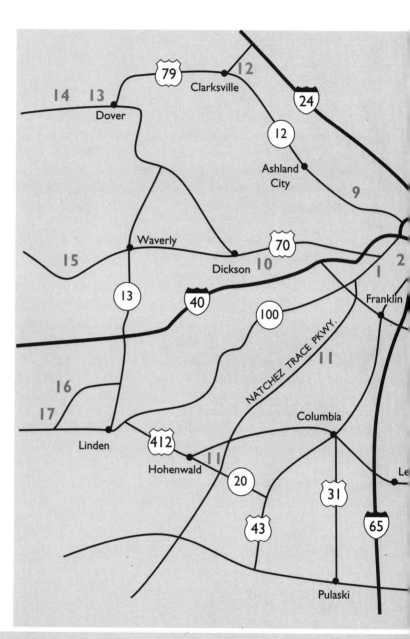

PART 1: HIKES IN THE WOODS

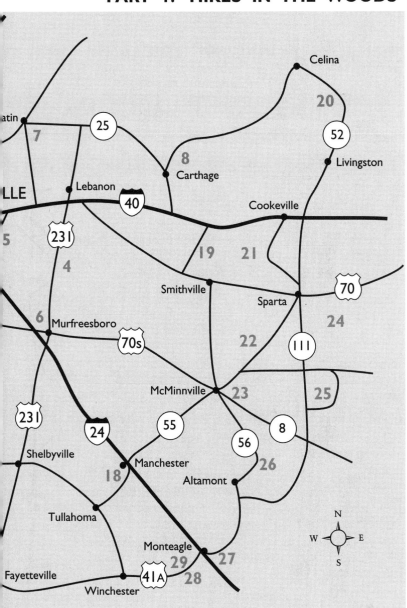

Lady Finger Bluff S. W. A.	21 Burgess Falls S. N. A.	26 Savage Gulf S. N. A.
Mousetail Landing S. P.	22 Rock Island State Park	27 Grundy For. S. N. A.
Old Stone Fort S. A. A.	23 Cardwell Mountain	28 Carter S. N. A.
Edgar Evins State Park	24 Virgin Falls Pocket W.	29 Univ. of South
Standing Stone S. P.	25 Fall Creek Falls S. P.	

LEGEND FOR MAPS

....   Hiking Trail / Country Road Walk

—————   Road

+—+—+—+   Railroad

P   Trailhead Parking

●   Landmark

▲   Point of exceptional interest / beauty

〰   Waterfall

⊼   Picnic Area

▲ (boxed)   Back-country Campsite

(284)   State Highway

(70)   Federal Highway

(40)   Interstate Highway

PART I

HIKES IN THE WOODS

HIKES
IN
THE

CENTRAL BASIN

WARNER PARKS

The incomparable Warner Parks would be a paradise for walkers wherever they might be located. But being near the heart of Nashville makes them even more inviting. At 2,665 acres, the combined parks make up the largest municipal park in Tennessee and one of the largest in the nation. Hiking trails, bridle paths, and scenic drives range over forested ridge tops, through deep, wooded hollows and open fields, along a river and smaller streams, and past wet-weather waterfalls.

The parks are in the Harpeth Hills, a cluster of mountainlike ridges along Nashville's southwestern border. Rising as high as 600 feet above the surrounding countryside, the Harpeth Hills are outliers of the Western Highland Rim that extend like fingers into the lower Central Basin. This makes for an extraordinarily diverse forest of trees and plants common to both the Central Basin and the Highland Rim, two of the three distinct physiographic regions that make up Middle Tennessee. There are more than 100 species of trees and shrubs in the Harpeth Hills, and the variety of wildflowers is enormous—more than 300 species.

Hikers can enjoy the parks' three long trails and five short nature trails, which are ideal for outings with small children. The 28 miles of scenic roads—especially the 5 miles closed to motor vehicles—are popular with walkers, too. In addition to using the trails and roads on your own, you can enjoy a variety of informative outings led by the parks' expert staff.

The Warner Parks date to 1926, when Nashville was fortunate to have a park board of five men dedicated to establishing one of the nation's premier park systems. Percy Warner, the new board chairman, was a wealthy, influential electric-utility pioneer with business interests throughout the South and in New York City. He was also an outdoor enthusiast. He wanted Nashville's park system to include a place that would remain in its natural state.

He found such a place in the Harpeth Hills. Warner's son-in-law, Luke Lea, was developing what would become Nashville's most prestigious neighborhood through his Belle Meade Park Company. Warner persuaded Lea to donate 868 wooded acres at the end of Belle Meade Boulevard for a nature preserve. This was the beginning of the Warner Parks.

Percy Warner died suddenly on June 18, 1927. Four days later, the park board voted to name the new park in his honor. Edwin Warner, Percy's younger brother, succeeded him on the board. For the next 20 years, Edwin Warner dedicated himself to expanding and improving Percy Warner Park. Edwin himself became the park-board chairman, a position he held until his death in 1949.

Under his leadership, land was added to the park. The final addition came in the early 1930s, when he donated funds to acquire over 600 acres south of Old Hickory Boulevard. In 1937, the park board honored him by calling this new acquisition Edwin Warner Park. Thus, there are two parks—Percy Warner and Edwin Warner—though they've always been managed as a single unit. To most people, they're simply "Warner Park."

The parks received a big boost during the Great Depression,

when extensive improvements were made by the Works Progress Administration (WPA), the agency President Franklin D. Roosevelt created in 1935 to provide relief to millions of unemployed Americans. In the WPA's eight years of existence, over 100,000 Tennesseans labored on a wide variety of public-works projects. Nowhere is the fruit of their labor more appreciated than in the Warner Parks.

Between 1935 and 1941, workers constructed seven limestone entrance gates, two limestone bridges, 9.5 miles of bridle paths, 5 miles of hiking trails, 37 picnic shelters, miles of stone walls, and the Iroquois Steeplechase, the only racetrack ever built by the United States government. The WPA used native materials in construction, and it's difficult to imagine any human alteration of the landscape that blends so well with the natural environment.

WARNER WOODS TRAIL

Highlights
Pleasant second-growth forest, views from Lea's Summit, historic Belle Meade Boulevard park entrance

Length
2.5-mile loop

Maps
"Hiking Trails of the Warner Parks"; USGS: Bellevue and Oak Hill.

Use
Hiking and day use only

Trailhead
The parking area is at the end of the road through the Deep Well

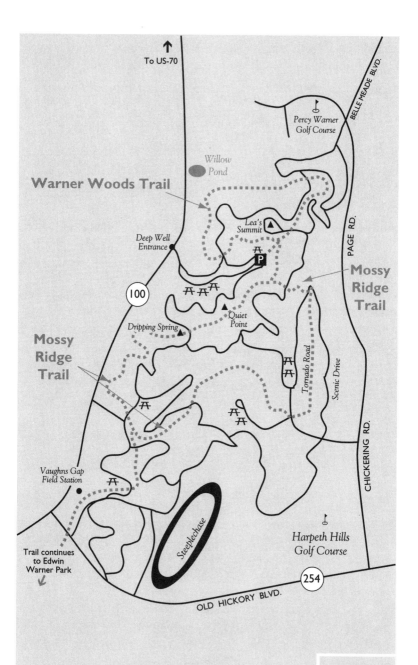

To US-70

BELLE MEADE BLVD.

Percy Warner
Golf Course

Willow
Pond

Warner Woods Trail

Lea's
Summit

Deep Well
Entrance

PAGE RD.

P

**Mossy
Ridge
Trail**

100

Quiet
Point

Dripping Spring

**Mossy
Ridge
Trail**

Tornado Road

Scenic Drive

CHICKERING RD.

Vaughns Gap
Field Station

Trail continues
to Edwin
Warner Park

Steeplechase

Harpeth Hills
Golf Course

254

OLD HICKORY BLVD.

WARNER PARKS

N
W   E
S

picnic area. To reach the road, drive 1.7 miles west on TN 100 from the TN 100/US 70 junction near Belle Meade.

Hike Description

This hike circles through the mature forest in the original part of the park, visiting Lea's Summit and its panoramic view and passing the formal Belle Meade Boulevard park entrance.

Take the short connector path from the parking lot to the official start of the white-blazed Warner Woods Trail. Go right to walk the loop counterclockwise, following the trail as it slices up the hill to the road to Lea's Summit. Walk left on the road to the overlook.

Much of Nashville spreads out in front of you from this 922-foot-high perch. The view is highlighted by the downtown skyline and Tennessee's historic State Capitol. The Highland Rim escarpment rises in the distance and lets you see how Nashville is on the very edge of the oval-shaped Central Basin that comprises the heart of the Midstate.

Lea's Summit is named for the financier who donated the original 868 acres for the park. A former senator and newspaper publisher, Luke Lea had visited Rock Creek Park in Washington, D.C., and Swope Park in Kansas City and was enthusiastic about a similar park for Nashville. It was not difficult for Percy Warner to convince his son-in-law to make the donation of land. Lea stipulated that it must stay in its natural state.

Return from the overlook to the Warner Woods Trail and turn left. Follow the trail's gradual descent to the main park and one of the many stone walls built by the WPA.

When you look down the hill to the left and see the same one-way road heading in the opposite direction, you'll appreciate how the road system was designed to take advantage of the contours of the land without disturbing its natural beauty. Percy Warner designed much of the network, and the city of Nashville completed cutting and grading the roads in 1931. The WPA paved them and added more mileage. Today, the road network totals 28 miles.

Where the road makes a hairpin curve, the trail swings to the opposite side of the ridge, descends slightly, and follows the contour of the hill to a point above the main entrance to the park. A short spur leads to an overlook.

Gates built of Sewanee sandstone and topped with stone eagles guard the Belle Meade Boulevard entrance. Locally prominent architect Edward Daugherty designed the gates, which were completed in 1930 with funds donated by Percy Warner's widow. From the gates, a stone-lined stairstep lane sweeps 875 feet up the hill. Built of rough, uncut fieldstone, it provides a transition between the extreme formality of the Belle Meade Boulevard entrance and the natural area. Nationally known architect Bryant Fleming of Ithaca, New York, designed the lane. It was completed in 1933.

Continue past the entrance overlook. After a short descent, cross the main park road diagonally and reenter the woods near a large cedar tree, taking care not to follow the parallel bridle path. The trail through here is part of the WPA's original trail

Lea's Summit, overlooking Nashville,
on the Warner Woods Trail

construction. It passes through an understory of shrubs as it eases down to a wet-weather stream that feeds Willow Pond on TN 100. The pond was created by the construction of the highway in 1930.

You can see along this stretch how non-native plants have invaded the Warner Parks and are threatening the competing indigenous species. The bush honeysuckle and ivylike creeping euonymus have just about taken over. Other parts of the parks are infested by Japanese honeysuckle and common privet. Park managers are engaged in an aggressive program to remove exotic plants. Several times each year, volunteers swarm over selected hillsides removing the pests.

As the trail continues along this level stretch, you will see the grounds of the Tennessee Botanical Gardens and Fine Arts Center—known to most people as Cheekwood, after the massive mansion that dominates it—off to the right. Mr. and Mrs. Leslie Cheek completed their home in 1929 and picked a name that included both their family names; she was a Wood. Bryant Fleming, the same New York architect who designed the stone-lined lane near the park entrance, designed the regal home. Cheekwood passed to the Cheeks' daughter, Mrs. Walter Sharp, who donated it to the state in 1969.

After crossing another wet-weather stream, the trail climbs, then levels off near a huge oak tree. A bench is provided for sitting and contemplating this tree. The white oak is 13 feet in circumference and four feet in diameter and rises to a height of 115 feet. It's thought to be at least 150 years old.

The trail climbs over a saddle and continues along the western side of the ridge, then turns sharply. You will cross the road and continue up the hill before the trail levels off and crosses the bridle path. It passes between two big tulip poplar trees, then heads past a grove of shagbark hickory before making a sharp right turn to climb to an old road.

This is one of Percy Warner's original roads, but one the WPA never paved. It's now called Farrell Road in honor of Charles E. Farrell, a Vanderbilt University zoologist for 23 years who, after retirement, worked at the Warner Parks Nature Center from 1977 to 1985. Many of the parks' outstanding nature programs began under Dr. Farrell's leadership. The museum at the nature center is named for him as well. Affectionately called "Chigger Charley," Farrell was an expert in acarology, the study of chiggers.

The trail follows the road up the hill, circles around its crest, then descends to the other side. In the gap just below Lea's Summit, it leaves the old road and curves down the hill to the right. After a steep descent, the Warner Woods Trail swings around the base of the ridge and reaches the beginning of the loop.

MOSSY RIDGE TRAIL

Highlights
Seasonal waterfall, moss-covered ridge, deep, rich forest, open fields, wildflowers

Length
4.5-mile loop

Maps
"Hiking Trails of the Warner Parks";
USGS: Bellevue and Oak Hill

Use
Hiking and day use only

Trailhead
Same as previous hike

Hike Description
This trail travels through coves that harbor unusually large trees, passes a lovely, two-tiered, wet-weather waterfall, and crosses the moss-covered ridge for which the trail is named.

From the parking area, a connector path leads less than 0.2 mile to the official beginning of the Mossy Ridge Trail. Go right to hike the loop counterclockwise.

The trail climbs out of the hollow, follows the contour of the ridge above the Deep Well picnic area, and threads through a garden of large, moss-covered rocks. The name Deep Well comes from a well, supposedly 300 feet deep, that provided water for a farm before the parks' creation. The well is now covered by the paved road.

After crossing the bridle path in a stand of impressive tulip poplars, the trail dips into a hollow, goes under another poplar grove, and then climbs steeply to a saddle.

The tulip poplar is also called the "tulip tree." Some people say the names come from the tree's greenish yellow tuliplike flowers, which bloom in May and June. Others say the names come from the tree's leaves, whose outline resembles a tulip. Whichever the case, the tulip poplar is a common tree throughout the Volunteer State and is Tennessee's state tree. Its wood is used for furniture, crates, toys, and musical instruments. It's not uncommon to see floors constructed of broad tulip-poplar boards in old houses.

Where the trail breaches the saddle at 0.4 mile, a short side trail ascends to Quiet Point, which overlooks the Deep Well hollow. A bench just over the crest of the saddle provides a nice place to sit quietly—on Quiet Point.

From the Quiet Point spur, the Mossy Ridge Trail descends slightly before climbing diagonally to the ridge crest and crossing the road. It then descends into a steep hollow and penetrates a patch of spring-blooming false rue anemone before reaching Dripping Spring at 1 mile.

This hollow is one of the nicest areas in the Warner Parks. If you suddenly found yourself here and didn't know where you were, you might think you were in a cove hardwood forest in the Great Smoky Mountains. The rich forest is dominated by large tulip poplar and beech. And Dripping Spring, when it's flowing, is a lovely, two-tiered waterfall. The falls are created by a spring, as the name suggests. Rainwater seeps through the soil and porous

Dripping Spring, a two-tiered waterfall on the Mossy Ridge Trail

rock until it reaches an impermeable layer of limestone. The water then migrates along the rock to the earth's surface, where it bubbles out of the steep hillside. It falls over bright green, moss-covered rocks, then drops eight feet in the second fall.

The false rue anemone next to the falls is just one of the many wildflowers that brighten a spring walk. The parks' staff lists 204 species of spring wildflowers. Purple phacelia covers the hillsides in places. You're also likely to see several kinds of violets, fire pink, spring beauty, Virginia bluebell, giant chickweed, dwarf larkspur, doll's eyes, May apple, toadshade, jack-in-the-pulpit, Indian strawberry, and Dutchman's-breeches, just to name a few. Dutchman's-breeches get their name from their flowers, which look like a pair of pantaloons hung out to dry. Some people call the flower "stagger-weed" because of its toxic qualities; animals seem intoxicated when they eat it.

The parks' wildflower list includes 274 summer species and 240 fall species. You can see why wildflower viewing and identification are popular activities in the Warner Parks.

The trail makes a slippery crossing on the rock ledge between the fall's two tiers, but you can avoid this maneuver by taking the short bypass that loops below the falls. It climbs steeply away from Dripping Spring and levels off past two giant sycamore trees.

The downed trees here are reminders of an experience Middle Tennesseans would just as soon forget: the ice storm of February 10, 1994. While the temperature hovered around freezing, a light drizzle fell throughout the night and froze to trees. The more it drizzled, the more ice accumulated. The night air was filled with the sounds of cracking limbs and of whole trees crashing to the ground. It was weeks before power was completely restored.

The trail levels off before turning sharply left to climb the ridge through a honeysuckle jungle and over layers of shale. Just short of the crest, it swings right and follows the undulating ridge through a forest that includes shagbark hickory and white oak. It then descends the southern side of the ridge in a large hairpin and follows the base to the edge of a wooded area. Here, in a belt of small trees, vines, and shrubs, you can witness the slow transformation of a field into a forest. Someday far in the future, this area will look like the woods you just left.

The trail descends through the meadow—fringed in April with a mix of bright redbud and white clouds of dogwood—crosses the road, climbs through the meadow beside a row of sycamore trees, and returns to the woods. It then follows the southern side of the ridge past a stand of cane.

You'll come to a junction with the Cane Connector Trail, which links the trails in Percy Warner Park to those in Edwin Warner Park. It extends a little less than a mile to the Warner Parks Nature Center across Old Hickory Boulevard. Part of the trail runs on what is believed to be the route of the Natchez Trace.

The connector trail is named for the cane growing here. Cane is a species of bamboo, a woody member of the grass family. When the early settlers came to Middle Tennessee, they found vast, almost impenetrable stands of cane they called "canebrakes." Not many of them are left today, but the word *cane* is found in countless natural features, evidence of how widespread it once was. The Caney Fork River is an example.

Past the junction, the trail enters the mossy area that gives the Mossy Ridge Trail its name. If you stop and look carefully, you'll notice how different the forest looks and feels from the north-facing hollows farther back. There are fewer trees here, and they are of different species. The drier, shallower soil here creates a different environment, so the vegetation is different.

After a steep climb, the trail levels off on the side of the ridge in a bed of bright green moss. It's beautiful throughout the year but is particularly outstanding in winter, when the late-afternoon sun lights up the moss like neon. Standing behind the moss are gnarled chestnut oaks rising above several varieties of shrubs: farkleberry, lowbush blueberry, and deerberry.

The trail continues around the contour of the ridge. After a slight climb, it reaches the road at 2.4 miles. Cross the road diagonally, staying on the Mossy Ridge Trail and off the bridle path, located just up the road. The trail follows the contour of the northern side of the ridge, crossing the bridle path, then crossing it again. At the second crossing, the rocky foot trail climbs steeply before leveling off on the ridge top.

The dense stand of small trees here—mostly sassafras and Hercules-club—indicates that this is a disturbed area. A 1979 fire burned about 150 acres in this part of the park.

The trail follows the nearly level ridge top before meandering down to a gravel road. Walk left on the gravel road. You will then cross the paved road, enter a field, and walk to the marker at the forest edge. Just inside the woods, the trail turns sharply right, then climbs to a saddle via a switchback. You will cross the bridle path that breaches the saddle, then climb the ridge on an old road. Soon, the trail levels off in a disturbed forest dominated by cedar trees. The trail here is called Tornado Road, after a storm that ripped up this part of the forest long ago.

The woods change abruptly as the trail reenters the old forest and continues along the crest of the ridge. This is some of the finest walking in the Nashville area. The nearly level trail follows the ridge through a forest dominated by beech and some unusually tall shagbark hickory. When the curtain of leaves has fallen, you can enjoy nice views of downtown Nashville to the right.

At 4.1 miles, the trail drops steeply through an eroded gully and reaches the main park road in a narrow gap. Walk left a short distance on the road, then follow the Mossy Ridge Trail to the right up a hollow. After a steep climb over the ridge and across the road, the trail descends into a hollow and passes a chimney, a remnant of a Boy Scout cabin built in the 1930s.

You will reach the beginning of the Mossy Ridge Trail just past the chimney. Turn right on the connector path to return to the parking area.

HARPETH WOODS TRAIL

Highlights
Spring wildflowers, original section of the
Natchez Trace, historic house

Length
2.4-mile loop

Maps
"Hiking Trails of the Warner Parks";
USGS: Bellevue

Use
Hiking and day use only

Trailhead
Warner Parks Nature Center, located off TN 100 just west of its junction with TN 254 (Old Hickory Boulevard)

Hike Description
On this walk, you'll enjoy a diverse forest environment, visit a fossil-filled rock quarry, see one of Nashville's oldest houses, and walk a stretch of the original Natchez Trace.

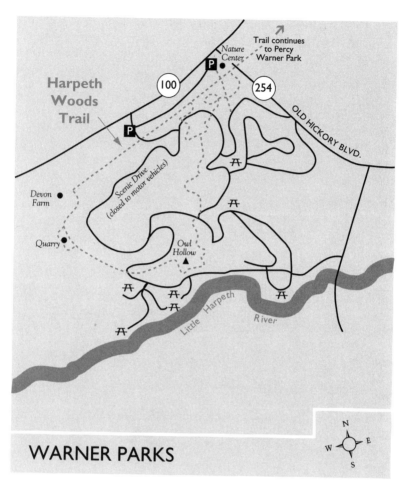

Harpeth
Woods
Trail

Nature Center

Trail continues to Percy Warner Park

Devon Farm

Quarry

Owl Hollow

Scenic Drive (closed to motor vehicles)

OLD HICKORY BLVD.

Little Harpeth River

WARNER PARKS

N W E S

The Harpeth Woods Trail and four short nature trails all begin at the Warner Parks Nature Center.

The nature center itself is worth a visit. The Charles E. Farrell Natural History Museum offers exhibits about native plants and animals and information about the prehistoric cultures that inhabited the area. An aquarium and a "touch and feel" table are also popular. The nature center's grounds are landscaped with native plants and contain an organic garden, a pond, a wildflower garden, beehives, and a weather station.

Access to the Harpeth Woods Trail and the nature trails is via a short connector path beginning at the trail information board. This path goes through a young wooded area alive with songbirds.

To hike the Harpeth Woods Trail clockwise, take the left fork where the loop begins. Follow the blue markings as the Harpeth Woods Trail intersects the nature trails before entering a meadow brightened in the spring by the purple tops of dead nettle and by blue ground ivy. As you cross the paved road at 0.1 mile, you may encounter people on foot, on bicycles, and in baby strollers, but not in cars. All the roads you will cross on this hike are closed to motor vehicles.

After crossing the road, you will climb the steep hill on a series of switchbacks. The numbers on the posts correspond to an informative booklet about the Nature Loop, the short trail that runs conjunctively here with the Harpeth Woods Trail. "Stop Two" is a big white ash tree, which, as the booklet notes, is the species that provides the wood used in baseball bats.

About halfway up the hill, the Harpeth Woods Trail and the Nature Loop part company. But before going left on the Harpeth Woods Trail, walk along the Nature Loop. You will soon reach a footbridge beneath a moss-covered bluff that holds a wet-weather spring. During very cold weather, particularly after soaking rains, the waterfall freezes, creating a sparkling ice display that reportedly prompted one youngster to exclaim, "Look at the popsicles growing!" During the spring, the bluff is covered with purple phacelia that has taken hold in shallow pockets of soil.

From the junction, the Harpeth Woods Trail climbs steeply before leveling off along the side of a ridge that still shows the effects of the February 1994 ice storm. The little creatures you hear scampering away from you are lizards, which seem to like the tangles of downed trees.

This and other stretches of the trails in the parks were built by the Youth Conservation Corps, which had camps here from 1974 through 1980. Its members helped build the Warner Parks Nature Center, too.

The trail circles around the hill past the springtime blooms of kidney-leaf buttercup, wild chervil, stinging nettle, Philadelphia fleabane, and saxifrage, then gradually ascends to a flower-covered saddle featuring the deep purple of dwarf larkspur. It follows the saddle and climbs to the ridge crest, which allows nice views of the Little Harpeth River Valley when there is no foliage. The Little Harpeth River—one of four rivers called Harpeth—rises in eastern Brentwood and meanders through the Nashville suburb before emptying into the Big Harpeth River just west of Edwin Warner Park.

The trail descends the dry, cedar-dotted southern face of the ridge. After some steep switchbacks, it reaches the circular park road. (The road leading off the circular road drops to the picnic areas along the river.) Cross the road diagonally to the right and reenter the woods.

The Harpeth Woods Trail follows the western flank of the ridge above Owl Hollow. When the leaves are down, you can see the ridges rising beyond the Harpeth River Valley. The trail then passes through a rock garden and descends among large cedar trees. Stop at the gigantic oak. If you look up, you'll see that its limbs have resurrection ferns growing on them. During dry weather, the ferns' leaves curl up and give the appearance of being dead. But when moisture returns, they come alive again.

The Harpeth Woods Trail reaches the Owl Hollow Trail and then the road at 1 mile.

Yes, owls live in Owl Hollow, as they do in the other Warner Parks hollows. Of the eight owl species in Tennessee, three are residents of this hollow: the Eastern screech owl, the barred owl, and the great horned owl. Because of their nocturnal habits, you're most likely to see owls as afternoon changes to evening. The screech owl screeches and the other two hoot. Listen quietly and you may hear one.

The two trails run conjunctively, rising through some shrubs and small trees before reaching the edge of the woods, where a brier patch divides them. Go left as the Harpeth Woods Trail levels off in a cedar grove along the base of the ridge and crosses the road at 1.3 miles. About 600 feet past the road, follow the path that leads to the left. It's a loop through the quarry that rejoins the main trail just ahead.

The region's earliest settlers quarried stone here. Some of it was used in the house you will visit down the trail. Much of the limestone for the entrance gates, walls, and bridges built by the WPA came from this quarry. It remains a popular place to look for fossils from the Ordovician geologic period, which occurred 450 million years ago.

After the quarry loop rejoins the Harpeth Woods Trail, the trail swings to the northern base of the ridge and wanders through an open forest featuring large, old beech trees. Some are den trees—live trees with holes or hollows large enough to shelter wildlife. Some are dead or dying.

Dead trees are important for a healthy forest. Without them, there would be no homes for cavity-nesting birds such as chickadees, titmice, and woodpeckers. Woodpeckers feed on insects found in dead trees. Mammals such as raccoons, foxes, and squirrels often nest or den in hollow trees. Small animals like lizards, salamanders, and snakes find food in dead trees and use the trees for cover, as do insects. When dead timber decomposes, it returns valuable nutrients to the soil to help feed young trees and other plants.

The trail turns sharply left. It then makes a sharp right through a honeysuckle jungle and past the remains of a gigantic oak before descending through a rocky area to an old road at 1.7 miles. The Harpeth Woods Trail goes right here, but you should take a short detour to the left to see one of the most historic houses in the Nashville area.

What is now known as Devon Farm is one of Middle Tennessee's oldest farms. It's uncertain who built the first brick house, incorporated as part of the home that stands today. Some believe it was pioneer surveyor John Davis, who came to the Middle Cumberland from North Carolina in 1788 and made his permanent home along the Harpeth in 1795. Others say Giles Harding, who settled here in 1798, built the house. Davis's daughter, Fanny, married Harding's son, Morris. The couple took over the farm and enlarged the house to nearly its current size.

You'll see a giant bur oak at Devon Farm. Its exact age is unknown, but some say it is one of the trees John Davis is known to have planted on his Harpeth property in 1795. The word *bur* refers to the fringed cap of the tree's unusually large acorn.

Edward D. Hicks II, the nephew of Fanny Davis Harding, had a passion for Devon cattle. After inheriting the farm in 1865, he imported Devon cattle and gave the estate overlooking the Harpeth River its current name. By 1888, he owned the largest Devon herd in the United States.

Hicks was an officer and director of the nearby railroad, the main line to Memphis. For many years, he maintained the pleasant custom of serving eggnog to the passengers and crews of passing trains on Christmas. Throughout the day and well into Christmas night, family members would follow the lane to the railroad, where the engineers would stop their trains in anticipation of the treat.

Part of the farm passed to Hicks's daughter, Fanny Hicks Woolwine, who sold the land that became Edwin Warner Park and expanded the Warner Parks to their current size.

Return from Devon Farm to the trail junction and continue as the Harpeth Woods Trail follows the old road.

This is part of the original Natchez Trace. The earliest trace came out of Nashville on the approximate route of today's West End Avenue/Harding Road/TN 100, crossed the Harpeth, and climbed Backbone Ridge. When the army relocated the Natchez Trace between 1801 and 1803 on orders from President Thomas Jefferson, the road swung away from the original route somewhere near here and struck south through the Harpeth Valley. (To learn more about the Natchez Trace, see the Natchez Trace Parkway chapter, pages 107–22.)

The last leg of this walk is on the old Natchez Trace as it parallels Vaughns Creek back to the Warner Parks Nature Center. Vaughns Creek goes nearly dry in the summer and fall, but it's a boisterous little brook during the wet season and after a good rain.

RADNOR LAKE STATE NATURAL AREA

Not many cities can claim a wilderness area within their boundaries. Tucked in the hills just 7 miles from downtown Nashville, this 1,060-acre preserve has an 80-acre lake, placid sloughs, creeks, grown-up fields, and a dense forest at elevations ranging from 774 to 1,160 feet.

This diverse ecological system accounts for Radnor Lake's incredible variety of plants and wildlife: five distinct plant communities, 18 species of mammals (including deer, bobcat, fox, weasel, otter, and mink), 17 species of reptiles, and 10 species of amphibians. Over 250 bird species have been observed at Radnor Lake, making the area one of the region's most popular bird-watching sites. More than 325 kinds of flowering plants put on a show nearly year-round.

You can enjoy it all on a 6-mile trail network accessible from the eastern and western entrances on Otter Creek Road. The road is closed to thru traffic, and it, too, offers pleasant walking, with sweeping views of the lake and the rugged hills surrounding it. The road provides a rare opportunity for the disabled to enjoy the solitude of the natural area. The park even has some all-terrain wheelchairs that can be used to negotiate the main trail.

Radnor Lake is not wilderness in the strictest sense. In fact, the lake itself is man-made. Much of its lower elevation was mowed until recently, and its woods have been logged several times. But the evidence of human intrusion is dim. There is no mistaking the feeling of wilderness, even though you are in the middle of a metropolitan area of over a million people.

Though it seems incongruous, it was heavy industry that caused this place to be so special. The Louisville & Nashville Railroad started building a major yard, a roundhouse, and shops just over the hills in 1915. To supply water for its steam locomotives, the L & N bought the basin that comprises the headwaters of Otter Creek and built a huge earthen dam. Water was piped 5 miles to the yard, which was named Radnor after the part of Nashville where it was located. The lake was filled by 1919, the same year the L & N completed the yard.

The isolated lake soon became a haven for migratory waterfowl and other birds. In 1923, Albert F. Ganier of the Tennessee Ornithological Society persuaded the L & N to designate Radnor Lake a bird sanctuary and prohibit hunting. Fishing continued on the lake, though on a small scale.

The advent of diesel locomotives ended the railroad's need for water. The L & N sold Radnor Lake to the Oman Construction Company in 1962. People living near Radnor Lake had grown accustomed to its solitude and knew what a treasure it was. So did faculty members at Nashville's many colleges and universities, who used Radnor Lake for field studies. Chief among them was Dr. Oliver Yates of David Lipscomb University. Yates began speaking out about the need for a plan to protect this special place.

Governor Winfield Dunn then took an active interest in making Radnor Lake a state natural area under Tennessee's Natural Areas Preservation Act of 1971. Dunn approached Oman executives, only to learn that the company had sold an option to a developer, who was planning a massive residential complex. When word of the proposed development spread, interest in preserving Radnor Lake intensified. A zoning change was needed to make the development economically feasible. By March 1973, thousands had signed a petition opposing the zoning change and calling for Radnor Lake's preservation.

Sensing rising opposition, the developer agreed to sell his option to the state. All that was needed was a payment of $3.5 million by August 16. Through some savvy maneuvering by Dunn and Congressman Richard Fulton—later Nashville's mayor—$3 million in state and federal money was acquired by July. The deadline of August 16 was fast approaching, and the fund was $500,000 short.

Nashville then embarked upon a remarkable grass-roots fund drive. In less than three weeks, citizen activists led by State Senator Doug Henry raised more than enough money. Stirton Oman, president of the company that owned the property, got the ball rolling by making the first major donation: a substantial $100,000. Within days, the whole city was astir with efforts to raise money to save Radnor Lake. McDonald's gave away burgers in exchange for contributions. An artist produced a limited-edition print and donated the proceeds from its sale to the preservation fund. Before it was over, Vanderbilt University, David Lipscomb University, Nashville's metropolitan government, and thousands of smaller donors made contributions. Radnor Lake became the first area acquired and managed under the Natural Areas Preservation Act.

The 1973 purchase of 940 acres left out a significant part of the Otter Creek basin, including a 133-acre farm and some hilltops. With assistance from the Nature Conservancy, acquisitions made in 1979 and 1989 completed the state's ownership of the entire basin and the hilltops. Smaller additions were made in the 1990s.

The lake is off-limits to boats except during canoe floats led by the park staff. The full-moon floats are particularly popular, and early registration is a must. Though a variety of organized activities is offered at Radnor Lake, most visitors come simply to enjoy a quiet, easy walk along the lake or to take one of the more strenuous trails to the ridge tops.

Be sure to stop at the visitor center at the western entrance. It houses a fascinating museum that tells the story of four periods in the history of the Radnor Lake area: early settlement, farming and timbering, railroading, and state ownership. Among the items on display are the original 1784 and 1793 North Carolina land grants given to Revolutionary War soldier Benjamin Reed and surveyor James Mulherrin. Another popular feature is the collection of Civil War artifacts found in the Radnor Lake area, some of them from the Battle of Nashville, fought just north of these hills in December 1864.

The man for whom the visitor center is named, Walter Criley, was the longtime planning director for the Tennessee Department of Conservation. The department developed the Radnor Lake master plan under his direction. Criley's competence and devotion are two of the reasons Tennessee once had one of the nation's premier state-park systems. He died of cancer in 1985 at age 54.

LAKE AND SOUTH COVE TRAILS

Highlights
Easy walk along Radnor Lake's northern shore, rich cove hardwood forest on the southern shore, wildflowers

Length
3.6-mile loop

Maps
RLSNA brochure; USGS: Oak Hill

Use
Hiking and day use only

Trailhead
The visitor center is on Otter Creek Road just east of its intersection with Granny White Pike. Otter Creek Road crosses Granny White Pike 1.7 miles south of Harding Place and an equal distance north of Old Hickory Boulevard (TN 254).

Hike Description
The trail along Radnor Lake's northern shore offers vistas of the lake and the steep, wooded hills surrounding it. It's gentle, well groomed, and accessible. It's by far the most popular trail in Middle Tennessee, suitable for anyone regardless of hiking ability. The return on the South Cove Trail is a strenuous walk through a deep, rich, north-facing cove, but if you like, you can do what most walkers do: return on Otter Creek Road.

You'll not find many spring wildflower walks better than this in all of Middle Tennessee. The variety of flowers is enormous. Some species—spring beauty, May apple, dwarf larkspur, purple phacelia, rue anemone, common blue violet, waterleaf—are common along much of the hike. Other species—blue phlox, celandine poppy, yellow violet, birdfoot violet, Dutchman's-breeches, wild hyacinth—are more localized.

To begin, walk from the visitor center to the Lake Trail on the short but interesting Spillway Trail. This trail follows Otter Creek, which is dry much of the summer and fall but can be a torrent of white water in winter and spring, when it tumbles toward the Little Harpeth River from the earthen dam.

River otters were once common throughout this area, but demand for their pelts and habitat degradation wiped them out of Middle Tennessee. These playful creatures need clean water and are considered a sign of a healthy environment. The Tennessee Wildlife Resources Agency (TWRA) started an otter restoration program in the 1980s. It was not successful at first, due to lack of knowledge about how to handle the delicate animals. The TWRA then turned to Lee Roy Sevin, owner of Bayou Otter Farm in Louisiana, a down-to-earth Cajun who seemed to be the only person in North America able to handle large numbers of otters in captivity. With Sevin's help, the first successful otter release occurred in 1984 at the Catoosa Wildlife Management Area near Crossville. In the next decade came successful releases in several river systems, including the Harpeth. Otters have found a home at Radnor Lake. But they are secretive little animals, and you're not likely to see one.

The Spillway Trail is marked with signs describing some of the park's natural features. One sign mentions coyotes. Most people identify coyotes with the American West, but they're in the East as well. Coyotes moved into Tennessee in the late 1960s. In *Tennessee's Wonders*, their superb pictorial guide to the state's parks, photographer John Netherton and Radnor Lake manager Mike Carlton explain that no one knows for sure how coyotes got here. One theory is that Western coyotes migrated east and inbred with domestic dogs. Eastern coyotes are larger than their Western cousins, but they are not as vocal, so you're less likely to hear them howling in the night.

The trail soon enters an old forest and crests a rise that offers a panoramic view of Radnor Lake. The Spillway Trail ends and the Lake Trail begins at the earthen dam.

The McElyea Nature Center, located across the dam, is named for the family that lived in the house and cared for Radnor Lake from 1946 until 1979. Jesse McElyea was the primary caretaker. Following his tragic death in an auto accident, his widow, Carrie, served as caretaker until her retirement.

Along the Lake Trail, you'll delight in the soft cushion of mulch that makes the walking so easy. It comes from Christmas trees. Each year, Nashvillians drop off their used trees at designated collection points, where they are ground into mulch that is brought here and spread on the Lake Trail.

The trail meanders along the shore, alternating between the hardwood forest and grown-up fields. This allows walkers to study forest succession, the process by which a disturbed area reverts

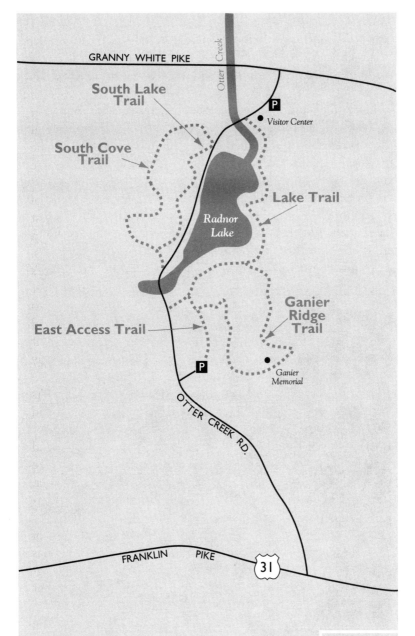

GRANNY WHITE PIKE

Otter Creek

South Lake
Trail

South Cove
Trail

P
Visitor Center

Lake Trail

*Radnor
Lake*

East Access Trail

Ganier
Ridge
Trail

P

*Ganier
Memorial*

OTTER CREEK RD.

FRANKLIN PIKE

31

RADNOR LAKE S. N. A.

to woods. The trail then crosses a seasonal stream in a cane-brake and passes an overlook above the lake. This is a nice place to pause and watch the multitude of ducks, geese, and other waterfowl.

Each fall, Radnor Lake welcomes waterfowl that spend much of the spring and summer in the North. In all, 22 species make the lake their winter home. Among the more common are the ring-necked duck, the lesser scaup, the bafflehead, the gadwall, and the American widgeon. The slate-colored, ducklike coot is also abundant. Wood ducks, mallards, and Canada geese all nest at Radnor Lake. In May, look for wood ducklings in the sheltered coves. Wood ducks migrate south about the time the Northern ducks come here for the winter.

Of course, waterfowl account for only a few of the bird spe-

Radnor Lake, tucked away in Nasville's suburbs

cies at Radnor Lake. There are dozens of others as well, including 36 types of warblers, 14 kinds of hawks, and seven different woodpeckers. Watching and identifying birds are popular activities at Radnor Lake. You can use a checklist available at the visitor center or take a park-sponsored outing.

The trail swings along a cove, then turns sharply right to cross a bog on a long bridge before entering an old forest that is returning to its former grandeur. It's particularly peaceful here. Except for an occasional aircraft overhead, the quiet is broken only by the singing of birds and chirping of insects. Or you might hear a woodpecker pounding away on a decaying tree. And you're seldom out of earshot of geese on the lake.

At 1 mile, the Ganier Ridge Trail—covered in the next hike—comes in from the left. Keep right on the Lake Trail as it follows the base of the ridge through a forest of large oak and tulip poplar with a sprinkling of black cherry and sycamore. This is a particularly good place to enjoy spring wildflowers. In April, you'll see patches of bright purple dwarf larkspur quaking in the breeze.

The trail swings away from the lake, passes through an area of small trees, and crosses another seasonal stream. It splits but soon rejoins before reaching the spur to the eastern parking area at 1.5 miles.

Continue on the Lake Trail as it approaches the lake and crosses a low-lying area; a long bridge carries the trail over the delta of Otter Creek as it gives its waters to the lake. At 1.7 miles, you will reach the end of the Lake Trail. Turn right on the road.

The walk now follows the paved road along the dike that separates the main body of the lake from the slough on the left. The term *pond scum* is taken as a pejorative in most contexts, but not here. The green plant on the slough is duckweed—aptly named, because this area is abundant with ducks in fall and winter. You'll see them diving for small aquatic plants and animals. The most numerous ducks here are the ring-necked duck and the lesser scaup. You can identify the ring-necked by the white ring on its bill. The lesser scaup is white with black at both ends.

In these shallow waters, you may also see green-backed herons. And if you're careful, the turtles sunning themselves on logs will stay put as you walk by. The slider and the soft-shelled turtle are two species commonly seen here.

At the end of the dike, you'll come to a drive leading into a farm that the state acquired in 1979. Here, you have a choice of how to return to the visitor center. Most people take the road, an easy route that follows Radnor Lake's southern shore and affords unobstructed views of the lake's rippling, ever-changing colors. This walk leaves the road, however, and takes to the high ridge south of the lake.

After climbing the steps away from the road, the trail levels off and traverses a bluff. You'll quickly come to a junction where the South Cove Trail splits from the South Lake Trail. Turn left on the South Cove Trail and climb. (The South Lake Trail stays along the base of the ridge and rejoins the South Cove Trail near the end of the hike.)

The South Cove Trail climbs steeply, then follows the ridge around the north-facing cove, which holds a rich forest dominated by tulip poplar, shagbark hickory, and sugar maple. Wildflowers flourish here in the spring. The trail starts to climb again above the cove before finally reaching the nearly level ridge top. It follows the ridge, then veers right on a spur jutting into the cove. The South Cove Trail returns to the crest of the main ridge, then angles right to descend to Radnor Lake. As it drops off the ridge on switchbacks, the trees get noticeably larger.

You will reunite with the South Lake Trail, which comes in from the right. Head downhill to Otter Creek Road. Walk left on the road a short distance to reach the visitor center.

GANIER RIDGE TRAIL

Highlights
Ridge covered with chestnut oaks, Nashville's
highest hills, wildflowers

Length
2.4-mile loop

Maps
RLSNA brochure; USGS: Oak Hill

Use
Hiking and day use only

Trailhead
The eastern parking area is on Otter Creek Road west of Franklin
Road (US 31). Otter Creek Road intersects Franklin Road 1.3 miles
south of Franklin Road's intersection with Harding Place (TN 255)
and 2.1 miles north of Old Hickory Boulevard (TN 254).

Hike Description
The Ganier Ridge Trail lets you sample a rare environment
on top of the highest hills in the entire Central Basin of Middle
Tennessee. Spring wildflowers are abundant. You'll see dwarf larkspur, purple phacelia, fire pink, rue anemone, toadshade, spring
beauty, birdfoot violet, May apple, jack-in-the-pulpit, Southern
dewberry, Indian strawberry, wild hyacinth, false garlic, saxifrage,
and many more.

The hike follows the steep, rocky access trail from the comfort station to a junction, where the Ganier Ridge Trail leads
right. Follow the trail along the contour of the flower-covered
ridge before it snakes steeply up and follows the crest, where spring
beauty seems to be just about everywhere in March and April.
This delicate white or pink five-petaled harbinger of spring opens

Radnor Lake at sunset

PHOTO BY JOE H. ALLEN

its blossoms only when the sun is shining.

After a dip, the trail enters an area dominated by an impressive grove of chestnut oaks. This ridge-top environment contrasts sharply with the cove on Radnor Lake's southern shore. The soil here is shallow and rocky. Though located in the Central Basin, these hills are geologically part of the Western Highland Rim, split from the main body of the rim by the erosion of the Harpeth River and its tributaries. If you're addicted to mountains, as many hikers are, come to Ganier Ridge for a quick fix. Or if you're just looking for a place around Nashville that's different, this is it.

These hills are part of the same Harpeth Hills that hold the nearby Warner Parks (see pages 3–20). But here, they are called the Overton Hills in honor of John Overton, the pioneer landowner who controlled much of the land in this part of Davidson County. Overton's historic home, Travelers Rest, located off

Franklin Road just over the hills, is open to the public. The oldest part of Travelers Rest dates to 1799.

A native of Virginia and a distant relative of Thomas Jefferson, Overton migrated by way of Kentucky to the Cumberland frontier at age 22 and started a law practice. He became friends with another young lawyer who had just arrived in Nashville, Andrew Jackson. Their lives were intertwined from then until Overton's death in 1833, during Jackson's second term as president.

Overton managed Jackson's campaigns for the presidency and was a trusted adviser to "Old Hickory" during his first term. A prominent man in his own right, Overton served as a trial judge from 1804 to 1810. The following year, he became a justice on the Tennessee Supreme Court. Overton and Jackson were partners in many land speculations. Along with James Winchester, they bought 5,000 acres on a Mississippi River bluff and laid out the town of Memphis in 1818.

Follow the Ganier Ridge Trail to a clearing that features a plaque honoring Albert F. Ganier, the man for whom this ridge is named. It was Ganier who in 1923 persuaded the railroad to make Radnor Lake a wildlife sanctuary.

From the Ganier memorial, the trail descends along the crest of the ridge through a saddle. If you're here when the leaves are down, look to the right to catch a glimpse of the concrete and glass of downtown Nashville, set against the backdrop of the Highland Rim escarpment.

The trail continues along the narrow, moss-covered ridge through chestnut oaks and beside the shining green leaves of mountain laurel before it starts to drop. The descent is steep at first but becomes more gradual as the trail threads its way through colonies of May apple, an umbrella-like plant that stays close to the ground. Its flowers bloom under its big green leaves.

After passing through an open area of large tulip poplar trees where the ground is peppered with yellow violets, then with rue anemone, then with phlox, then with waterleaf, the Ganier Ridge

Trail reaches an old road and turns left. It intersects the Lake Trail at 1.6 miles.

Walk left on the Lake Trail to its intersection with the East Access Trail at 2 miles. Follow the access trail to the eastern parking lot.

SHELBY BOTTOMS GREENWAY

Shelby Bottoms offers a unique opportunity to enjoy nature right in the heart of Nashville. Starting on the edge of Shelby Park, just minutes from downtown, the 810-acre greenway stretches 3.5 miles along the Cumberland to a point across the river from Opryland. Its multiuse paved paths and unpaved walking trails wander through an area being opened to the public in phases. The hike below is in Phase I, which opened in 1997. Other phases will open as funding and staffing permit.

Its central, urban location makes the preserve attractive, to be sure, but the bottoms are a special place to visit for other reasons as well. Most all of Middle Tennessee's trails are in upland forests, but here you have the rare opportunity to explore a river bottom with a wide variety of habitats: riverbanks, ponds, marshes, open bottom land, moist ravines, and uplands.

There are some huge trees at Shelby Bottoms. You can find Tennessee's largest basswood, Carolina hickory, green hawthorn, swamp privet, and shellbark hickory. You can also find Davidson County's largest swamp chestnut oak, silver maple, shagbark hickory, and sweet gum. A shingle oak located here is tied for the largest in the whole United States.

The more than 180 species of birds recorded at Shelby Bottoms range from the great blue heron to the tiny ruby-throated hummingbird. You'll find all kinds of herons, ducks, geese, hawks, sandpipers, gulls, woodpeckers, flycatchers, and sparrows, along with no fewer than 37 different warblers. Birds are abundant year-round, but particularly so during the spring and fall migrations.

As wild as the bottoms are, they are not wilderness in the truest sense. The rich Southern swamp forest that blanketed the lowlands was cut long ago, and a substantial part of the bottoms was cleared for farming. As late as the 1980s, the rich land was leased to farmers, who grew soybeans, wheat, and corn. This led to a condition called "forest fragmentation." It's a bad news, good news story. Animals needing big chunks of uninterrupted forest interior cannot live at Shelby Bottoms. Yet edge-loving species such as deer, raccoons, and opossums thrive in the mixture of woodlands and fields.

How is it that this remarkable, crescent-shaped patch of urban land has stayed free of development? Flooding. The Cumberland River gets outs of its banks every now and then, covering much of the bottom with water. Construction in the flood plain has not proven feasible and is not allowed under current regulations.

During his first term as Nashville–Davidson County mayor, Phil Bredesen concluded that if the bottoms were not put into public ownership soon, the opportunity to preserve them would be forever lost. So he persuaded the Metro Council to appropriate funds to buy Shelby Bottoms. Under the plan approved by Nashville's award-winning parks department, construction will be limited mostly to trails, overlooks, and a nature center, in keeping with the area's wild character. Some of the open land will be left to return to forest, a long-term process that will provide a good opportunity to study forest succession.

TREES TRAILS LOOP

Highlights
Marsh, riverbank, and forest habitats

Length
1.8-mile loop

Maps
Shelby Bottoms Greenway map;
USGS: Nashville East

Use
Hikers and cyclists may use the paved trail.
Access is limited to day use only.

Trailhead
The parking area is at the eastern boundary of Shelby Park. Take Exit 84 off I-65 and go east on Shelby Avenue to South Fifth Street. Turn right (south) on South Fifth and go to where it ends at Davidson Street. Turn left on Davidson Street. After entering Shelby Park, follow the park road to the Shelby Bottoms parking area, located past the railroad trestle. You can also get there by entering the park at the end of Shelby Avenue and following the winding road to the main park road off Davidson Street.

Hike Description
This easy walk circles the first phase of the greenway opened to the public. It's called the Trees Trails Loop because it follows four trails named after trees: Maple, Hickory, Poplar, and Sweetgum. Part of the hike is on the paved trail that will eventually run the length of the entire greenway, and another part is on mulched trails.

From the parking area, walk to the circular trailhead. Go left on the paved Maple Trail and follow it as it curves past a moist, tree-covered ravine and emerges into an expansive wetland.

With the rumble of a train crossing the trestle, the roar of jets overhead, the sounds of boats on the river, and your view of the houses bordering the natural area, you might initially feel a twinge of disappointment. After all, you came here to enjoy the natural experience. But your glass is half full, not half empty. The ever-present hum of urban life merely serves to prove how special Shelby Bottoms is and how fortunate Nashville is to have this place forever preserved in its natural state.

At 0.3 mile, the Hickory Trail veers left. Before you follow it, though, continue through the field on the Maple Trail to the overlook. Rising above the bottom near two ponds, it provides an opportunity to study a wetland and its abundance of birds.

Return to the Hickory Trail and follow it deeper into the bottom, where the birds are more abundant. You're likely to encounter mockingbirds and bobwhite quail here. The mockingbird, Tennessee's state bird, is fairly easy to spot, with its gray body and the white patches on its wings. It's certainly easy to detect by its mimicking song. A mockingbird will rapidly repeat a phrase several times before going on to another one. By contrast, the quail stays so well hidden in the grass and underbrush that you may not see one. But you'll know it by its unmistakable "bob-white!" call.

The Hickory Trail turns right to follow a line of willow trees

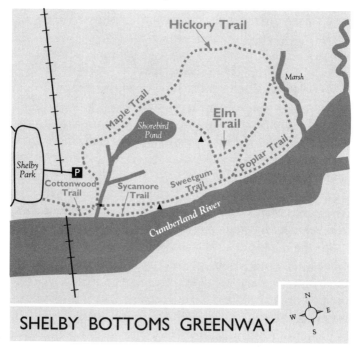

SHELBY BOTTOMS GREENWAY

bordering a marsh. Marshes—islands of water surrounded by higher ground—are formed when water settles in a depression. One intriguing aspect of marshes is the way their habitats vary with the slightest rise in elevation. The nutrient-rich center is home to plants called "emergents," which grow with their roots and often their bases in wet soil or water; the cattails in this marsh are a good example. Then, as you move away from the center, the drier, higher ground supports a growth of hardwood trees that includes cottonwood, willow, sycamore, and green ash.

Marshes attract a variety of wildlife, particularly birds. The rich habitat provides them with abundant food and with nesting sites protected from ground predators. Just as marsh plant life varies with slight elevation changes, so does the population of birds. Some birds take to the watery center of the marsh, some thrive in the grass and sedge around the edge, and others prefer the trees on the border.

Amphibians are also present. Salamanders usually prefer the wettest part of the marsh and toads the driest. Frogs are somewhere in between—except for the bullfrog, which likes the water. Turtles are the most abundant reptile. All kinds of invertebrates—insects, snails, and crustaceans—make up the core of the marsh food chain.

You'll soon reach the paved trail that ends at the edge of the Phase I development; eventually, it will penetrate farther into the natural area. Go right. After walking a few hundred feet, take the unpaved Poplar Trail as it angles left. The Poplar Trail hugs the line of trees before meeting the riverbank and following it downstream.

Much of the trail work at Shelby Bottoms is done by volunteers organized by the Metro Greenways Commission and a citizen support group called Greenways for Nashville. The Alpha Kappa Alpha sorority at Fisk University, greenway supporters, and local residents spread the mulch that provides such nice, soft footing on the unpaved trails.

Paths lead from the Poplar Trail to the edge of the river at several points. Look carefully at the bluff across the river and you'll see a cave blocked by a gate. Jacques-Timothe De Montbrun—later called Timothy Demonbreun—is often honored as Nashville's first citizen. This French Canadian came to the Cumberland country as early as 1769 and spent several winters trading for furs. In escaping an Indian attack, he once took refuge in this cave, which has been called Demonbreun's Cave ever since. He moved to Nashville for good in 1790 and lived until 1826. An imposing statue of Demonbreun stands guard over the Cumberland River on the bluff next to the courthouse.

The Poplar Trail ends at the paved trail. Go straight on the Sweetgum Trail, which offers a rare opportunity for strolling along the bank of the Cumberland River. Before long, you'll come to an impressive overlook built out over the river and shaded by an enormous silver maple.

It was a Virginian, Thomas Walker, who gave the Cumberland River its name. Walker was hired in 1750 to explore beyond the Great Valley of Virginia and today's East Tennessee. He gave the name Cumberland—in honor of the duke of Cumberland, son of and prime minister to England's King George II—to the mountains he explored, to a gap through them, and to a small river he encountered. From its beginnings as the tiny mountain stream Walker named, the Cumberland picks up water as it dips into Tennessee, winds through Carthage, Nashville, and Clarksville, and returns to Kentucky to empty into the Ohio River.

Standing in the river is an intriguing stone-and-brick structure with a conical roof. Built in 1892, this is the old intake tower for Nashville's waterworks, constructed a few years before that. The waterworks is still Nashville's principal source of water, though the intake tower is no longer in use.

Past the overlook, a short footpath—the Sycamore Trail—runs closer to the riverbank and returns to the paved trail at a bridge over a moist ravine. Ravines like this are one of the distinctive habitats at Shelby Bottoms. Native trees include box elder, locust, hackberry, and walnut, but as the forest matures, the ravine will likely hold oak, hickory, elm, and sycamore.

Just across the bridge, turn right to return to the trailhead.

CEDARS OF LEBANON STATE PARK

On the trails at Cedars of Lebanon, you'll experience an ever-changing environment of eerie rock formations, disappearing streams, sinks, caves, oak-hickory forests, cedar woods, and cedar glades, which are rocky openings with plant communities like no others on earth. The combined state park/forest/natural area preserves samples of the cedar glades unique to Middle Tennessee.

The vast stands of big cedars that once covered parts of the Central Basin so impressed pioneer settlers that when they needed a name for the seat of newly created Wilson County in 1801, they chose Lebanon, after the biblical cedars of Lebanon. For the next 100 years, local residents cut cedars for cabins, shingles, fences, and furniture, yet the forest remained intact. Large-scale commercial harvesting ended that. Red cedar makes good pencils, and Middle Tennessee became a pencil-manufacturing center. Logging was widespread and wasteful. By 1910, the vast cedar forests were just about gone.

Because crops won't grow in the rocky cedar glades, most people considered them wasteland and treated them as such. That has changed now, thanks largely to the work of two scientists separated by several generations.

Dr. Augustin Gattinger was a German-born physician and botanist who immigrated to Tennessee in 1849. During the Civil War, his Northern sympathies prompted a move to Union-occupied Nashville, where military governor Andrew Johnson appointed him state librarian. Gattinger spent the rest of his life studying the plants of Tennessee and was among the first to recognize the unique life of the cedar glades. Several cedar-glade plants bear his name.

Starting with her 1948 dissertation at Duke University, "Plant Communities of Cedar Glades of Middle Tennessee," biologist Elsie Quarterman of Vanderbilt University studied, wrote about, and talked about the glades for nearly half a century. Her unyielding devotion to the glades contributed to their preservation at Cedars of Lebanon and elsewhere. Cedar glades are now protected at scattered sites in Davidson, Rutherford, and Wilson Counties, some of which were acquired with the help of the Nature Conservancy. Private landowners, too, are starting to recognize the value of the glades and protect those on their property.

Middle Tennessee's cedar glades are home to three federally listed endangered species: Tennessee coneflower, Guthrie's ground plumb, and leafy prairie clover. Thirty-three state-listed rare plants are associated with the cedar glades.

Cedars of Lebanon Park and Forest was created by a New Deal conservation and public-works program, the Lebanon Cedar Forest Project. The idea was to convert submarginal lands from agriculture to other uses—in this case, reforestation and recreation. The project got under way in 1935 and was largely completed within two years. Local men hired by the Works Progress Administration constructed roads, buildings, and picnic areas and planted 792,000 cedars in the badly eroded land. The federal

Cedar glades on the Hidden Springs Trail harbor plants
unique to Middle Tennessee.

government leased the area to the state of Tennessee in 1939
and gave the state absolute ownership in 1955.

The state forest now takes up 6,943 acres, the park 831 acres,
and the natural area 1,043 acres. In 1977, the United States Department of the Interior designated the natural area a National
Natural Landmark. One way to learn more about the cedar glades
is to participate in the park's annual wildflower pilgrimage, held
in April. The pilgrimage features faculty members from local in-
stitutions who are experts on the cedar-glade environment.

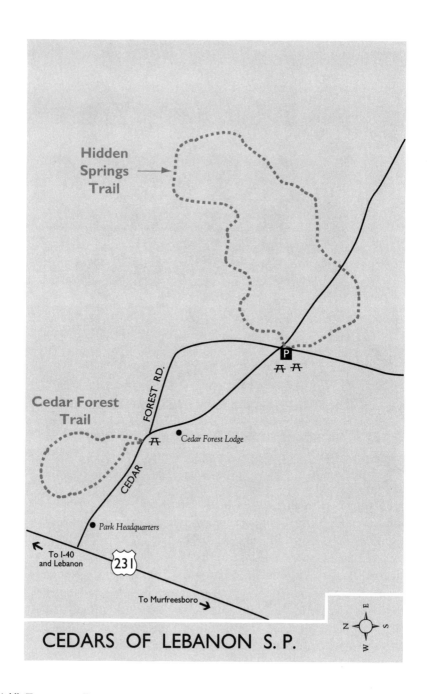

Hidden
Springs
Trail →

FOREST RD.

Cedar Forest
Trail

⛉ Cedar Forest Lodge

CEDAR

⛉ Park Headquarters

← To I-40
and Lebanon

231

To Murfreesboro →

CEDARS OF LEBANON S. P.

N E S W

HIDDEN SPRINGS TRAIL

Highlights
Sinks, caves, rock formations, cedar forest and glades, wildflowers

Length
4.4-mile loop

Maps
CLSP&F trail map; USGS: Vine

Use
Hiking and day use only

Trailhead
The trailhead is just off Cedar Forest Road 2 miles inside the park. After tuning into the park off US 231 south of Lebanon, follow Cedar Forest Road 1.9 miles to a fork. Take the right fork. The trail starts on the left across from a picnic area.

Hike Description
Hikers on the Hidden Springs Trail experience an environment unlike any other in the United States. The trail passes deep sinks and caves, threads its way through limestone rock gardens and cedar glades, and goes into forests of cedars and hardwoods.

Winter is a good time to take this walk. The absence of green underbrush highlights the green moss on the rocks and enables you to get a better look at the rock formations. But spring and summer are good times, too, because of the wildflowers. You can see spring flowers common to Middle Tennessee's woods: cutleaf toothwort, rue anemone, giant chickweed, toadshade, spring beauty, May apple, false garlic, violet, and Solomon's-seal, to name only a few. Giant chickweed is known by other names: starweed, winterweed, and birdseed. It has starlike flowers and begins growing as winter turns to spring. Its seeds are eaten by several species of birds. Solomon's-seal is named for the biblical king

Solomon of Israel, who was noted for his wisdom. The rootstock of the flower has scars that are shaped like a signet, used as a royal seal. As the story goes, it was Solomon who placed his seal of approval on the plant.

Along this hike, you can also see flowers that stick to rocky, open areas like the cedar glades: rose verbena, star grass, hoary puccoon, Nashville breadroot, and others. And you'll see flowers endemic to the cedar glades, like Tennessee coneflower, white or yellow glade-cress, pale yellow Tennessee milk vetch, glade violets, and white-flowered sandwort. The glades are ablaze in summer with Spanish bayonet, Gattinger's lobelia, glade larkspur, Gattinger's prairie clover, and lots and lots of daisies.

From the road, a path leads a few feet into the woods to the sign announcing the beginning of the loop trail. Take the left fork to hike the trail clockwise.

After a short walk among hardwoods dominated by hickory and maple, the trail crosses Cedar Forest Road and passes to the right of the first of many sinks. At times, the route of the Hidden Springs Trail can be confusing because there are so many paths leading to sinks and caves. Stay alert to the directions.

One of the challenges of the trail is identifying the six different plant zones you'll hike through. They range from exposed rock where no plants grow to hardwood forests dominated by oak and hickory. Between the two extremes are cedar woods, shrubs, grassy glades, and gravelly glades. The depth of the soil is the primary factor that determines these plant zones.

At 0.2 mile, you'll come to a path that leads left to the 0.5-mile Limestone Sinks Self-Guided Nature Trail. Stay to the right on the Hidden Springs Trail, which travels through shallow, rocky soil. At 0.3 mile, you'll reach another path leading to the Limestone Sinks Self-Guided Nature Trail. Go left to see the big oak located 60 feet down this side path.

The huge bulge on the tree is an oak gall. Strange as it seems, oak galls are caused by insects. Insects often lay their eggs inside the tissue of plants, and galls develop as the eggs hatch into larvae.

Return to the Hidden Springs Trail, which now wanders

through an area of large rocks and bright green moss and passes a row of four large sinks.

Geologists gave the name *Lebanon limestone* to thin-bedded rock of the Ordovician age, which occurred from 430 to 500 million years ago. This topography is known as *karst*, after a similar place in Slovenia and Croatia. It's characterized by sinks, caves, springs, disappearing streams, and underground drainage. Sinks are created by the flow of water. Slightly acidic surface water flows through cracks and crevices in the limestone, carrying away soluble material. The cracks and crevices continue to grow until sinks or caves are formed. Sinks usually terminate at the underground water table. There are a total of 18 caves here at Cedars of Lebanon.

From the row of four sinks, continue on the Hidden Springs Trail. At 0.5 mile, the trail rises to higher ground, where there is a noticeable change in the forest. This is a good place to observe a transition between plant zones. You're entering an area where hardwoods prevail over cedars—where the soil is less rocky, deeper, and better at holding moisture.

Where a path leads left to a sink, the trail makes a sharp right turn and descends back into the rocky area. It then comes to a low, moist spot that holds an open forest of large hickory and sugar maple. The Hidden Springs Trail crosses the horse trail and an old road before entering an area covered with bright green moss. It starts to climb, passes a sink guarded by a large oak and sugar maples, then wanders across rough terrain before gradually descending the northern side of the low ridge. The pines you are walking through were planted, as pines are not native to the Central Basin. Between 1955 and 1966, the state planted 289,600 loblolly pine seedlings at Cedars of Lebanon.

After passing through the pines, the trail enters a large, grassy glade that is covered with flowers much of the year. Look carefully and you'll see that what looks like wasteland is actually alive with all kinds of life.

The trail leaves the glade, crosses a wet-weather stream on a short bridge, then crosses Burnt House Road. It widens through an oak-hickory forest along the park boundary before returning to the rocky cedar woods and turning right to reach an open area of bedrock at 2 miles. The trail then veers left a short distance to the hidden spring for which it is named. A well has been dug to the underground stream, located about 30 feet below the surface.

The trail passes left of the fenced-in spring en route to a rocky streambed that's dry except after heavy rains. Turn right along the streambed. You'll see why there are so few year-round streams in this karst landscape: on the left in the streambed is a deep crevice that robs the stream of its water.

After a short distance in the streambed, the trail leads to the right near a huge, downed oak. Past the creek where the trail makes a sharp right turn is a short path to a huge sink with a cave opening. Openings like these are havens for animals, which take refuge among the layers of rock and in the cave itself. Birds nest in crevices near the entrance. Raccoons and rodents move into and out of the cave. The cave itself is inhabited by gray bats, salamanders, cavefish, and blind cave crayfish. The rare Tennessee cave salamander is found only in a handful of the state's caves.

The trail recrosses Burnt House Road, then meanders through a cedar glade covered with flowers, passes a sink covered with deep moss, reaches another flower-filled glade, crosses an old road at 2.7 miles, then alternates among cedar woods, hardwood forests, and open glades.

Cedar glades are actually minideserts, severe environments subject to extremes of light, temperature, and moisture. Surface temperatures are often 10 to 30 degrees warmer than in the adjoining woods. About 350 species of plants grow in the glades, some of them found nowhere else in the world.

Take time to study each glade and you'll see they're all different. Some are grassy, some gravelly, and some both. Notice, too, the different plants in each glade. Some glades have hardly any flowers and others are ablaze with color. The blue-gray growth is reindeer moss, so named because it comes from the far North.

It's a sun-loving, long-growing lichen that thrives in dry areas, one of the more than 3,600 lichen species in the United States and Canada.

At 3.1 miles, you'll cross an old road before continuing through the forest. The trail breaks into another large, open glade, goes into the cedars, crosses the horse trail, goes through another open glade, and crosses Cedar Forest Road at 3.6 miles. It then curves around a small wetland created by a spring and continues through the cedar forest, which is broken intermittently by stands of large oak and hickory. You will cross the horse trail at 4 miles, then cross it again. After passing through another open glade, you will return to the trailhead.

CEDAR FOREST TRAIL

Highlights
Forest of cedars and hardwoods, interesting rock formations

Length
2-mile loop

Maps
CLSP&F trail map; USGS: Vine

Use
Hiking and day use only

Trailhead
Across Cedar Forest Road from a picnic shelter,
0.8 mile from the US 231 entrance

Hike Description
This forest trail alternates between hardwoods and cedars and crosses the park's highest elevation.

Before beginning the trail, take time to visit the Cedar Forest Lodge and Jackson Cave. They're just down the right fork in the road past the picnic area on the right. The lodge was built in 1937 of native stone and rough-hewn cedar logs in the rustic style promoted by the National Park Service during the New Deal. In 1997, the lodge was renamed for Dick Huddleston, one of the park's first rangers; Huddleston worked here for 42 years. Behind the lodge, two scenic overlooks offer views of the Jackson Cave entrance.

Hike the Cedar Forest Trail counterclockwise. The rocky path climbs away from the road before leveling off behind a housing development adjoining the park. It meanders through a forest dominated by oak and large shagbark hickory, then wanders through some rocks before turning right and cresting the park's highest elevation: 806 feet. The hardwood understory here makes for beautiful colors in the fall.

After descending through a mixed forest and moss-covered areas, the trail reaches a sink at 0.8 mile. This sink looks different from most others in the park. The huge rocks have collapsed inward toward the cave opening at the bottom.

From the sink, the trail goes through a jumble of rocks, then through an oak-maple forest. It passes several sinks and follows a power line for a short distance before turning sharply left. On the mostly level contour of the southern side of the hill, it alternates between rocky cedar woods and hardwoods. At several places, the trail picks its way through large fields of broken boulders.

After a short climb, it reaches an old road that once led to a lookout tower. Turn right and follow the old road down the hill to the trailhead.

LONG HUNTER STATE PARK

Long Hunter State Park protects 2,400 acres of classic inner Central Basin landscape on J. Percy Priest Lake in fast-growing southeastern Nashville-Davidson County. The park's oak-hickory forests, cedar woods, cedar glades, and bluffs are on land the Corps of Engineers took for the lake in the 1960s, then made available to the state for the park.

Long Hunter's diverse environments, its 30 miles of lakeshore, its 20 miles of hiking trails, and its accessibility make it one of Middle Tennessee's outdoor treasures. Good hiking is available on three long trails and several short ones. A popular paved trail circles 2 miles around 110-acre Couchville Lake. Because this trail is barrier-free, it provides a great opportunity for the disabled to enjoy the freedom of being outdoors.

Walking is just one activity at Long Hunter. Visitors also enjoy swimming, fishing, boating, and wildlife viewing. The visitor center houses a display on cedar glades featuring stunning wildflower photography by Byron Jorjorian and Tony Myers. Children will like the wildlife exhibit, and everyone will enjoy the wild-flower garden on the grounds. The park offers all sorts of programs, some tailored for the disabled and the elderly.

The name *Long Hunter* honors people like Uriah Stone, the man for whom the dammed-up river is named. The rich land around today's Nashville was explored and hunted by American colonists for several decades before James Robertson planted a permanent settlement on Christmas 1779. The earliest recorded exploration was made in 1766 by James Smith. Uriah Stone was in his party. Smith's group and those that followed stayed in the Cumberland wilderness for long periods—often for years at a time—which is why they were called long hunters.

These hardy, resourceful men were always on the move, looking for game in the vast, uninhabited forest. While making his way up the Cumberland River from the Great Salt Lick—today's downtown Nashville—Uriah Stone discovered a large tributary. Intrigued by it, he navigated 40 miles upstream to where the river forks, hunting and trapping along the way. That waterway has been called the Stones River ever since.

The lake is named for J. Percy Priest, who represented the Nashville area in Congress in the 1940s and 1950s.

VOLUNTEER AND DAY LOOP TRAILS

Highlights
Sweeping bluff-top views of J. Percy Priest Lake, interesting rock formations, rich oak-hickory forests

Length
4.1-mile loop

Maps
LHSP trail map; USGS: LaVergne

Use

Hiking and day use only

Trailhead

The trailhead is at the Baker's Grove Road park entrance. Baker's Grove Road intersects TN 171 (Hobson Pike) 0.7 mile north of the main park entrance. The park is on TN 171 southeast of Nashville. It can be reached by taking Exit 226 off I-40 or Exit 62 off I-24.

Hike Description

This hike penetrates a mature oak-hickory forest, threads through rocky cedar woods, and crests craggy bluffs above the submerged channel of the Stones River. It follows the Day Loop Trail and part of the longer Volunteer Trail, which leads 6 miles to designated back-country campsites.

From the trailhead, you'll follow an old road through a cedar-hackberry thicket, where you're likely to startle a deer or two. The trail then turns right, enters the old oak-hickory forest, and crests a rise covered with green creeping euonymus.

The vast primeval wilderness that once covered Middle Tennessee is gone, but the forests have made a remarkable recovery at Long Hunter and other places. The canopy of this relatively pristine forest is made up mostly of several kinds of oak—white, shumard, chinquapin, and scarlet—mixed with four types of hickory—shagbark, bitternut, mockernut, and pignut. The understory is mostly dogwood.

All these trees produce "mast," an important component of the diet of wildlife. Oak and hickory produce "hard mast"—nuts, acorns, etc.—and dogwood produces "soft mast"—berries, etc. For squirrels in particular, but also for wild turkeys, ruffed grouse, bobwhite quail, raccoons, and small rodents, oak is the most important mast-producing tree.

The Volunteer Trail leaves the oak-hickory forest and picks its way through a jumble of limestone outcrops to the cedar-covered shore of J. Percy Priest Lake.

Tennessee is the Volunteer State. Just how it got that nickname is unclear. Some say it honors the large number of Tennesseans

Prickly pear amongst the cedars on the Day Loop Trail

TENNESSEE DEPARTMENT OF ENVIRONMENT AND CONSERVATION

who volunteered to fight in the War of 1812. Others say it honors those who volunteered during the Mexican War, which broke out in 1848. There is no uncertainty, though, about how this fine trail got its name. Volunteers—Boy Scouts, mostly—built this and other trails at Long Hunter.

You will come to a junction at 0.6 mile where the Day Loop Trail splits from the Volunteer Trail. Go left on the orange-blazed Day Loop. You'll immediately cross a usually dry steam in a rocky area typical of the karst landscape of the inner Central Basin.

The trail parallels the edge of the lake and passes through a rocky cedar forest that includes patches of green moss and bluish gray reindeer moss. It then turns away from the lake and picks its way through jumbles of bright green, moss-covered rocks that look like giant velvet cushions. After passing some sinks, it abruptly reenters the hardwoods and zigzags back to the shore, offering nice views of the lake and the high bluffs on the opposite bank. The trail then reaches some cedars and cuts through a bed of moss dotted with prickly pear.

The prickly pear is Middle Tennessee's only true cactus. It's found in the cedar forests' dry, rocky areas. This accounts for the

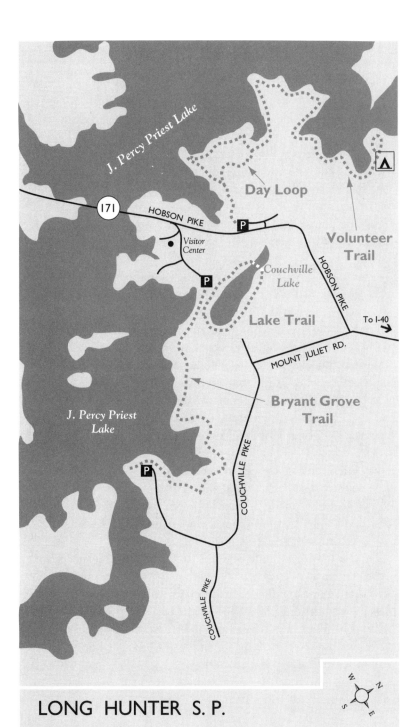

J. Percy Priest Lake

Day Loop

171

HOBSON PIKE

Visitor Center

Couchville Lake

Volunteer Trail

HOBSON PIKE

To I-40

Lake Trail

MOUNT JULIET RD.

J. Percy Priest Lake

Bryant Grove Trail

COUCHVILLE PIKE

COUCHVILLE PIKE

LONG HUNTER S. P.

W N E S

prickly pear's green pads, which help the plants store water. The plant produces beautiful flowers in May and June.

The trail eventually rises through a rugged rock garden, crosses a rocky area with some deep crevices, and comes to a cedar-crested bluff above the lake. From the bluff, you can hear the sound of water lapping against the rocks and see up and down J. Percy Priest Lake. When the weather is clear, the Overton Hills of Radnor Lake State Natural Area are visible on the western horizon. The bluff will give you a sense of the rich diversity of Middle Tennessee's landscape. You are in a craggy inner-basin cedar forest above a large lake, but just a few miles away is the altogether different environment of the green hills of the Highland Rim outliers.

The bluff provides excellent animal habitat. Small openings make good dens for Long Hunter's fox and bobcat populations.

Just because you don't see bobcats doesn't mean they aren't around. Wary, shy, and solitary, they're usually active only after twilight and before dawn. Bobcats are similar in appearance to domestic cats, except that they're larger and are distinguished by the short "bobbed" tails that give them their name. They feed mostly on small animals, rabbits making up over half their normal diet. If you look carefully in mud or snow, you might see their tracks, which look like those of domestic cats, only larger.

The red fox is more abundant in Middle Tennessee today than it was when the first settlers arrived. This cousin to the dog prefers open country mixed with woodlands. Foxes are opportunistic feeders whose diet is made up of whatever they can find, including rats, mice, rabbits, groundhogs, opossums, birds, insects, eggs, fruits, and grasses.

As you leave the bluff, you'll notice that the transition from cedars to hardwoods is so sudden that it looks man-made. The abrupt change is evidence of the major role that soil properties play in determining the composition of a forest. The constant shifting back and forth between these two environments is an intriguing aspect of walking in the inner basin at Long Hunter and at nearby Cedars of Lebanon.

The trail swings back near the lake, curves around a point, and follows a cove through a forest harboring some large oaks. After passing a cave on the right, it leaves the lake, climbs through a splendid grove of shagbark hickory, curves around the head of a rocky ravine, and picks its way through rocks before rejoining the white-blazed Volunteer Trail at 2.7 miles.

Turn right on the Volunteer Trail to return to the trailhead. (Note that the 5-mile walk to the campsites at the end of the Volunteer Trail is a nice one, though. It passes through cedar and hardwood forests and along lakeside bluff tops. Because it's so easy and so accessible, the Volunteer Trail makes a great place to backpack with children.) From the junction, the trail climbs through hardwoods next to a rocky wet-weather steam, crosses the remains of an old stone fence, turns right, and continues its gradual ascent. Near the crest, it goes through a stand of tulip poplars that are all about the same size, a sight more common on the Highland Rim than here in the inner basin.

The trail then curves through an impressive oak-hickory forest. The understory of sugar maple brightens the woods in mid-fall, and the waxy, crimson leaves of scarlet oak stand out against the deep-blue sky of late fall. Next, the trail enters a cedar-hackberry thicket loaded with songbirds and passes a giant oak on the left.

After crossing some mossy bedrock, you will make a rocky descent back into the hardwoods and reach the first Day Loop–Volunteer Trail junction at 3.5 miles. Retrace your steps to the trailhead.

BRYANT GROVE TRAIL

Highlights
Cedar woods and glades, wildflowers, lake views

Length
4 miles one-way

Maps
LHSP trail map; USGS: LaVergne

Use
Hiking and limited bicycling are allowed.
Access is limited to day use only.

Trailhead
From the park entrance on TN 171, follow the road to Couchville
Lake. The trailhead is on the right edge of the parking lot. Bryant
Grove Recreation Area, where the trail ends, can be reached by
turning off TN 171 onto South Mount Juliet Road north of the park
and then following the signs. Note that the park trail map indicates
that the Bryant Grove Trail follows the paved Couchville Lake Trail
for a short distance; in truth, the two trails do not run together.

Hike Description
This is an easy, nearly level walk around the curving shore of
J. Percy Priest Lake and through some fantastic cedar glades and
cedar woods. It's not a loop, so you'll have to run a shuttle or
retrace your steps.

The trail takes off through the woods and soon turns right
onto an old road bordered by beautiful cedars. You'll emerge onto
the lakeshore, where, when the wind is up, you'll hear the
white-capped waves sloshing onto the muddy, denuded layers
of limestone.

Couchville Lake, located adjacent to J. Percy Priest Lake, has
an interesting history. When J. Percy Priest Dam backed up the
Stones River, lake water flowed through underground passages
and filled a depression in the limestone-rich land, creating a second, small lake, which was named for the nearby community.
The level of Couchville Lake always matches that of the main
lake, for J. Percy Priest Lake is the source of Couchville Lake's
water.

The Bryant Grove Trail curves broadly left, passes to the right of a moss-covered layered limestone sink, climbs a gentle grade into hardwoods, and turns left off the old road at 0.6 mile. The gravel trail then passes through a forest dominated by large shagbark hickory. The understory is quite colorful in the fall, thanks to its population of sugar maples. It's also colorful in early spring, when redbuds give the look of a pink cloud hanging beneath the canopy of taller trees. You might be startled by a large black, white, and red bird sweeping from the crown of one tree to another. It's a pileated woodpecker.

After passing an old stone fence on the right, you'll enter an area of moss-covered, velvet-looking rocks and pass an open, grassy cedar glade on the left. The trail then penetrates a tangle of cedars, hardwoods, and shrubs where the ground is covered with mossy rocks and glade privet is the most common shrub. The contrast of winter colors is striking: bright green moss, dark green cedars, tan grass, blue-gray lichen, gray tree trunks. In spring, color is provided by an abundance of wildflowers, including Nashville mustard, buttercups, and toadshade.

After weaving through this jungle, the trail crests a slight elevation before returning to the lake and curving left to follow the shore of a large cove. This sheltered cove is a good place to see some of the 20 species of waterfowl that winter here, as well as resident shorebirds such as the great blue heron, Tennessee's largest nesting bird. You'll see lots of gulls, too. The ring-billed gull is the most common, but others spotted here are the Bonaparte's gull, the laughing gull, the herring gull, and the extremely rare great black-backed gull.

You will cross a wet-weather stream at 2 miles and curve through a grassy cedar glade. The trail turns sharply right and returns to the lake, curving around an inlet past several glades. It crosses Bryant Creek on a bridge at 2.8 miles, then swings right to follow the creek to where it pours into J. Percy Priest Lake. You will pass an open prairie on the left before entering a dark cedar thicket.

At 3.4 miles, you'll come to a huge, gravelly cedar glade that looks like someone has taken a sledgehammer to a concrete parking lot. Glades like this are havens for flowers from March to November. Among the spring flowers here are rose verbena, buttercup, Nashville mustard, Nashville breadroot, and glade phlox. The thickets around the glade provide ideal habitat for birds. You're sure to see and hear lots of them.

The trail goes through a more open forest of cedars mixed with hardwoods, picks its way through a rock garden, and reaches Bryant Grove Recreation Area at 4 miles. The recreation area is located on a point in a big bend of the lake. A short trail leads from the picnic shelter along the bluffs above the river channel to the end of the point.

Sherrod Bryant was a free black man who came to this area from North Carolina before 1840. Through his hard work, he is believed to have become the wealthiest black in Tennessee by 1850. The Bryant Grove community takes its name from him. His descendants still live in the Mount Juliet area.

STONES RIVER
NATIONAL BATTLEFIELD

This unit of the National Park Service preserves a small but important part of the fields and forests fought over in one of the Civil War's greatest battles. That blood-soaked land is now a pleasant green island in Murfreesboro's sea of suburban growth. In the winter—the season of the battle—green cedars color the drab landscape. In the spring, they provide a dark backdrop for splashes of redbud around the edges of the fields. Here, too, you'll find some of the cedar glades that are unique to Middle Tennessee.

A hiking trail skirts the park's perimeter, visiting sites crucial to the outcome of the "Battle in the Cedars," which took place from December 31, 1862, to January 2, 1863. The walk on the 2-mile auto-tour road through the cedars and fields is also popular with people in the fast-growing Murfreesboro area. Another great place to walk is the Stones River Greenway, a 3-mile paved path along the tree-shaded riverbank. This cooperative project of the National Park Service and the local parks department includes battle sites, as well as fortifications the Union army later built to protect its huge Murfreesboro base. The path starts at Old Fort Park off Old Fort Parkway (TN 96) and runs to

McFadden's Ford, the scene of fighting on the second day of the battle. There are access points along the way. Long-range plans call for a spur linking the greenway and the national battlefield.

Christmas 1862 found the two principal Western armies 30 miles apart in Middle Tennessee, the Confederates headquartered at Murfreesboro and the Federals at Nashville. The respective commanders thought they knew each other's intentions. Confederate general Braxton Bragg did not believe the Union's Army of the Cumberland would mount an offensive before spring and had his Army of Tennessee dangerously spread out over a 20-mile front on either side of Murfreesboro. Major General William S. Rosecrans, the Federal commander, believed that if he started an offensive, Bragg's Confederates would retreat south rather than fight. They were both wrong.

Rosecrans launched an offensive on December 26. He divided his army into three parts, sending them southeast from Nashville by different routes. When the surprised Bragg realized what Rosecrans was up to, he concentrated his troops along the western fork of the Stones River. Rosecrans, too, realized the danger of a fragmented army. When he brought his three wings together near Murfreesboro, a fight was inevitable.

Bragg's Confederates assumed a defensive position and waited for a Federal attack. When it didn't come on December 30, Bragg decided to launch his own strike. At dawn on December 31, the Confederate left struck the Union right in the vicinity of where TN 96 crosses I-24 today. Bragg's plan was to push the Federals across the Nashville Pike and the Nashville & Chattanooga Railroad, severing their line of supply and retreat.

Bragg's plan worked, at least at first. The Confederates wheeled the disorganized Federals close to the Nashville Pike. The rocky terrain and dense cedar forests made it difficult for the Southerners to maintain their momentum, however. They were exhausted, and the attack faltered. The Federals rallied and made a stand. When darkness fell over the bloody ground on New Year's Eve, the armies faced each other near the Nashville Pike.

Bragg wired Confederate president Jefferson Davis that his

troops had won a glorious victory. Indeed they had, to that point. But the battle was not finished.

Thinking the Federals would retreat, Bragg kept his army in place the next day. But he misjudged Rosecrans. The Ohio engineer decided to dig in and make a stand. The Army of the Cumberland didn't budge on New Year's Day. On January 2, Bragg decided to try something different. He threw his right flank against the Union left near McFadden's Ford. This turned out to be a suicide mission. The Federals occupied the high ground along the river and used their ample artillery to repulse the Confederate charges.

Now it was Bragg who was in a difficult position. The Stones River was rising from heavy rain, which increased the risk that his men would be trapped between the river and Rosecrans's army. Bragg received reports—erroneous reports, it turned out—that heavy Federal reinforcements were arriving from Nashville. Bragg, who had 34,000 troops, already thought Rosecrans had 70,000 men. In truth, the Federal commander had 44,000. Acting on the false information, Bragg decided to retreat. Near midnight on January 3, the soldiers of the Army of Tennessee marched south in a cold winter rain from what they thought was a victory.

The suffering at Murfreesboro was staggering. The Federals lost 1,636 killed, 7,397 wounded, and 3,673 captured, a casualty rate of 29 percent. For the Confederates, it was 1,236 killed, 7,766 wounded, and 868 captured, a casualty rate of 25 percent.

The Battle of Stones River was not a clear-cut win for either side. But in time, it proved to be an important victory for the North. Since the Confederates retreated south to the Tullahoma area, the huge Federal base at occupied Nashville was secure. The real victory, though, was political. The war hadn't been going well for the North. War-weariness was setting in. The victory helped shift public sentiment toward continuing the conflict.

Incidentally, you might see historical makers entitled "Battle of Murfreesboro." No, there were not two battles. The Union and the Confederacy gave different names to many battles. The Confederates tended to name battles after the town that served as their base. The Federals generally favored a landmark—often a river or stream—on their side of the line. Hence, what the Confederates called the Battle of Manassas the Federals called Bull Run, after a creek. The Confederates' Sharpsburg was the Federals' Antietam, also after a creek. Shiloh was Pittsburg Landing in the North. When the state of Tennessee erected historical markers here, it used the Southern *Murfreesboro* rather than *Stones River*. In naming national battlefields, the National Park Service uses the Northern version in some instances—as here at Stones River—and the Southern version in others—as at Manassas and Shiloh.

STONES RIVER BATTLEFIELD TRAIL

Highlights
Important battle sites, the nation's oldest Civil War monument, cedar forest and glades

Length
3.8-mile loop

Maps
SRNB trail map; USGS: Murfreesboro and Walterhill

Use
Hiking and day use only

Trailhead
The trailhead is across from the visitor center by the picnic tables, just north of the Chicago Board of Trade artillery battery. The entrance to the national battlefield is northwest of Murfreesboro off US 41/US 70S. It can also be reached from Thompson Lane, which intersects TN 96 in the commercial strip just east of the I-24 interchange.

Hike Description

The trail follows the perimeter of the park through hardwood and cedar forests, past cedar glades, through open fields, and to the national cemetery. Though it has no official name, some old maps call it the "Five Mile Trail."

After entering a grove of large cedars, the trail makes a sharp left turn to follow the park boundary south. A marker notes the location of a Federal infantry trench, the only Union fortification remaining from the battle. After the Confederate advance faltered on the first day, the Federals dug earthen fortifications on this high ground as protection from the attack they were sure would come the next day. But the Confederates didn't attack on New Year's Day. On January 2, the fighting shifted north to McFadden's Ford on the Stones River.

The trail continues along the boundary through a forest dominated by cedar and hackberry. If you're here in the spring, keep an eye out for wildflowers, particularly spring beauty, rue anemone, phlox, and Nashville breadroot.

At 0.4 mile, you'll reach a trail junction. Follow the path to the left a short distance through a cedar forest and a rock garden to the road and the auto tour's second stop. A marker describes the Confederates' impossible task of fighting through these thick cedars during action that took place between 10 A.M. and 11 A.M. on the first day of the battle. After driving the Federals back nearly 3 miles, the Confederate advance stalled here.

Return to the trail junction and continue along the boundary. After 300 feet, you'll reach another junction. The path to the left leads through patches of bright green moss, through a rock garden, and past a cedar glade to the park road. Continue on the trail along the boundary as it curves past a concrete marker and passes through classic Middle Tennessee cedar-glade country.

The trail turns right and wanders south, then east, then south again before reaching a cannon sitting alone in the woods. This is where Captain David D. Waters of Mobile parked his Alabama battery after a day of supporting the infantry as it wheeled the Federals toward the Nashville Pike. The path to the left leads to the road.

Federal artillery along the Stones River Battlefield Trail

The trail continues south along the park boundary, passes a grove of large shagbark hickory, returns to the cedars, and reaches the southern park boundary at 1.3 miles. A sign announces the location of the Blanton log house. A pile of limestone rocks that made up the foundation is all that remains of the house, which stood during the Civil War.

The trail meanders east through an area invaded by privet, then passes among intermittent cedars and hardwoods before reaching some rugged limestone outcrops and two abandoned guns at 1.8 miles. A marker points out the difficulty of moving artillery over this rough terrain and notes that the Federals abandoned guns as they retreated.

One of the most important parts of the battle—the stand of Brigadier General Philip H. Sheridan's division—occurred in this area. Most of the divisions on the Union right were unprepared for the Confederate attack at dawn on December 31, but not Sheridan's. His men held firm during the early phase of the Confederate advance and retreated to this point only when the front to their right collapsed. By holding off successive waves of advancing Confederates, Sheridan gave the rest of the Army of

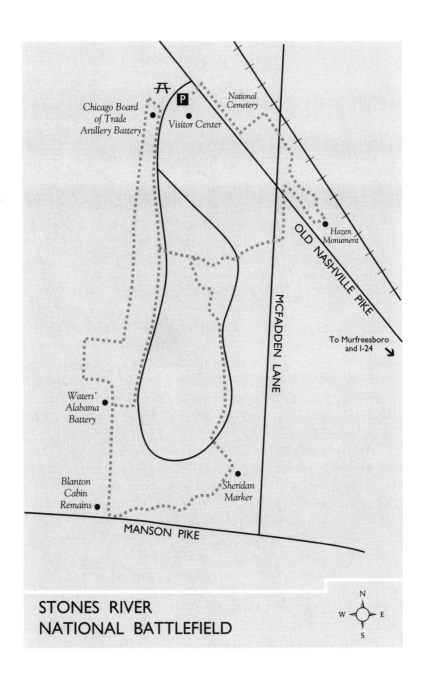

STONES RIVER
NATIONAL BATTLEFIELD

Chicago Board
of Trade
Artillery Battery

P
Visitor Center

National
Cemetery

Hazen
Monument

OLD NASHVILLE PIKE

To Murfreesboro
and I-24

MCFADDEN LANE

Waters'
Alabama
Battery

Blanton
Cabin
Remains

Sheridan
Marker

MANSON PIKE

N
W — E
S

the Cumberland valuable time to assume more secure positions closer to the Nashville Pike. Eventually, Sheridan was forced to fall back nearer to the road. The fighting here was so intense that the area came to be called the "Slaughter Pens."

Sheridan emerged from the Civil War a hero in the North, his stature right behind that of Ulysses S. Grant and William Tecumseh Sherman. He remained in the army after the war and became its commanding general in 1884.

From the abandoned guns, the trail follows a paved path out of the woods to a parking area and a historical marker erected by the state of Michigan in honor of its soldiers who fought at Stones River. This is a good place to see several wildflowers that have adapted to the mowed fields. Hugging the ground are grape hyacinth, purple dead nettle, bluets, dandelions, and several types of violets, including the tiny field pansy.

The trail follows the paved road to the right as it enters the cedars and comes to stop five on the auto tour at 2.2 miles. It then leaves the road and veers left into the woods. When you reach a fork, bear left. Before long, you'll come to a **T** junction on the edge of a field bordered by a split-rail fence. Turn right.

By leasing this land to farmers, the National Park Service keeps the fields open, just as they were in 1862. This was a cotton field back then.

When the advancing Confederates managed to get through the woods to the edge of this field, their goal was in sight: the Nashville Pike and the railroad are across the fields to the right. But this is as far as they got. One Federal division commander told a brigade commander to hold his line "until hell froze over," and that's exactly what the Union men did. They formed in a stronger position near the road and—aided by the killing fire from two regular-army artillery batteries and the Chicago Board of Trade Battery—repulsed the Confederates.

One of the Confederates killed here was James E. Rains of Nashville. The death of this citizen-soldier was typical of the many thousands of tragedies in the great American conflict. At age 21, Rains had finished Yale Law School and begun a law practice in Nashville. He had been elected city attorney in 1858 and district attorney for Davidson, Sumner, and Williamson Counties in 1860. When war broke out, he enlisted as a private in the 11th Tennessee Infantry. It was common on both sides for units to elect officers, and Rains was elected colonel. He commanded a brigade here at Stones River. The death of this 29-year-old deprived Middle Tennessee of a man who was sure to have been a leader in the traumatic postwar period.

The trail goes to the right along the edge of the field. This was the scene of indescribable misery as dying and wounded men littered the no man's land between the lines on New Year's Eve 1862, which remains the bloodiest day in Tennessee history.

At another **T** junction, go left along the fence, then curve right and cross the park road. The guns to the left represent the positions of the Federal artillery that helped stop the Confederate advance.

Across the road, the trail enters a field and crosses McFadden Lane. It follows the lane, then crosses the Old Nashville Highway—known as the Nashville Pike in 1862. It's a busy thoroughfare now, so be careful. A tollhouse located here served briefly as the headquarters of Major General Thomas B. Crittenden, the Kentuckian who commanded one of the three wings of the Army of the Cumberland.

Across the Old Nashville Highway, turn right and walk to the parking area. Follow the paved sidewalk to the left past some huge trees to the Hazen Monument.

Some of the battle's fiercest fighting took place here, around a clump of trees called the "Round Forest." While the Union line west of here swung around like a door, this part of the line—the door hinge—stood firm against a succession of Confederate attacks. "Hell's Half Acre," it was also called.

The brigade of Colonel William B. Hazen was one of the Federal units that held this spot. After the battle, while Union troops occupied Murfreesboro, Hazen's brigade built this stone memorial. Completed in 1863, it is believed to be the nation's oldest Civil War monument. Plaques erected by the park service give the text of the faint inscriptions on each side of the sturdy masonry. The remains of 35 soldiers are buried within the enclosure.

When you leave the enclosure, turn right and walk parallel to the railroad through a transitional forest to McFadden Lane. This, too, is a public road, so be careful crossing it.

The battle at Murfreesboro began nearly two years of fighting along the railroad linking Nashville to Atlanta by way of Chattanooga, a lifeline for both armies. Although the war in the East got more attention at the time—and has ever since—many historians believe that the outcome of the Civil War was decided along the railroad in Tennessee and Georgia, rather than in Virginia. Stones River, Chickamauga, Lookout Mountain, Missionary Ridge, Resaca, Kennesaw Mountain, Peachtree Creek, and Atlanta were all battles fought on or near this railroad.

The line through here, the Nashville & Chattanooga, was Tennessee's first successful railroad. Thru trains began running between the two Tennessee towns in 1854. Part of the CSX system today, it is still an important line.

A marker along the railroad notes the spot where Lieutenant Colonel Julius P. Garesche—Rosecrans's chief of staff—fell. The general and his staff made conspicuous targets as they rode along the front urging the men to resist the Confederate thrust. A shot took off Garesche's head. His horse ran another 50 feet before the officer's headless body fell to the ground.

After crossing the lane, follow the edge of the field next to the railroad to the rock wall enclosing the national cemetery. Walk left along the wall, which will return you to the Old Nashville Highway. Turn right, then turn into the cemetery entrance.

This cemetery was set aside in 1865 as a burial ground for Union soldiers who died at Stones River and other places in Middle Tennessee. It's still an active cemetery where veterans are buried.

Follow the Old Nashville Highway past some large trees inside the cemetery wall. Leave the cemetery through the gate and cross the highway to return to the visitor center.

BLEDSOE CREEK STATE PARK

This small park on Old Hickory Lake's Bledsoe Creek embayment offers a variety of habitats, among them the lakeshore and a hardwood forest. The shore is a good place for viewing waterfowl, particularly during migration season, and the forest offers a fine display of wildflowers. You can enjoy the park on a 4-mile trail network that runs along the edge of the lake and through the upland forest.

The naming of Bledsoe Creek dates to Middle Tennessee's earliest recorded history. Brothers Anthony and Isaac Bledsoe were leaders of the Cumberland settlements. Each had a fort, or "station," near here. Isaac was one of the Virginia long hunters who arrived along the Cumberland River in 1771, then returned in 1772 to camp along the creek that is still called Station Camp Creek today. (For more about the creek, see the Station Camp Walk, pages 310–12.) Other tributaries of the Cumberland also got their names from that 1772 expedition. Mansker Creek was named for Kasper Mansker and Drakes Creek for Joseph Drake. Bledsoe Creek was named for Isaac Bledsoe.

In 1784, Isaac Bledsoe built a fort near today's village of Castalian Springs. Anthony Bledsoe then followed his younger brother to the Cumberland settlements, built his station—called Greenfield—a few miles north of Isaac's, and quickly became one of the area's most prominent leaders before Tennessee's statehood. He served in the North Carolina Senate and was one of the founders of Davidson Academy, which eventually became Peabody College, now part of Vanderbilt University.

From the time the first settlers arrived in the Cumberland country in 1779 until Tennessee's statehood in 1796, the scattered settlements were under the constant threat of Indian attack from the south. Anthony Bledsoe and his family took refuge in Isaac's fort during one such attack in 1788. A ball from an Indian's musket killed Anthony. The Indians killed Isaac, too, in 1793. The site of Isaac's fort is now Bledsoe's Fort Historic Park.

Zieglers Fort Road, which leads to Bledsoe Creek State Park, is another reminder of the fierce Indian attacks. In a 1792 attack on Ziegler's Station, Jacob Ziegler and four others were killed, four settlers were wounded, and 18 were taken prisoner. Militia led by General James Winchester pursued the attackers and prisoners past a big spring where Lebanon's public square is today. But they discontinued the pursuit for fear of harming the prisoners in a fight. All the prisoners were eventually freed, though one child, Sarah Wilson, remained with the Creek tribe for many years.

SHORELINE, HIGH RIDGE, BIG OAK, AND BIRDSONG TRAILS

Highlights
Wildlife observation points on Old Hickory Lake, diverse forest

Length
3.1-mile loop

Maps
BCSP trails; USGS: Bethpage, Hunters Point

Use
Hiking and day use only

Trailhead
The trailhead is in the park's picnic area. From TN 25 east of Gallatin, turn south onto Zieglers Fort Road and drive to the park entrance. Go 0.4 mile on the park road, then turn right on Raccoon Creek Road into the picnic area. Go to the end of the road. The Shoreline Trail enters the woods at the wildlife observation area on the lakeshore.

Hike Description
This hike follows the Shoreline Trail along Old Hickory Lake past several wildlife observation areas, then circles back on the High Ridge, Big Oak, and Birdsong Trails.

It starts on a quiet, shallow backwater of the lake, where a bench provides a nice place to observe Canada geese, mallards, great blue herons, and black-crowned night herons, all of which are common here. Bald eagles and osprey are occasionally seen here, too. Keep an eye out for big turtles sunning on logs.

Follow the Shoreline Trail to the left into a mixed forest of large cedars and small hardwoods. In summer, you'll find the low, creeping wildflower called heal-all here. As its name might lead

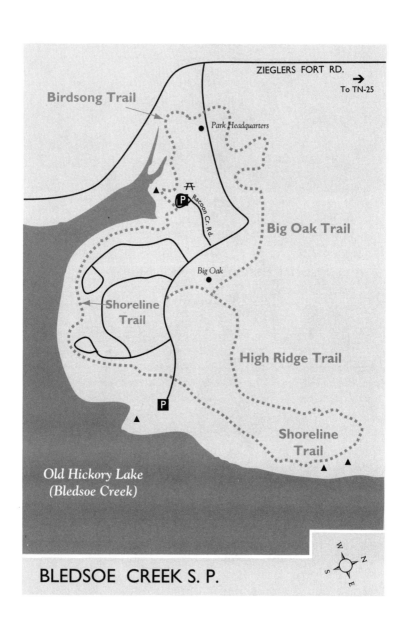

Birdsong Trail

ZIEGLERS FORT RD.

To TN-25

Park Headquarters

Big Oak Trail

Racoon Cr. Rd.

P

Big Oak

Shoreline
Trail

High Ridge Trail

P

Shoreline
Trail

Old Hickory Lake
(Bledsoe Creek)

BLEDSOE CREEK S. P.

W N S E

you to expect, this flower was once used in medicines, particularly for diseases of the mouth. Take a close look and you'll see that the small opening between the flower's upper and lower petals resembles a mouth.

The trail soon turns left at a small inlet. It turns sharply right where a path from the picnic area comes in, then crosses a seasonal stream on rocks at the head of the inlet and continues along the lakeshore. It skirts the campground and passes a playground, staying close to the edge of the lake.

At 0.5 mile, the trail reaches the main body of the Bledsoe Creek embayment and turns left to follow its western shore. After going through a power-line cut, it reaches a boat landing. A designated wildlife observation spot is located here—a handicapped-accessible pier jutting into the lake.

Walk up the hill to the corner of the parking lot. The trail reenters the woods on the right.

The Shoreline Trail passes farther from the lake now as it follows an old road through a grove of large cedar trees before angling closer to the shore. The stone fence on the left serves as a reminder that this was once cleared farmland. The trail wanders along the flat area next to the lake, crosses a gully, and climbs to the top of a bluff that offers fine views up Bledsoe Creek.

From the overlook, the trail follows the contour of the steep ridge above the lake through a lovely hardwood forest dominated by sugar maple, hickory, and oak. It then drops back to the lake before reaching another wildlife observation point at 1.3 miles.

If you look up the lake, you might see some big white birds wading in the shallows. Great egrets are making a comeback here, thanks to the removal of pesticides. They like to wade in marshes and shallow bays, where they feed on fish. Great egrets migrate north into Middle Tennessee in March and depart by late November. They are usually seen in the largest numbers in August and September.

The trail leaves the lake and climbs steeply up the ridge to a rock outcrop. When there is no foliage, you can look up Bledsoe Creek from points along the trail between the lake and the rock outcrop and catch a glimpse of Cragfont, the magnificent stone house completed in 1800 by General James Winchester.

After serving as an officer in George Washington's army during the American Revolution, Winchester came to the Cumberland country in 1787 and quickly became one of the most influential men on the frontier. He was a founder of Cairo, a once-important river port just south of the state park. With Andrew Jackson and John Overton, he also founded Memphis.

In 1798, Winchester set out to build the finest house on the Cumberland frontier. He selected a site on a bluff high above Bledsoe Creek and brought stone masons, carpenters, and joiners 600 miles through the wilderness from his native Maryland. Cragfont still stands in excellent condition. A state historic site open to the public, it can be reached off TN 25 just east of where it crosses Bledsoe Creek.

From the rock outcrop, the trail makes a rough descent through a cedar thicket, recrosses the gully, and climbs again. At 1.5 miles, it reaches what appears to be a **T** junction. But the trail coming

Cragfront, atop a Bledsoe Creek bluff, is worth a side trip from the state park.

in from the right is just an alternate climb up the hill. Turn left here; if you came up the alternate path, go straight.

The route continues to be a bit confusing. Originally, the Shoreline Trail dropped off the ridge and formed a loop, and the High Ridge Trail climbed the ridge from that point. But the Shoreline Trail's descent has been closed, and a new trail has been blazed across the ridge to join the High Ridge Trail. The Shoreline Trail's descent toward the lake and the High Ridge Trail's climb from the lake have been eliminated. The map on the front of the park office shows these changes, but some of the park's trail maps don't.

The old route to the lakeshore leaves the trail less than 100 feet from the **T** junction. There, the new trail veers right and stays on the side of the ridge, running parallel to an old stone fence. It's an easy walk along the ridge. Where the trail veers right at 1.7 miles in an open oak grove, the old trail comes in from the left.

The High Ridge Trail gradually descends through an area where walkers often come upon browsing deer. The mixture of field and forest here is perfect for edge-loving deer. If you look closely, you'll see deer paths running through the woods.

At 2 miles, the High Ridge Trail ends at a junction with the Big Oak Trail just short of the park road. Turn right on the Big Oak Trail. You will soon pass the massive oak that gives this trail its name. If you're here in the spring, don't be surprised to see wild turkeys picking their way through the forest.

The trail meanders along the base of the ridge and crosses a wet-weather stream. In summer, you'll see a nice blue display of tall bellflowers here. After crossing another stream, the trail climbs to the top of a hill in a cedar grove, then descends to a trail junction near the road at 2.5 miles. Continue straight on the Big Oak Trail as it swings away from the road among cedars infested with bamboo grass. After several curves, the Big Oak Trail ends at the road just inside the park.

Cross the road onto the paved Birdsong Trail. After less than 300 feet, angle off the pavement onto the trail that leads right.

The trail reaches a creek and follows it toward the lake. In spring, this bottom is dotted with wildflowers like spring beauty, phlox, and violets.

The trail swings away from the creek, passing between an inlet and a ball field on the left. Take the steps up to the ball field, turn right, and skirt the field to reach the parking lot. If you turn right and walk a short distance, you'll be where you started your hike.

CORDELL HULL LAKE

This narrow, winding, 72-mile-long reservoir squeezed between steep hills retains the flavor of the Cumberland River. The lands acquired for the lake are devoted to many public uses: a wildlife refuge, a waterfowl refuge, a wildlife management area, a county park, and eight recreation areas.

The magnificent Bearwaller Gap Trail follows the outside of giant Horseshoe Bend between Tater Knob Overlook and Defeated Creek Recreation Area. The trail's location—where the Central Basin's lowlands merge with broken pieces of the Highland Rim—makes for an ecologically rich transition forest and abundant wildlife. And the views from the bluffs towering over the bend are among the most dramatic in the Central Basin.

Cordell Hull was born in a log house in Pickett County but later moved with his family to Carthage, where his father prospered in the lumber business. Hull studied law at Cumberland Law School in Lebanon and practiced in several Upper Cumberland towns before heading for Washington and a 21-year career in Congress. Though he served as a member of the United States House of Representatives, as a senator, and as secretary of state under President Franklin D. Roosevelt, Hull never forgot his Upper Cumberland roots. Honored as the father of the United Nations and as a Nobel Peace Prize recipient, he remained until his death in 1953 a modest man, always proud of his Middle Tennessee heritage.

Completed near Carthage in 1973, Cordell Hull Dam was the last big dam the Corps of Engineers built on the Cumberland River.

BEARWALLER GAP TRAIL

Highlights
Panoramic bluff-top views, cascading streams, diverse forests, abundant wildlife

Length
5.7 miles one-way

Maps
BWG hiking trail; USGS: Carthage

Use
The trail is for hiking only. Camping is allowed at a designated campsite.

Trailhead
The trailhead is at Tater Knob Overlook, located off TN 263; the overlook is 3.6 miles north of the TN 25/TN 263 junction in Carthage. The trail ends at Defeated Creek Recreation Area, off TN 85 north of Carthage. To reach the trail's terminus from Tater Knob, continue on TN 263 to TN 85, turn right, and go 2.1 miles to the recreation-area entrance. The end of the trail is on the right after 1.4 miles.

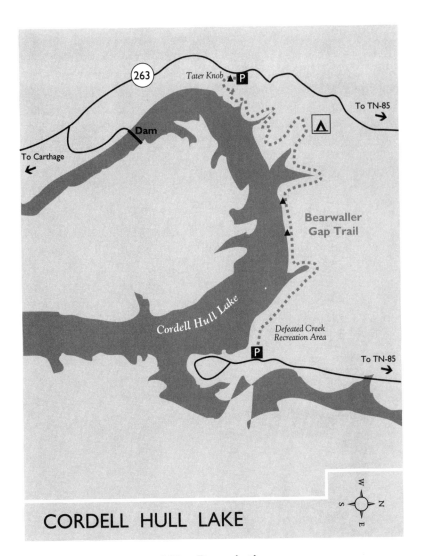

CORDELL HULL LAKE

Hike Description

This dramatic trail is strenuous in places as it climbs to the tops of bluffs high above Cordell Hull Lake. The endless parade of small, wet-weather waterfalls and the abundance of seasonal waterfowl make this a good winter hike, but it's nice in early spring, too, thanks to the variety of wildflowers.

From Tater Knob Overlook, the trail descends through cedar-dotted shallow soil, passes among hardwoods, and returns to the scruffy cedar woods before crossing a fern-covered ravine and passing a bed of club moss.

The grapefruit-size balls you'll see on the ground are the fruit of the Osage orange tree. Because it's often used for hedge plantings, the tree is also called hedge apple. Its durable wood was used by Indians for bows, which accounts for its other common names: bowdock and bowdark.

At 0.4 mile, you'll come to a wet-weather stream. Turn left and follow the bluff above the Cumberland River impoundment. After some nearly level walking through a wooded area of oak, tulip poplar, beech, locust, and dogwood, you'll climb over the top of a cedar-capped bluff that offers views of the dam off to the right. Turkey vultures and black vultures often roost on this bluff.

The trail swings around an inlet above a deep, damp ravine lined with layers of mossy, velvet-looking limestone and returns to the bluffs above the lake. It then makes a sharp right next to a sugar maple and follows an old road around a cove and through a bed of ivy below rock ledges.

The start of Bearwaller Gap Trail overlooks Cordell Hull Dam.

The trail veers right off the old road at 1.3 miles and picks its way through a rocky, north-facing slope covered with beech and ironwood. As you round a bend, you'll see a waterfall, then another, then another, and on and on. The creek tumbles off the ridge and makes more than a dozen falls over layers of limestone.

You will then curve around the cove, cross the creek, and climb through a mixed forest of cedars and hardwoods among layers of rock until you reach a narrow, cedar- and oak-covered ridge spine. The trail descends, turns left, and passes some stacks of rocks left from when this land was cleared for farming. It then runs inland along the narrow spine. You will come to a junction at 2.3 miles. Follow the old road down the hill to the right.

After the road makes a curving descent into the head of Martin Hollow, it comes to the designated campsite, set in an open area beneath tulip poplars. Picnic tables, metal grills, a spring, and an outhouse are provided. This and other areas along the trail benefit from regular maintenance by several Boy Scout troops.

The trail leaves the campsite and goes through a cedar thicket where the ground is covered with moss and lichen and where, after a big rain, water seeps out of the hill in a number of impromptu springs. It then follows a stone fence before making a rocky descent into Twin Prong Cove. The trail runs upstream into Ashhopper Hollow, turns sharply right, crosses the creek, passes a brier patch and a canebrake, reenters the woods, crosses a series of gullies, and curves around the point to run along the main part of the lake. It then begins its climb through the oaks to a rock outcrop from which you can look downstream and see the route you have walked from Tater Knob. The rocks here are loaded with fossils.

In a sensational but difficult stretch, the trail makes a steep, rocky climb between oaks on the left and cedars on the right and crests the bluff at 3.7 miles. You can take in the entire sweep of Horseshoe Bend from this spectacular, 300-foot-high overlook.

The area where you're standing and the lowlands across the lake are part of the Cordell Hull Wildlife Management Area, owned by the Corps of Engineers but managed by the Tennessee Wildlife Resources Agency. The Defeated Creek embayment—where this hike ends—is a waterfowl refuge.

Ducks seen here between October and May include the bafflehead, the canvasback, and the greater scaup. The Canada goose is a year-round resident. You may glimpse an osprey in the spring, and you're sure to see a great blue heron most any time. The osprey is a large, water-loving, eaglelike hawk noted for the way it hovers on beating wings before plunging feet-first for a fish. Its keen eyesight enables it to spot fish from 100 or more feet above the water. Nesting bald eagles are found on Defeated Creek.

Between the 1820s and the 1920s, this stretch of the Cumberland River was an important commercial route. Railroads were late in penetrating the remote Upper Cumberland. Until the highway construction boom of the 1920s, steamboats were the main source of transportation. This is where Captain Tom Ryman, the man for whom Nashville's Ryman Auditorium is named, made his fortune.

Standing on this bluff around 1900, you would have seen huge collections of logs floating downriver. "Rafting" was the method used to get the vast Upper Cumberland timber harvest to Nashville's two dozen sawmills. The industry started in the 1870s and lasted well into the 20th century, until most of the merchantable timber had been harvested.

As the trail descends steeply on a narrow backbone between a deep hollow on the left and a sheer drop to the lake on the right, you'll see a gap to the left where an old road runs. When settlers came to the Cumberland country in the late 1700s, they found cool, shady places like this where bears liked to "waller." That is how this trail got its name.

The descent grows steeper and the trees smaller as the narrow backbone starts to give out. You will pass a rock outcrop and pick your way through a rock garden. Follow the trail as it turns left up a cove in the lake. At 4.2 miles, you will come to a junction in a recovering field. Go left.

The trail enters a mowed area and passes a spring and a waterfall on the left, just up the hill from a willow tree. Take a look at the base of the tree and you'll see that a beaver has chewed through about half of it. This is a delightful place to stop and rest. Looking past the dark cedars out into the main channel, you'll see bright green pastures sweeping up to the forested hilltops.

Past the head of the cove, the route can be a little confusing, as there are several divergent paths. Take the one closest to the lake. Where two tumbling creeks come together, cross one and then the other. Walk down the opposite side of the cove through the rocky, south-facing cedar forest and across several cascading wet-weather streams. As the trail reaches the point of land at the end of the cove, it climbs, then runs along the steep-sided hill next to the lake.

The trail then makes a strenuous climb up the near-vertical face of the bluff on several demanding switchbacks before reaching a broad plateau on the side of the ridge. The descent back to the lake alternates between rough walking through layers of exposed, cedar-covered limestone and easier walking among hardwoods.

After crossing a short footbridge, the trail goes among some cedars and through a brier patch before reaching the parking lot at Defeated Creek Recreation Area.

People are intrigued by the names of the twin communities of Defeated and Difficult, located nearby. The names have a common origin. In the winter of 1786, a party of hunters from the Cumberland settlements was camping along the creek when it was attacked by Indians. All but one hunter was wounded. The men *defeated* by the attackers had a *difficult* time getting back to their homes in today's Sumner County, and thus the names were born.

HIKES

ON

THE

WESTERN HIGHLAND RIM

BEAMAN PARK

Acquired by Nashville's parks department in 1996, this 1,500-acre preserve on the edge of the Western Highland Rim northwest of downtown will offer yet another opportunity for a wilderness experience within the city. It was not open to the public as of this writing, but the planning was moving along swiftly. Eleven miles of unpaved hiking trails will penetrate the deep forest, pass crystal-clear streams cascading down the hollows, and circle over the oak- and hickory-covered ridge tops. There will be a mostly level 2.5-mile paved loop trail along the contour of one of the main ridges.

The late Alvin G. Beaman, the man for whom the park is named, was a member of Nashville's parks board from 1955 to 1963. His widow, Sally Beaman, gave the money to buy this huge tract. Just how she came to know about it is an interesting story. A group of doctors had owned the land for 25 years. In the early 1990s, they started discussing a sale to the parks department, offering to sell it for less than half the appraised value. Jim Fyke,

Nashville's parks director, immediately realized the potential. Steve Henry and other area residents took an interest, too, as did Nashville mayor Phil Bredesen and members of the Greenways Commission.

Interest in buying the land grew rapidly. Bob Brown, a veteran hiker, trails activist, and commission member, accompanied a newspaper reporter and photographer to the site. A few days later, Brown and his faithful dog, Trouble, were pictured exploring the site in an article in *The Tennessean*. Lee Beaman, Alvin Beaman's son, saw the article and discussed it with his mother. Within days, Sally Beaman donated the entire $650,000 to buy the land.

The entrance to Beaman Park will be located in the valley of Little Marrowbone Creek off Little Marrowbone Road. The road runs between TN 12 (Nashville-Ashland City Highway) and Eatons Creek Road, which also runs off TN 12.

MONTGOMERY BELL STATE PARK

This popular resort park not far from Nashville on the Western Highland Rim has something for everyone: boating, fishing, golf, tennis, swimming, archery, and, of course, hiking in the back country. Nearly 20 miles of trails wind through one of Middle Tennessee's most impressive hardwood forests, beside sparkling streams, next to scenic lakes, and to historic sites associated with the iron industry and the founding of the Cumberland Presbyterian Church. And if you visit Montgomery Bell between February and November, you can count on finding some of its more than 250 species of wildflowers in bloom.

The Montgomery Bell Trail is the park's main trail. It follows the park's perimeter in places, goes around three lakes, and visits Hall Spring. It makes for a good hike on any occasion, but it's particularly well suited for beginning backpackers because of its gentle grade, its accessibility, and its three back-country shelters. This book divides the trail into two sections: the eastern section and the western section. There are five shorter trails ranging from

0.25 mile to 1.7 miles in length. And if you like to walk in the woods but don't care for hiking on trails, the park roads provide a nice alternative.

Though Montgomery Bell never owned any of the land that now comprises the 3,782-acre preserve, his influence can still be felt here and elsewhere in Middle Tennessee. More than anyone, Bell was responsible for developing the iron industry that flourished for more than a century on the Western Highland Rim.

The person credited with getting the iron industry going is James Robertson, the same man who led settlers into what is now Middle Tennessee in 1779. Robertson discovered brown iron ore while surveying at nearby Bartons Creek. The ore was close to the surface and could be easily mined. Robertson bought some land and established Cumberland Furnace, the area's first ironworks, in 1797. He sold his works to Montgomery Bell in 1804.

Bell came to Middle Tennessee from Pennsylvania by way of Kentucky. Before long, he had several furnaces going and won a lucrative contract with the army. Legend has it that cannonballs molded at Bell's works were used by General Andrew Jackson's troops at New Orleans during the War of 1812.

Montgomery Bell was an eccentric and controversial fellow who remains a mystery to this day. Though he was one of Tennessee's wealthiest men, he lived most of his life in a run-down one-room cabin. He never married but is thought to have fathered over 100 children by both white and black women. He reportedly never paid a debt without being sued but was charitable enough to donate money to start the Nashville school that bears his name. He was widely regarded as a cruel taskmaster of his slaves, yet his most intimate friend, James Worley, was a slave. Late in his life, Bell offered freedom, money, and passage to Liberia for any of his slaves who wanted to emigrate to the African resettlement. Half his slaves took him up on it.

In 1850, Bell moved to a grand plantation mansion, Ashlawn, which still stands on Franklin Road in Brentwood. He let the house fall into disrepair and eventually returned to his cabin in the Dickson County hills. He died there in 1855 at age 86. His most impressive achievement is the tunnel his slaves cut through the Narrows of the Harpeth River, where Bell established a massive iron forge. (Located off US 70 between Nashville and White Bluff, the Narrows are well worth a visit.)

The iron industry reached its peak in the 1850s and had its ups and downs after that. Cumberland Furnace finally closed for good in 1936. The site of Laurel Furnace is in Montgomery Bell State Park.

The state park began the way most Tennessee parks did: as a New Deal public-works project. It took some finagling to get it started. The Resettlement Administration's mission was to acquire submarginal farms and remove the owners to more fertile land. The National Park Service, on the other hand, was looking for land with the potential to provide outdoor recreation.

When Resettlement Administration officials came to investigate, local civic leaders took them to a farm said to be so badly eroded that you couldn't get a quarrel started on it. But when National Park Service representatives arrived, the locals took them to where a lovely creek meandered through a hollow, the site of today's Lake Woodhaven. As a result, both agencies saw potential for their missions.

When World War II ended construction, only two lakes and two group camps had been completed. The park was deeded to the state during the war. In the late 1940s, development resumed. The swimming beach on Lake Acorn was completed in 1950, the same year Tennessee's first state-park inn opened. The state added a golf course and a third lake in the 1970s.

The park's visitor center, located just inside the US 70 entrance, has an interesting display about Montgomery Bell, the iron industry, and the development of the park. Among the items on display is the original 1938 National Park Service master plan.

A seasonal highlight at the park is the April wildflower festival. During the festival, you can also learn about the animals that inhabit Middle Tennessee and do a little stargazing.

MONTGOMERY BELL TRAIL, EASTERN SECTION

Highlights
Mature hardwood forest, cascading creek, Creech Hollow Lake, abundant wildflowers, brilliant fall colors

Length
6.2-mile loop

Maps
MBSP trails map; USGS: Burns

Use
The trail is for hiking only. Camping is allowed by permit at a designated back-country shelter.

Trailhead
The park is off US 70 between White Bluff and Dickson. Where the park road forks at the visitor center, turn left toward the inn, then turn left again into the picnic area, where you'll find the trailhead.

Hike Description
This easy, white-blazed trail through a mature oak-hickory forest is a treat in the spring because of its abundant wildflowers and in the fall because of the brilliant foliage.

From the picnic area, follow the paved path across Wildcat Creek to the charming sandstone cottage that was once the park's headquarters. It's now an outlet for original local arts and crafts produced by members of the Five Rivers Arts and Crafts Association.

Start the hike by scrambling up the steep hill to the sign across from the arts-and-crafts shop. In the spring, this mossy patch is covered with bluets, pussy-toes, violets, and spring beauty, which take to the sun-drenched embankment.

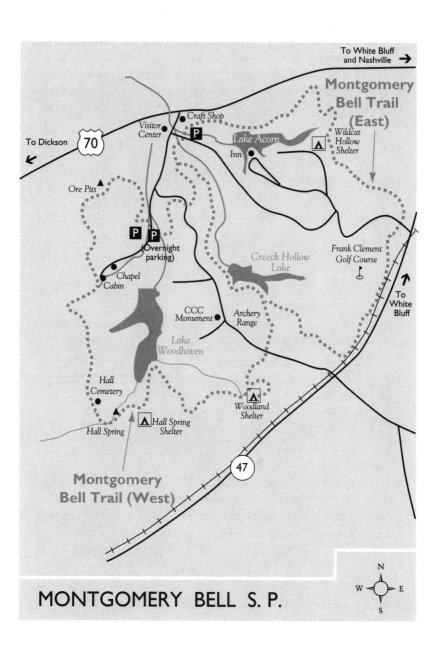

MONTGOMERY BELL S. P.

The trail climbs on the old White Bluff–Dickson wagon road. After it levels off on the wider ridge crest, you can look through the trees down the hill to the right and catch a glimpse of Lake Acorn, one of the pair of lakes created when the National Park Service made this a recreation demonstration area in the 1930s.

At 0.8 mile, the trail veers to the right away from the old road and goes around the edge of a huge sink, then around another sink, then still another. This is a beautiful place in early spring. The subdued landscape is colored by redbuds, which seem to be everywhere, and by the flowers of a few isolated red maples. Beneath the towering oak, hickory, and tulip poplar, the understory is so thick with dogwood that it looks like snow. Come back in late October and you'll be treated to another color show. Crimson dogwood mixes with iridescent pink sourwood and yellow-and-orange sugar maple, all below a canopy of yellow hickory and reddish brown oak.

When Vanderbilt University biologist Elsie Quarterman studied this area in the 1970s, she reported that the forest here on Wildcat Ridge is the best example of a Western Highland Rim oak-hickory forest. As you walk along the easy trail, you can see why. The huge trees have the appearance of never having been cut. This is called an oak-hickory forest for a very simple reason: those are the dominant trees. Oak and hickory account for 88 percent of the trees on this ridge.

There are many different kinds of oak, among them bur, red, black, and white—11 in all at Montgomery Bell. It's often difficult to tell them apart. White oak, the most common, is valuable to the forest-products industry on the Western Highland Rim, as its wood is used for furniture and flooring.

The trail curves right and descends through an understory of beech trees, crossing a ravine lined with Christmas ferns and a small stream on its way to Wildcat Creek. It then crosses the sparkling creek and follows it as it falls over layers of bedrock to the headwaters of Lake Acorn.

At 1.6 miles, you'll reach a spot where a branch comes in from the left and merges with Wildcat Creek. The Wildcat Hollow shelter is on the rise straight ahead. Lake Acorn's backwater comes right up to where the creeks merge.

Take time to explore Wildcat Hollow. The ground is carpeted with wildflowers in the spring. The variety is enormous. You'll find crested dwarf iris, rue anemone, spring beauty, violet wood sorrel, phlox, violets, giant chickweed, and toadshade, just to name a few. The moss-covered bluff rising above the branch across from the shelter is a haven for flowers, too—particularly for patches of phlox. Phlox leaves were once used as a laxative and in a potion for upset stomach, sore eyes, and skin diseases.

Stroll down the path next to the lake and look into the clear pool. You're sure to see lots of minnows and fish and perhaps a water snake as it slithers away from you and swims for cover under a rock ledge. As you make your way down the shore, you'll also hear the *ker-plop* of frogs as they jump into the lake. Tennessee is home to 21 frog and toad species, and if you stay around until sunset, you'll hear them croaking. Look for turtles, too, on the trees that have fallen into the lake; you'll have to approach cautiously or they'll slide into the water. And if you happen upon a great blue heron fishing in the shallows, you might be startled by its squawking as its giant wings lift it away from you.

After visiting Wildcat Hollow, continue on the trail as it climbs gently along the crystal-clear branch that tumbles into Wildcat Creek. The trail crosses the branch several times before turning right to climb out of the hollow.

Along this stretch and throughout the park, you'll walk through areas of bramble and small trees that have the appearance of recently cleared land. These areas were indeed cleared recently, but not by man. The infamous February 1994 ice storm toppled many huge trees. Because of the disruption in human activities the storm caused, it was viewed as a disaster. But it's part of the way nature manages a forest. Openings left by fallen trees create opportunities for new growth, which needs more sunlight than can penetrate a mature forest canopy.

As it runs along the side of the ridge, the trail passes three of the original National Park Service markers before reaching a park maintenance road at 2.6 miles. Walk left on the road for 250 feet. Just before the gate, turn right and reenter the woods.

The highway just beyond the gate is now designated TN 47, but it was US 70 before the park was established. When Tennessee started building modern paved highways following the passage of the State Highway Act of 1923, one of the first projects was the construction of the Memphis-to-Bristol Highway, which ran from one end of the state to the other. Most of it was designated US 70 in 1925. Today's US 70, located on the other side of Montgomery Bell, was built as part of the park's development.

The trail now follows an old road along the top of a ridge where the soil is poorer and the trees are noticeably smaller.

As you pass the beautiful golf course, don't be surprised to see the white tails of deer hurtling away from you. Deer like to browse the edge, where the field meets the forest. White-tailed deer are so plentiful in Tennessee today that it's difficult to imagine that there were probably no more than 250 in the whole state in the 1930s. Restocking started in East Tennessee in the late 1930s and moved to Middle Tennessee in the 1950s. It's now estimated that the statewide deer population tops 800,000.

The golf course is named for Frank Clement, the Dickson County native who was Tennessee's governor in the 1950s and 1960s and who served longer than any governor save one, William Carroll.

The busy railroad that parallels the trail was originally the Nashville & Northwestern Railroad, which was to run west from Nashville to the Mississippi River. It made it only 25 miles out from Nashville by the time the Civil War halted construction in 1861. The Union army completed it to the Tennessee River for the purpose of transporting men and materiel to the huge base in occupied Nashville. (If you're interested in hiking at the site of the Tennessee River Civil War port, see the chapter on Johnsonville State Historic Area, pages 151–58.)

The old road makes a series of roller-coaster dips and rises. In the middle of one of them, at 3.7 miles, the Montgomery Bell

Trail turns right off the old road. The walking becomes more pleasant as you descend along a small stream through groves of large oak, hickory, and tulip poplar. The hickories in Montgomery Bell's splendid forest are mostly pignut and mockernut. Their wood is valuable as fuel; it is used as firewood and converted to charcoal. It is also used in products ranging from flooring to baseball bats to skis.

The trail crosses a branch before arriving at a junction at 4.3 miles. Take the right fork. Starting here, the Montgomery Bell Trail runs conjunctively with the Creech Hollow Trail. The combined trails soon begin following the shore of Creech Hollow Lake.

You can tell by the size and type of trees that the narrow strip between the deep forest and the lake was bulldozed to make way for the lake. Cedar and tulip poplar are pioneer species, some of the first trees to return to cleared land. Pure stands of tulip poplar often take over former fields. One day, this lakeshore will look like the more mature forest to the left. The cedars, which need sunlight, will be crowded out.

After swinging around a cove in the lake, the trail passes through a mowed field and reaches the dam. Go around the left end of the dam and follow the trail back into the woods.

The trail follows the hollow downstream along the creek. After crossing a ravine, it runs along the top of the bluff above the creek. You will ascend a gradual hill before reaching a trail junction at 5.6 miles. Go right. (You'd take the left fork if you were walking the western section of the Montgomery Bell Trail, the next hike.)

The trail continues through the heart of the park, crosses a ridge, and descends on some steps into a depression. This was the quarry that produced rock for some of the construction in the park. It's now covered by a pine plantation. The park road will come into view on the left before you reach a trail junction across from the visitor center at 6.1 miles. Turn right. The Montgomery Bell Trail runs conjunctively with the blue-blazed Wildcat Trail here. After meandering through a cedar thicket and crossing the creek in a bottom covered with spring beauty and phlox, the combined trails climb to the road. Just across the road is the picnic area where the hike started.

MONTGOMERY BELL TRAIL, WESTERN SECTION

Highlights
Ore pits, birthplace of the Cumberland Presbyterian denomination, Hall Spring, scenic Lake Woodhaven

Length
7.2-mile loop

Maps
MBSP trails map; USGS: Burns

Use
The trail is for hiking only. Camping is allowed by permit at designated back-country shelters.

Trailhead
The trailhead is at the picnic area in Church Hollow. After entering the park from US 70 between Dickson and White Bluff, stay on the main park road past the visitor center. The road forks just past the campground entrance; take the right fork. Where the road splits again, take the right fork into Church Hollow. The trail crosses the road just inside the woods. Note that if you plan to hike the Montgomery Bell Trail overnight, you should leave your car at the parking area reached by taking the left fork—the fork that leads to Group Camp One—at the last split.

Hike Description
This interesting walk passes through a variety of forest environments and leads to historic sites, a huge spring, and an overlook on Lake Woodhaven.

The western section of Montgomery Bell Trail visits the reconstructed Samuel McAdoo cabin.

From the picnic area, cross the road and enter the woods at the trail sign. Through here, the white-blazed Montgomery Bell Trail runs conjunctively with the Ore Pit and Wildcat Trails.

The trail curves up the hill through a forest dominated by white oak and soon enters eroded gullies left behind by the extraction of iron ore in the first half of the 1800s. At 0.25 mile, in the middle of the ore pits, the Wildcat Trail turns right on its 1-mile journey up Wildcat Creek to Lake Acorn, but you should continue on the combined Montgomery Bell Trail/Ore Pit Trail, which zigzags through the ore pits.

You'll notice huge tulip poplars growing out of the pits. Trees that sprouted on the waste were simply left to grow, because ore mining left the land worthless for other uses. These trees could easily be more than 100 years old.

The ore mined here was shuttled on a trestle to the nearby Laurel Furnace, where it was forged into iron. Richard Napier, who married a daughter of pioneers James and Charlotte Robertson, started the furnace here in 1815. In 1855, its last year of operation, Laurel Furnace produced 657 tons of pig iron.

After descending from the ridge and the ore pits, the trail comes to a paved road and a log cabin at 1 mile. The log cabin and the charming sandstone chapel just beyond it mark the birthplace of the Cumberland Presbyterian denomination. Its creation grew out of the Great Revival, an evangelical movement that swept across the frontier like wildfire in the early 1800s. Preachers drew crowds too large for church buildings. Before long, revivals evolved into great outdoor camp meetings. Worshipers came from near and far and stayed for days.

Presbyterian leaders became alarmed about the movement's emotional excesses and about the ordination of uneducated preachers. They ordered a halt to the ordinations. When a number of preachers felt moved to continue the practice, a rift developed between the evangelists and mainline Presbyterians.

Samuel McAdoo of Dickson County was a leading evangelist. In 1810, he and a group of colleagues met at his log cabin on this spot. They decided to renounce the authority of the Presbyterian Church and continue the ordinations. This was the beginning of the new Cumberland Presbyterian Church. The replica of McAdoo's cabin was built in 1956 and the chapel in 1961.

Walk behind the cabin in the shade of four huge, old sugar maples. The pioneers who settled Middle Tennessee valued maples not only for their shade and beauty, but also for their sap. It takes about 32 gallons of sap to make a gallon of syrup and 4.5 pounds of sugar. Big trees like these can yield as much as 60 gallons of sap per year. Maple wood has its uses, too, in flooring, boxes, crates, and veneers.

Follow the trail to McAdoo Spring. You will cross a branch on a bridge and climb slightly to where the Montgomery Bell Trail and the Ore Pit Trail go their separate ways. Go right on the Montgomery Bell Trail, which heads upstream on an old road along a branch. In places, the branch cascades in a series of miniature waterfalls over moss-covered bedrock. At one point, the trail climbs over a bluff and descends along a green slope covered with Christmas fern.

After curving around the base of the hill, the old road that carries the trail straightens out in a young forest of cedar, oak, sycamore, and black cherry. At 1.9 miles, the trail crests a ridge and crosses another old road. You can rest here on a comfortable bench and listen to the birds. You're sure to hear the familiar *caw-caw-caw* of crows as they navigate around the crowns of the tall oaks.

Continue on the white-blazed old road as it skirts the park boundary through an edge environment. You're likely to startle some deer here. The trail passes through some tall pines growing from seedlings planted to control erosion on this once-depleted farmland. After dipping into a bottom and crossing a creek on a sturdy footbridge, it passes woods white with dogwood in April. At 2.6 miles, it crosses the sugar maple–flanked entrance to Hall Cemetery, which is just to your left in a grove of tall, symmetrical cedars.

The old road stays near the boundary past the cemetery road and drops into a bottom, passing a huge, old oak on the right. Black vultures like to roost on this ancient tree, so don't be startled by the flapping of wings as the birds fly away from you.

If you walk here in the spring, you'll appreciate the contrast between the cedar grove you just left and the creek bottom you've just entered. What little color there is in the cedars is muted. But the bottom is a carpet of color. Wildflowers are everywhere— phlox, Virginia bluebell, Jacob's-ladder, spring beauty, violets, toadshade, giant chickweed, kidney-leaf buttercup, and toothwort. And if that's not enough, the forest understory is brightened by redbud, dogwood, and wild plumb.

The trail fords Hall Creek, which flows to Lake Woodhaven. At 2.9 miles, it leaves the old road, turns left, and follows the wildflower carpet to Hall Spring and one of the park's three backcountry camping shelters. The spring, guarded by tall sycamores, produces 1,100 gallons of cool, clear water per minute. A multitude of seeps in this area ooze water during wet weather.

Behind the shelter, the trail runs along the ridge, then drops into a wetland created by beaver dams that block the flow from the spring. Because of the value of their fur, used in hats, beavers were hunted nearly to extinction in Middle Tennessee. But they have made a strong comeback—too strong, some say. Their dams often flood valuable forests and farmland, and many consider them nothing more than pests. They returned here to Hall Creek in 1971.

You're not likely to see one of these wary creatures, as they work mostly at night. But you can see where they have gnawed trees along the creek. Beavers fell trees to get at the succulent leaves, twigs, and bark in the canopy. They work extremely quickly. A beaver can fell a tree three inches in diameter in less than 10 minutes, and a pair of them can build a two-foot-high, 12-foot-long dam in two nights. They build dams to create ponds, which provide protective cover for their lodges.

At one point on the trail, a boardwalk leads out into the wetland. The boardwalk was designed to let hikers experience this rich environment firsthand. Unfortunately, it has fallen victim to the lack of maintenance that plagues many of Tennessee's state parks. Though still in use as of this writing, it is in poor repair.

The trail curves around to a peaceful, open, mossy spot overlooking beautiful Lake Woodhaven. Linger here. If it's late fall or winter, you'll see lots of migratory waterfowl on the lake. Resident wood ducks and Canada geese are common, too. River otters and muskrats are here, but you probably won't see these shy creatures. The water's surface is often broken by fish. You may see fishermen on the distant bank or in boats trying for largemouth bass, bluegill, catfish, and crappie. Outboard motors are not allowed in the park.

If you look down the main stem of Lake Woodhaven, you'll see the dam that created the lake. The earthen dam has a large, carefully laid masonry spillway. An all-black company of the Civilian Conservation Corps (CCC) stationed here from 1935 to 1940 built the spillway. The CCC was segregated, as was the rest of society then. The all-black company and two all-white companies that worked in the park are memorialized on a marble monument on the main park road and by a plaque at the visitor center. The museum at the visitor center displays some fascinating photos of the "CCC boys."

The trail departs the lake, follows the ups and downs of the ridge, and passes through several forest types. You'll notice some pines that were hit hard by the February 1994 ice storm. It was only through the heroic effort of the park staff and dedicated volunteers that the Montgomery Bell Trail was reopened through the tangle of downed trees.

The trail climbs through some gullies that demonstrate how the land was badly eroded before it was made into a park. At 4.4 miles, you'll come to a junction. The path to the right leads 0.5 mile to Woodland Shelter, which sits on a rise above a spring. Continue on the Montgomery Bell Trail as it climbs into the oak-hickory forest and reaches the park road at 4.7 miles.

Along here and at other places, you'll walk past the root network of downed hardwoods. These rootcaps and the disturbed soil make good homes for burrowing animals like chipmunks, so don't be surprised to see one scampering into a hole as you approach a fallen tree. These members of the squirrel family always seem to be busy gathering nuts, seeds, and grain—often in quantities of a bushel or more—to store in their complex underground homes.

The woods at Montgomery Bell also host their share of one of Middle Tennessee's most common animals. The opossum doesn't get much respect—most people know it only as road kill—but it's actually quite an interesting animal. Though it looks like a giant rat with grayish white fur and tail, it's not a rodent but rather a marsupial—the same kind of mammal as Australia's kangaroo. The female opossum delivers a litter of newborns that are barely past the embryonic stage. They crawl into a pouch in the mother's belly that contains 13 mammary glands.

Opossums have 50 teeth, the most of any North American mammal. When they feel threatened, they hiss or grin—thus the saying "grin like a possum." They will also feign death, lying limp and motionless with their eyes and mouths open, which accounts for an even better-known slogan, "playing possum."

Walking through this area, you'll appreciate the white blazes on the trees. Oak leaves don't care where they fall. They create a uniform brown carpet that makes it difficult to see where the trail runs in fall and winter.

After crossing the road, the trail drops off the ridge, skirts an archery range, and follows a ravine before crossing a spur and reaching a trail junction at 5 miles. From this junction to the next—a distance of 1.3 miles—the trail follows the same route along Creech Hollow Lake as does the eastern section of the Montgomery Bell Trail (see pages 94–100).

Go left at the next junction, following the sign that points to Hall Spring. Before reaching the park road, the trail turns back to run parallel to the way you just came.

In the deep oak-hickory forests of Montgomery Bell, you may be startled by a large, crow-sized, red-headed bird sweeping from the crown of one tree to another. This is the magnificent pileated woodpecker, distinguished by its flashing black-and-white coloration and its red crest. Its call is a common sound in the Middle Tennessee forests.

You will cross the road and go into and out of a steep hollow, then circle around some bluffs covered with mountain laurel. After a steep descent, the trail crosses Four Mile Creek—which flows out of Lake Woodhaven—then follows the creek downstream a short distance. This is a particularly pleasant stretch. Tall, laurel-covered bluffs rise on the opposite bank, and the tiny flood plain is covered with wildflowers in early spring.

The trail goes left past the maintenance area and the overnight parking area. After returning to the woods, it passes a bed of evergreen club moss and crosses the paved road to Group Camp One. It then circles over a short rise above the site of Laurel Furnace and passes through some gullies covered with tulip poplar and large cedar.

The Montgomery Bell Trail reunites with the Ore Pit Trail at 7.1 miles. The combined trails descend through beds of May apple and ferns to the picnic area where the hike started.

NATCHEZ TRACE PARKWAY

The Natchez Trace Parkway is a 445-mile-long park that follows the route of the once-important overland road between Nashville on the Cumberland River and Natchez on the Mississippi. The parkway's environments range from Mississippi swamps to mountainlike ridges near Nashville. Over 100 kinds of trees, 215 species of birds, 57 species of mammals, and 89 species of reptiles and amphibians live along the parkway. The variety of spring wildflowers is enormous.

Walkers can combine pleasant short hikes with visits to historic sites on parts of the Old Trace near Leipers Fork and at the Grinder cabin, where famed explorer Meriwether Lewis died under mysterious circumstances.

The Natchez Trace has been known by a series of names that reflect its evolving uses: the Chickasaw Trail, the Boatman's Trail, the Mail Road. There was once an attempt to give the path an official name—the "Road from Nashville in the State of Tennessee to Grindstone Ford of the Bayou Pierre in the Mississippi

Territory"—but that mouthful never took hold. It's curious that during the late 1700s and early 1800s—when the road was most heavily used—it was rarely known as the Natchez Trace. No one knows for sure how it got that name, but the term *trace* was a familiar one on the frontier. It meant a dim path through the wilderness.

When explorers first came into the Cumberland country in the mid-1700s, they found broad paths beaten down by buffalo and other animals traveling to the Great Salt Lick, located near present-day Bicentennial Mall in Nashville. No Indians lived in Middle Tennessee at that time, but tribes that came into the region to hunt used those ancient buffalo paths. One path went from the Great Salt Lick to the Chickasaw towns near what is now Tupelo, Mississippi, where it intersected a trail leading to the Spanish town of Natchez.

What was then known as the Chickasaw Trail followed the route of today's West End Avenue, Harding Road, and TN 100 to Backbone Ridge, then followed the ridge's narrow spine south. It stayed on ridge tops and watershed divides to avoid impassable streams and swamps.

The Chickasaw Trail took on new life when the trans-Appalachian region started filling with settlers after 1780. The pioneers needed a place to sell the harvest from their fields and forests, but it was not feasible to haul goods back east over the Appalachian Mountains. So they turned to the long-established towns of New Orleans and Natchez. Settlers in Tennessee, Kentucky, Ohio, and Pennsylvania loaded their flatboats with produce, furs, flour, and iron and floated down the great inland waterways to the Spanish towns on the Mississippi. Returning the boats upstream was next to impossible, so the boatmen sold them for lumber and returned north on the Chickasaw Trail.

Called "Kaintucks" regardless of where they were from, the boatmen usually traveled in companies of from 15 to 20 men and camped along the way, as there were no accommodations. The Chickasaw Trail thus became the Boatman's Trail. Its use by Kaintucks started to decline in 1811, following the introduction of steamboats. It was much easier to hitch a ride on a steamboat than to walk through the wilderness. The boatmen were just about gone from the trace by 1820.

When the Mississippi Territory—today's Alabama and Mississippi—became part of the United States in 1798, the trace took on a different role: it became an official national road. Not long after the territory was established, the Walton Road opened, connecting Nashville to Knoxville. Also about that time, the young nation established Washington as its capital. The Natchez Trace became a link in the communication chain that ran from Washington through Knoxville and Nashville to the territorial capital at Natchez.

To improve what was a weak link in the chain, President Thomas Jefferson ordered the army to improve the Boatman's Trail. Between 1801 and 1803, it upgraded 264 miles of the trace. The army began its work where Nashville's Warner Parks are today. But instead of following the Backbone Ridge route of the Boatman's Trail—the route of today's parkway—the army road (or government road) stayed in the valley of the Harpeth River, following the route of today's Old Natchez Trace and Old Hillsboro Road in Williamson County. This new route connected with the high road at Garrison Creek. (You can walk the army road on the Old Natchez Trace Walk; see pages 285–91.)

The Natchez Trace was designated a post road in 1800, with one monthly Nashville-to-Natchez mail delivery. That number steadily increased. By 1816, there were three deliveries per week. The route out of Nashville shifted often to meet changing needs. Starting in 1802, postriders did not leave Nashville on the trace at all. Instead, they went straight south to the new town of Franklin, then cut over to the trace. When a post office was established at Columbia in 1808, postriders went there before turning west to pick up the trace.

Eventually, it made more sense for travelers and mail to get to and from the Mississippi Territory on steamboats. Use of the Natchez Trace started to decline. Then a new, shorter road to the Old Southwest was completed in 1820 under the direction of General Andrew Jackson. This military road ran from Columbia through what are now Mount Pleasant and Lawrenceburg and on to New Orleans. Thru travel on the Natchez Trace had just about ended by 1830.

The Natchez Trace probably would have been forgotten had it not been for the Daughters of the American Revolution (DAR). Prompted by a 1905 magazine article about the trace, the DAR marked the route with 21 monuments between Natchez and Nashville. One of the markers stands at the corner of the Old Natchez Trace and Old Hillsboro Road in Williamson County, and the northernmost marker is in Nashville's Centennial Park. A DAR plaque is on Golf Club Lane in Nashville.

The Natchez Trace Parkway started as a New Deal public work during the Depression. Though Congress authorized the parkway in 1938, construction was slow. It was not until 1996 that the final segment opened near Nashville. The parkway's northern terminus is on TN 100 west of the Warner Parks.

In 1983, Congress authorized the Natchez Trace Scenic Trail, a hiking and equestrian trail running the length of the parkway. So far, the only substantial part in Tennessee is the 25-mile stretch from Garrison Creek to the Duck River. The trail is well maintained by volunteers affiliated with the Natchez Trace Trail Conference.

GARRISON CREEK TRAIL, OLD TRACE

Highlights
Original section of the Natchez Trace, scenic overlook, rich forest

Length
3.7-mile loop

Maps
NTP map and guide; USGS: Theta

Use

The trail is open to hikers and horseback riders
during the daytime only.

Trailhead

The trailhead is at the Garrison Creek parking area at
milepost 427.6 on the parkway. The parking area is 1 mile south of
the TN 46 parkway entrance near Leipers Fork, west of Franklin.

Hike Description

This hike is on the northern end of the 25-mile trail that
extends along the parkway from Garrison Creek to the Duck
River. Because part of it is actually on the Old Trace, walkers
can experience what it must have been like to travel the historic
route when it was in use.

The hiking trail takes off behind the comfort station at the
Garrison Creek parking area, splits from the horse trail, and cuts
up the hollow through a brier patch that is taking over a field.
This is a popular spot for bird watchers, as birds love thickets
like this one.

The trail leaves the old field and climbs steeply into the woods
through a stand of even-aged tulip poplar, a sure sign that this
was once cleared land. It makes a sharp right turn in a bed of
large ferns beneath the beech understory, then angles up the side
of a steep ridge covered with oak, beech, black cherry, and
hickory. This moist, north-facing slope is rich in wildflowers in
the spring. You'll see spring beauty, violets—both yellow and
white—May apple, toadshade, doll's eyes, wake-robin, violet
wood sorrel, rue anemone, and the fiddleheads of young
Christmas ferns.

At the crest of the ridge at 0.5 mile, the trail passes through a
split-rail fence and comes to an overlook above Garrison Creek.
You're looking down into quintessential outer Central Basin landscape. Like dozens of other streams flowing off the Western Highland Rim escarpment, Garrison Creek has carved out a fertile
valley that holds some of the most prized land in Middle Tennessee; you can tell that from the fine houses. Green pastures

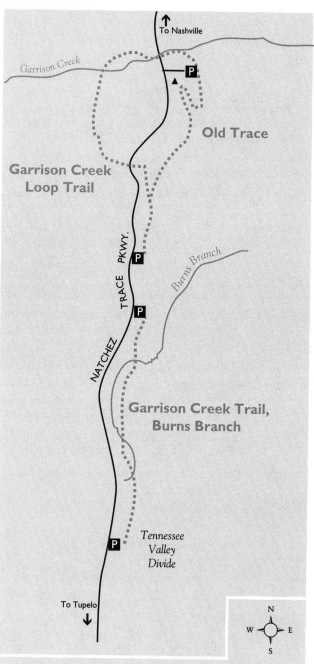

To Nashville

Garrison Creek

Old Trace

Garrison Creek
Loop Trail

TRACE PKWY.

Burns Branch

NATCHEZ

Garrison Creek Trail,
Burns Branch

Tennessee
Valley
Divide

To Tupelo

N
W — E
S

NATCHEZ TRACE PARKWAY

sweep up the hills to woods that shine with redbud and dogwood in the spring and glow with sugar maple in the fall.

Standing on this ridge, it's not unusual to see a hawk soaring above the edge of the woods, looking to make a meal of a rabbit, chipmunk, or mouse. The red-tailed hawk is the most common bird of prey in Middle Tennessee and is often seen perched on tree limbs beside the road. The hawk's name comes from its rusty red tail.

If you're here at dusk on a summer evening, you'll probably hear the unmistakable call of the whippoorwill. This common summer resident likes wooded areas near open fields, such as those you see below.

The trail leaves the overlook and runs along the ridge to a junction with the Old Trace at 0.7 mile. Turn right. For the next mile, you'll be walking on the longest stretch of the Old Trace in Tennessee.

During the army's improvement of the trace between 1801 and 1803, soldiers camped along the stream and gave it the name Garrison Creek. The earliest route of the trace came south over Backbone Ridge, just as the parkway does today, but the army took the route off the ridge and ran it through the Harpeth Valley. The trail coming in from the left here is the 1801–3 army road climbing from the valley to rejoin the older, high-ground route. The ridge is named for Captain Thomas Butler, one of the two army officers in charge of the troops who worked on the trace.

Autumn is a fine time to make this ridge-top walk. When the late-afternoon sun streams into the forest, it'll make you think you're seeing millions of leaf-shaped light bulbs. And there's a reason beyond the natural beauty of the forest to take this hike in the fall. Because it drains poorly and is used more by horseback riders than hikers, the trail is quite muddy in wet weather, giving you a touch of historic realism you might prefer to avoid. But in the fall, instead of oozing through ankle-deep mud, your boots will rustle through crisp, newly fallen leaves of tulip poplar, sugar maple, oak, beech, hickory, black cherry, and dogwood.

You'll get the feeling the forest looks much as it did to the lonely postriders making their way to Natchez.

Black cherry like you see here is a valuable component of Middle Tennessee's forests. Its wood is prized for furniture, paneling, scientific instruments, toys, and handles.

The trail passes a massive three-trunk oak on the left, then a large four-trunk oak a bit farther, then another three-trunk oak a bit farther still. In a beech grove at the head of a tulip poplar–filled hollow at 1.5 miles, you'll pass a junction with the Garrison Creek Loop Trail. Continue on the Old Trace; you'll return to this junction in a few minutes. Butler Ridge bends broadly to the left before making a straight path to the Old Trace parking area at milepost 426.2.

The hike turns around here. Retrace your steps to the junction and angle left off the Old Trace onto the Garrison Creek Loop Trail. Before long, a whisper from above will tell you that you're in a stand of tall pines. As you walk among conifers interspersed with equally tall tulip poplars, you'll see evidence of the February 1994 ice storm.

The trail leaves the pines and circles around the head of a beech- and poplar-studded hollow before running along the side of the ridge above the motor road. After a broad curve, it leaves the deep woods, passes a row of sycamores on the left, and goes under the road in a tunnel; if you have children along, they're sure to enjoy this passage.

If you're traveling the Natchez Trace Parkway in the warm months, you may see furry animals perched next to the road. These are woodchucks—or, as some call them, groundhogs. These big vegetarians make their homes in burrows that usually have two or more openings and can be as deep as four or five feet and as long as 25 or 30 feet. Their extensive tunnels often provide homes for other animals. This largest member of the squirrel family in Tennessee is the only one that is a true hibernator. Woodchucks start storing fat in the summer and retreat to their burrows in October. They remain until February—until around Groundhog Day, in fact.

The trail climbs the hill and bears right through a lush thicket between redbud-lined woods and a mowed right of way. This transitional area is recovering from the road excavation. If it is left alone, it will someday look like the deep woods up the hill. Typical pioneer trees here include black locust, cedar, and sassafras. The many shrubs and vines include blackberry, bush honeysuckle, and sumac. Among the herbaceous plants are goldenrod, Queen Anne's lace, and broomsedge.

The mosaic created by the mowed right of way, the shrub-sapling thicket, the forest, the pasture, and Garrison Creek makes this an ideal wildlife habitat. Of particular interest is the edge between the thicket and the forest, which supports a distinct community of birds and mammals that move from the cover of the deep woods into the thicket. Of course, the red-tailed hawk you may have seen from the overlook knows this.

Songbirds love thickets like these. You're sure to see and hear plenty of them. One common bird is the beautiful indigo bunting, a Neotropical migrant seen from March through October. Keep an eye out, too, for the ruby-throated hummingbird, a tiny bird no bigger than your thumb. It's Tennessee's smallest nesting bird.

If you're walking through here in the fall, you may see gray, cone-shaped, paper-looking objects hanging from young trees in the bramble. They're hornet's nests.

After the trail drops steeply, you'll discover a third reason to take this walk in the dry autumn: you have to cross Garrison Creek without benefit of a bridge. When the water is low, there are some rocks you can hop across just upstream from the horse trail. During the rest of the year, plan on getting your feet wet.

Once you're across the creek, follow it downstream next to a pasture on the left. If you take this walk in spring, you'll enjoy a nice display of phlox, buttercups, Jacob's-ladder, and purple phacelia. In the flood plain next to the creek, a lone red maple stands among the stream-loving sycamores. This small tree is bright red in both spring and fall. It's not nearly as common in Middle Tennessee as its cousin, the sugar maple. Red maple is also called swamp maple because it prefers moist soil, like here along the stream.

The hackberry trees here let you know that you're on the border between two of the Midstate's physiographic regions. Hackberry is rare on the Highland Rim, where you've been walking, but is common in the lower Central Basin.

The trail recrosses the creek and follows it around the edge of the mowed field before passing under the graceful span that carries the motor road across Garrison Creek's flood plain. At 3.5 miles, you'll climb a short rise, pass the trail sign, and come to the paved loop in the horse-trailer parking area. Follow the paved road to the right to where the trail started.

GARRISON CREEK TRAIL, BURNS BRANCH

Highlights
Spring wildflowers, tumbling creek

Length
1.4 miles one-way

Maps
NTP map and guide; USGS: Theta

Use
The trail is open to hikers and horseback riders during the daytime only.

Trailhead
The trailhead is at the Burns Branch parking area, located at milepost 425.4 on the parkway. The parking area is 3 miles south of the TN 46 parkway entrance near Leipers Fork, west of Franklin.

Hike Description
This walk on a short stretch of the 25-mile Garrison Creek

Trail offers a display of spring wildflowers that rivals any in the region. The trail follows tumbling Burns Branch up to the Tennessee Valley Divide, the imaginary line separating the watersheds of the Cumberland and Tennessee Rivers. (Note that if the state completes the western part of TN 840 South, it will cut across Burns Branch and probably end this as a place to walk.)

From the parking lot, follow the trail upstream past the redbuds and dogwoods that extend their branches over the creek. If you look up the creek during the spring, you'll see endless patches of phlox beneath the green, moss-covered bluff on the opposite bank.

After going through a meadow dotted with bluets and buttercups, the trail crosses a small tributary and comes to a dirt road. Turn left, cross the creek, then veer right off the road into the woods. After crossing the creek again, the trail runs beside a perfectly laid stone wall that supports the motor road. In addition to the phlox that's everywhere, you'll come across foamflower, doll's eyes, purple phacelia, rue anemone, giant chickweed, toadshade, crested dwarf iris, and lousewort. You'll see some cattails, too, growing next to the creek.

Early settlers believed that cattle grazing among lousewort got covered with lice, which is how the plant got its name. The settlers brewed a tea from the plant to treat upset stomach.

Following a crossing in a grove of beech trees, Burns Branch falls off one ledge after another. You will cross the creek on a slick, flat slab of bedrock and head up the other side. As you make yet another colorful creek crossing, you might conclude that, for wildflower viewing, Burns Branch is about as good as it gets.

You will soon pass a deformed beech tree on the right. Its trunk rises straight, bends parallel to the ground for a few feet, then reaches straight up again. If you have children along, they'll enjoy climbing on this saddlelike trunk.

The trail makes a last dip to cross a seasonal stream before its final climb through a forest dominated by oak, beech, and tulip poplar. It bursts out of the woods into a field covered with tan broomsedge and passes clumps of sumac that turn crimson in the fall.

The walk ends at the paved Tennessee Valley Divide overlook. The divide wanders the ridge tops diagonally across Middle Tennessee from the Kentucky border at Land Between the Lakes to near Monteagle on the Cumberland Plateau. It then snakes north back to the Bluegrass State at Cumberland Gap. Along here, water flowing north of the divide makes its way via the Harpeth River to the Cumberland, and water flowing south goes by way of the Duck River to the Tennessee. The Cumberland and the Tennessee empty into the Ohio River just 10 miles apart near Paducah, Kentucky.

LITTLE SWAN TRAIL, OLD TRACE

Highlights
Cascading streams, historic Meriwether Lewis site, Old Trace

Length
4.3-mile loop

Maps
NTP map and guide; USGS: Gordonsburg

Use
Hiking and day use only

Trailhead
The trailhead is at the Grinder cabin at the Meriwether Lewis site. Turn into the site at milepost 384.9, follow the signs toward the pioneer cemetery, and park in the lot next to the log cabin. The site can also be reached from TN 20 between Summertown and Hohenwald.

Hike Description
This trail in the rugged headwaters of Little Swan Creek takes you through a narrow, 250-foot-deep valley lined with bluffs

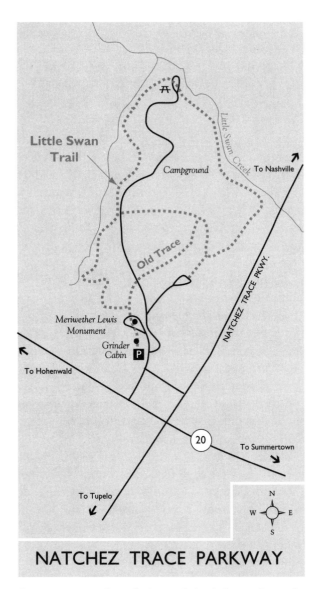

Little Swan Trail

Campground

To Nashville

Little Swan Creek

Old Trace

Meriwether Lewis Monument

Grinder Cabin

To Hohenwald

NATCHEZ TRACE PKWY.

20

To Summertown

To Tupelo

N
W E
S

NATCHEZ TRACE PARKWAY

covered in mountain laurel. Part of the hike is through a registered state natural area.

The cabin where the hike starts is a reconstruction of the house occupied by Robert and Priscilla Grinder when they were thrust into one of the most mysterious events in American history: the death of famed explorer Meriwether Lewis in 1809.

Accommodations started to spring up on the Natchez Trace after it was made a national road. But even then, the lodgings didn't amount to much. They were mostly "stands" run by pioneer families to make a little extra money.

Meriwether Lewis was a man of "undaunted courage," noted historian Stephen E. Ambrose in his best-selling 1996 book of that title. In 1803, President Thomas Jefferson selected the gifted young Virginian to lead an expedition through the newly purchased Louisiana Territory and on to the Pacific Ocean. Lewis and his coleader, William Clark, returned in late 1806. The following year, a grateful Jefferson rewarded Lewis with the governorship of the territory. St. Louis was then the territorial capital.

When accusations of financial irregularities were leveled against him in 1809, Lewis decided to travel all the way to Washington to defend himself. He and his party floated down the Mississippi River to the site of today's Memphis, then traveled overland to the Natchez Trace, intent on heading to Nashville, then on to Washington.

Lewis, who had a history of what we now know as depression, was a disturbed man when his party wandered into Grinder's Stand. There was talk that he had tried to kill himself twice on the difficult journey from St. Louis.

John Grinder was away the night Lewis stayed. In the early-morning hours, a pistol shot awakened Priscilla. As she peered into the darkness, she saw a man stagger to her cabin door. He tried to open it. Too afraid to do anything, she watched him stumble away. He tried to get some water from the well, then disappeared from sight.

At sunup, Lewis's servants found him in bed with part of his skull blown away. He also had a wound in his chest and slashes on his throat. He died shortly after dawn.

Was it murder or suicide? Most historians, including Ambrose, believe it was suicide. But no one really knows for sure, and the controversy continues to this day.

To start the hike, walk behind the Grinder cabin through an oak grove to where the sunken Old Trace—worn by the feet of thousands of men and animals—emerges from the scrub woods on the left. Turn right and follow the Old Trace as it curves along the edge of the woods past some towering oaks and crosses the paved loop road. You'll have to look carefully in the grassy median for the markers that let you know this is an old cemetery. Meriwether Lewis is buried here.

Walk through the cemetery to the stone monument that honors Lewis. In 1848, the state of Tennessee erected this monument, a broken shaft symbolizing the great explorer's premature death. In 1925, Meriwether Lewis National Monument was established with funds raised from the modern states through which the Lewis and Clark expedition passed. The 300-acre park is now incorporated into the Natchez Trace Parkway.

Cross the other end of the paved loop onto the Old Trace. At a forked cedar tree, a sign marks the beginning of the Little Swan Trail, which leads left into the woods. The moss-covered trail curves through a forest of small oaks, descends via switchbacks into a hollow, and runs past stands of oak and tulip poplar rising above beds of Christmas fern. The Little Swan Trail is not blazed and is sometimes difficult to follow.

The trail rises above the creek on some bluffs topped with beech trees, then makes a sharp right to climb out of the hollow. After passing through a blackberry bramble below an overlook, it comes to the paved road to the campground at 1 mile. The Little Swan Trail doesn't cross the road, but instead veers back into the woods. (The trail sign across the road marks a connector path that cuts through the Little Swan Trail's loop.)

The Little Swan Trail follows the narrow strip between the road and a steep hollow. The dogwoods in the hollow put on quite a show in April, when they bloom, and again in the fall, when their leaves turn crimson.

The trail swings left along a narrowing ridge dominated by a variety of oaks. When the ridge gives out, the trail drops back into the hollow along the creek. At 2 miles, in a beautiful spot where the creek squeezes between the ridges, the trail passes through a picnic area and comes to the paved loop road. Walk through the grove of big cedars in the grassy median to pick up the trail again behind the comfort station.

The next stretch is unusually scenic, as the trail follows beautiful Little Swan Creek on its narrow passage through the Western Highland Rim. The trail alternates between the soggy bottom next to the creek and bluffs where mountain laurel spreads its branches over the moss- and fern-covered edges. In places, it dips through ravines carved by Little Swan Creek's many pretty little feeder streams. The remarkable diversity of vegetation in the moist bottom is a stark contrast to the oak-hickory forest on the dry heights above.

At 3 miles, the trail arrives at two signposts missing their signs. It then turns right, away from Little Swan Creek. The trail climbs to a tributary that cascades over layer after layer of bedrock, then crosses the creek a few times on large, flat, well-placed rocks. Because this trail is not heavily used, much of it is covered with moss, which makes for comfortable walking.

The trail junction at 3.5 miles is where the connector path comes in. The Little Swan Trail ends just ahead in a picnic area, so take the connector path, which slices to the right up the hill.

The connector path reaches the top of the ridge and the Old Trace at 3.6 miles. Turn left and follow the Old Trace. You can see that the buffalo that beat down this road and the Indians who later used it stayed to the ridge tops as much as possible. The word *trace* is certainly appropriate here, as the route at times is hardly more than a faint break in the trees.

Cross the campground road and continue on the Old Trace. You won't have any trouble following it now, since the park service keeps it cleared. This makes for nice walking, but it's not much like the Natchez Trace. You'll see plenty of birds, for this is the type of edge environment they love. One common bird you're likely to come upon is the blue jay, a rather large bird of striking blue, black, and white coloring.

When you come to the forked cedar tree where the Little Swan Trail began, retrace your route to the Grinder cabin.

DUNBAR CAVE
STATE NATURAL AREA

*D*unbar Cave State Natural Area provides for Clarksville what Radnor Lake and the Warner Parks provide for Nashville: a peaceful oasis packed into ever-growing suburbs. The park contains a lake, an old oak-hickory forest, and a young forest recovering from farming. All this makes for diverse habitats rich in wildlife and plants, which may be enjoyed on a trail network of slightly more than 2 miles. Added to this is the cave itself—8 miles of caverns beneath the Western Highland Rim within the Clarksville city limits.

For a natural area, Dunbar Cave has an unnatural history. During much of the 20th century, it was known more for its music and entertainment than for its nature. A mineral-springs resort complete with a hotel was here as early as 1900, but it faded along with other such resorts in Middle Tennessee. Dunbar Cave's glory years as an entertainment venue started in 1931 with the construction of a new hotel, a swimming pool, tennis courts, summer cottages, and a bowling alley. The concrete pavilion, the bandstand, and the concession stand you'll visit at the cave entrance were built then, as was the dam that creates the lake.

Dunbar Cave became a popular big-band tour stop for such renowned stars as Benny Goodman, Tommy Dorsey, and Kay Kyser. World War II ended the big-band era. In 1948, country-music star Roy Acuff acquired Dunbar Cave and built the golf course across the lake. For a brief time, the place flourished again. It started to decline once more in 1950, when the hotel burned. The swimming pool closed in 1969.

Its latest life began in 1973, when the state acquired Dunbar Cave for its new natural areas system. Regularly scheduled tours of the cave are offered most of the year. Space is limited, so call early for reservations. You can learn about birds, animals, stars, and wildflowers on other organized outings.

LAKE, RECOVERY, AND SHORT LOOP TRAILS

Highlights
Cave entrance, scenic lake, upland forest

Length
1.7-mile loop

Maps
DCSNA brochure; USGS: Clarksville

Use
Hiking and day use only

Trailhead
The trailhead is at the visitor center on Dunbar Cave Road. Turn onto Dunbar Cave Road from US 79 between downtown Clarksville and Exit 4 off I-24.

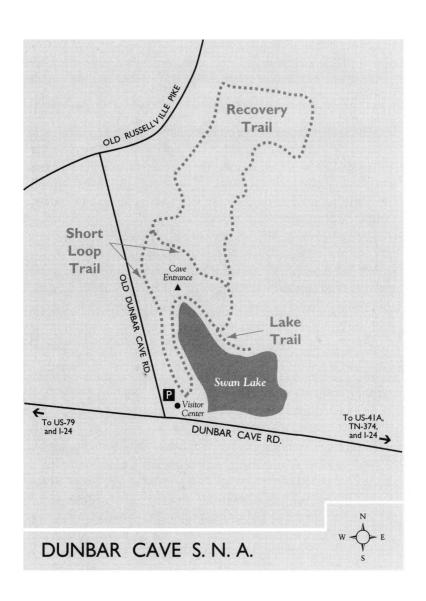

Recovery
Trail

Short
Loop
Trail

Cave
Entrance

Lake
Trail

OLD RUSSELLVILLE PIKE

OLD DUNBAR CAVE RD.

Swan Lake

P

Visitor
Center

To US-79
and I-24

DUNBAR CAVE RD.

To US-41A,
TN-374,
and I-24

DUNBAR CAVE S. N. A.

N
W — E
S

Hike Description

This hike takes in the park's three trails as it circles Swan Lake and crosses the forested ridge.

From the visitor center, take the paved path along the lake. The turtles sunning on the logs may stay put as you walk past. Then again, they may not. They shy away from people and often slide into the lake when hikers approach.

As you walk toward the ridge ahead, you'll be treated to a honking serenade by Swan Lake's Canada geese and other waterfowl. Don't be surprised if a flock of coots skitters away as you approach. Coots are slate-gray, ducklike birds with nearly black heads and white bills. They can also be recognized by the way they patter over the water before taking off. Coots are common in Middle Tennessee from September to May.

The trail follows the lake under splashes of April-blooming redbud below the steep, oak-covered hillside before reaching the grotto that holds the cave entrance. Climb the stairs. The opening is tucked beneath a tall bluff of sedimentary rock. The big concrete deck served as a dance floor when Dunbar Cave was a popular entertainment venue.

After visiting the entrance, return to the lakeside and go through the arches under the concrete deck. Follow the trail around the lake to where it turns left to ascend the ridge. The name now changes from the Lake Trail to the Short Loop Trail.

The trail climbs the hill past several beds of May apple, one of the most common wildflowers on the Highland Rim—and also one of the most interesting. May apple usually grows in colonies, as you see here. The plant has two umbrella-like leaves and a single flower that blooms under the leaves. Parts of the plant are prized for medicines. Indians used them as laxatives. Today, May apple is being studied as a source of anticancer medications.

As the rocky trail through the oaks crests the ridge, you will reach a junction where the Short Loop Trail goes left and the Recovery Trail goes straight; follow the Recovery Trail. It drops off the ridge and out of the big timber into a newer forest of cedar, dogwood, tulip poplar, and sassafras. Here, the land is slowly recovering from farming.

The trail curves through a bottom covered with straight, tall tulip poplars mixed with a few sycamores, then circles broadly around the foot of the ridge before making a gentle climb. After tunneling through some cedars bent from an ice storm, it turns and tops out on the ridge. The trail then eases down through a mix of dogwood and redbud before running straight as a yardstick through a cedar thicket. Here, you'll find year-round splotches of green provided by the cedars, some holly trees, and thick mats of club moss.

After curving through a showy display of dogwood, the trail dips into the head of the tulip poplar–covered cove you traversed earlier, then rises through still more dogwood to the top of the hill. This stretch is abundant with cardinals, whose bright red color makes them easy to spot among the dark cedars. Cardinals are among the most common year-round birds in Tennessee. They are often seen in scrubby thickets like this one.

The trail passes a large oak, reenters the old forest, and descends gently through more May apple. Where the Recovery Trail ends at the Short Loop Trail at 1.1 miles, go straight, continuing the gentle descent. When you reach the grotto holding the cave entrance, go right on the old paved road, then walk past a grove of straight, tall oaks to the visitor center, where you started the hike.

FORT DONELSON
NATIONAL BATTLEFIELD

Resting beautifully above the Cumberland River at Dover, this park preserves some of the rugged hills and hollows fought over in February 1862. The fields and woods are so peaceful today that it's difficult to imagine the carnage and suffering here during the Civil War.

You can combine history and nature on an easy, well-maintained trail that circles from the heights down to the river and back. You'll pass Confederate fortifications, artillery batteries that guarded the river, a wildlife management area, and a mature hardwood forest containing diverse plants.

Most of the 537-acre national battlefield lies between Hickman and Indian Creeks, now backed up by Lake Barkley. In addition to the hike described here, a 1-mile trail follows the Confederate fortifications from Grave's Battery, located near the visitor center, to stop number eight on the driving tour, French's Battery. You can also enjoy pleasant walking on the park roads.

The Union campaign against Fort Donelson boosted sagging

morale in the North and profoundly affected the outcome of the Civil War. This was the first successful campaign combining land and naval forces. It opened the Tennessee and Cumberland Rivers for Union advances into the Confederate heartland and led to the surrender of Nashville, one of the South's most important cities. The battle also propelled an unknown Confederate cavalry officer into the spotlight. And the Union victory put a Federal officer on the road to the presidency.

One of the five original full generals in the Confederate army, Albert Sidney Johnston was assigned an impossible task early in the war. His mission was to defend the vast Confederate territory from the Appalachian Mountains west to what is now Oklahoma. It was only a matter of time before the Federals attempted to penetrate Johnston's thin gray line.

In those days before good roads, and in a part of the country where there were few railroads, the rivers—the Mississippi, the Tennessee, and the Cumberland—were the obvious routes for Northern invasion. After a Federal attempt to advance on the Mississippi failed, it was time to try the Tennessee and the Cumberland.

To defend against river advances, the Southerners built two forts near the border of neutral Kentucky: Fort Henry on the Tennessee and Fort Donelson on the Cumberland. It took awhile, but Brigadier General Ulysses S. Grant and Flag Officer Andrew H. Foote finally convinced their superiors to let Grant's soldiers and Foote's gunboats assault the forts. On February 3, 1862, a flotilla steamed up the Ohio from Grant's headquarters in Cairo, Illinois. It navigated up the Tennessee and easily captured poorly situated Fort Henry on February 6. (You can hike through part of Fort Henry at Land Between the Lakes; see pages 139–50.)

Fort Donelson would not be so easy. It was built in a stronger position, on a hill above the river. And as the Federals advanced from Fort Henry, the Confederates hastily built more extensive fortifications in a large crescent on the high ridges around the river town of Dover.

Grant's soldiers marched across the narrow strip of land between the two rivers while Foote's fleet navigated the Cumberland. It was balmy and springlike, and many Federal soldiers discarded their coats and blankets, unaware of Tennessee's fickle weather. Meanwhile, Johnston faced a difficult choice. Should he send most of his troops to Dover to combat the Federals, or should he retreat into Tennessee and make a stand at a more secure place? He chose the latter, ordering four brigadier generals to take their troops to Dover to slow Grant's advance while the rest of the Confederate forces slipped from the Kentucky border into Tennessee.

Johnston's decision was badly flawed. Instead of going to Dover to take command himself, he sent four subordinates of equal rank. The line of authority among them was blurred, and they disagreed on how to confront Grant. As steamboats chugging down the Cumberland from Clarksville brought a steady stream of Confederate reinforcements, one of the generals made a boastful prediction. Columbia's Gideon Pillow, a political general with limited military experience, wired the governor in Nashville, "I will never surrender the position, and with God's help, I mean to maintain it."

Grant's troops had nearly surrounded the entrenched Confederates by nightfall on February 12. The next day, Grant ordered his division commanders to probe the Confederate lines. In violation of his orders, they launched more forceful attacks. At the same time, Foote's gunboats shelled Confederate positions. But at the end of the day, the adversaries were in about the same positions as they had been at dawn.

The weather then became a factor. A bitter wind blew in a cold front laden with sleet and snow. Though temperatures that night plummeted to near 10 degrees, leaders on both sides prohibited campfires for fear of drawing enemy artillery. More than a few soldiers froze to death. The suffering was particularly bad among the wounded who lay in the no man's land between the lines.

On February 14, most of the action was on the river, and it went the Confederates' way. Grant thought Foote's gunboats could steam past Fort Donelson, but he was wrong. The Southern gunners sent them fleeing downriver. But even with that success, the situation for the men in gray was desperate. The cold, surrounded troops were running out of food. Something had to be done.

Though they initially disagreed about the next step, the four Confederate brigadiers finally decided to attempt to break out. On the morning of February 15, Pillow led an attack against the Federal right south of Dover. The goal was to clear the road to Nashville and allow the trapped Confederates to escape. Unknown to the Southern brigadiers, Grant was not at the front, but was on the river conferring with Foote. Now it was the Federals who suffered from lack of leadership.

Pillow's attack was a dramatic success. In intense fighting that turned the snow-covered ground a bloody red, his men pushed the Federals back far enough to clear the road to Nashville.

When Grant heard the distant sound of fighting, he returned and organized a counterattack. Meanwhile, Pillow and Simon Bolivar Buckner—another of the four brigadiers—argued about what to do next. Buckner wanted to lead the troops on to Nashville right then, but Pillow favored returning them to their original positions to retrieve baggage, artillery, supplies, and the rest of the men. They turned to the senior brigadier, John B. Floyd, a Virginian who had been secretary of war under James Buchanan, Abraham Lincoln's predecessor in the White House. A politician turned general, Floyd first agreed with Buckner, then sided with Pillow, ordering the troops to give up their hard-won positions and return to where they had been that morning.

On the night of February 16, Floyd wired Johnston, the Confederate commander, by then in Nashville, that the Southerners had won a great victory. Floyd ordered an evacuation to Nashville by the road secured by Pillow's advance. But then the full effect of the divided Confederate command surfaced. Reports came in during the night that Grant's troops had reoccupied their original positions and closed the escape route. The generals debated what to do next. Someone mentioned surrender, the course finally agreed upon. Pillow and Floyd took to the river and fled, leaving Buckner to surrender.

Buckner sent a message to Grant asking to discuss terms. The West Point–educated Kentuckian was offended by Grant's response—"Unconditional surrender"—but was in no position to bargain. On Sunday morning, Grant accepted Buckner's surrender at the Dover Hotel. Nearly 12,000 Southerners prepared to be led away to prisons north of the Ohio River.

There was one Confederate officer who insisted he had not come to Fort Donelson to surrender. Nathan Bedford Forrest, who had joined the army as a private and was by then a cavalry colonel, led his brigade of horse soldiers and some infantry through the frozen waters of Lick Creek and away to safety. By the end of the war, Forrest was a lieutenant general and one of the most respected and feared cavalry officers on either side.

"Unconditional Surrender" Grant became a hero in the North. He was promoted to major general and was eventually given command of all Union forces in the West, which included Tennessee in those days. After Grant's success at Vicksburg and Chattanooga, President Lincoln made him the first lieutenant general in the United States Army since George Washington. It was only then, fairly late in the war, that the Ohio native went east to face Robert E. Lee in Virginia.

Interestingly, Grant had been a failure in the old army. After graduating from West Point, he had served in the Mexican War. Then drinking got the best of him. While stationed in Oregon in 1854, he was allowed to resign his commission rather than face a court-martial for habitual intoxication. He borrowed money for passage to New York. While there, he became destitute. His hotel refused him credit and even seized his baggage. He asked a friend, a fellow officer, for help. That friend restored his credit at the hotel and financed Grant's trip back to the Midwest. The friend was Simon Bolivar Buckner.

Before Buckner was taken north after the capture of Fort Donelson, Grant made a kind gesture to his humiliated opponent. "You are, I know, separated from your own people, and perhaps you need funds," he told Buckner. "My purse is at your disposal." Buckner declined the offer.

When Grant died in 1885, Buckner was a pallbearer at the funeral.

DONELSON TRAIL

Highlights
Civil War sites, overlooks above the
Cumberland River and Lake Barkley, rich forest

Length
3.4-mile loop

Maps
FDNB map and guide; USGS: Dover

Use
Hiking and day use only

Trailhead
The trailhead is at the park entrance, across from the visitor center.
Enter the park off US 79 on the western outskirts of Dover.

Hike Description
On this trail, you can learn about one of the turning points in the Civil War while you enjoy a splendid natural setting overlooking the Cumberland River.

The trail starts just inside the park entrance, across the road from the visitor center; it is not blazed but is well marked with signs. At first, it passes beneath the big oaks along the northern extreme of the Confederate earthworks. Except for a slight intrusion at the Jackson Battery, the route stays outside the earthworks. If you enjoy dogwoods blooming in April, this is the place for you, as the blossoms create a white cloud along the edge of the woods.

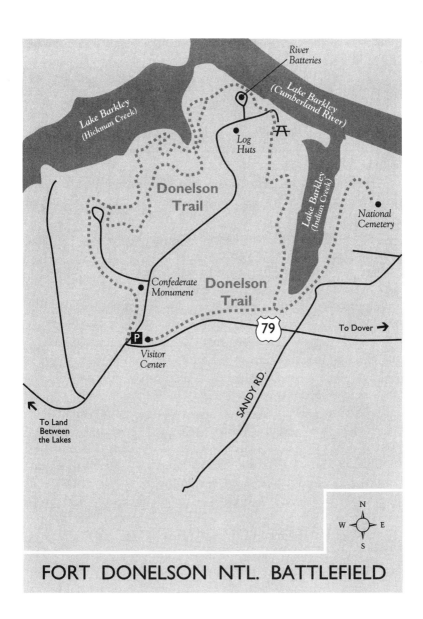

FORT DONELSON NTL. BATTLEFIELD

After Grant returned from his meeting with Foote on February 15 and discovered that his right flank had been defeated in Pillow's breakout, he decided to attack here, where the Confederate line was weakened by the movement of troops to support Pillow. The Federal left was commanded by Brigadier General C. F. Smith.

"General Smith," Grant said, "all has failed on the right. You must take Fort Donelson."

"I will do it," Smith proclaimed. He then went off to personally lead the assault.

Imagine the young flatlanders who had never tasted combat assaulting these steep slopes, which were covered with snow and ice and protected by an abatis—a barricade of felled trees. The Federals overran the weakened and poorly armed Southerners, pushing them off the earthworks.

Continue walking to the end of the Confederate earthworks above the Hickman Creek embayment of Lake Barkley. You will come to a trail sign that points to the Cumberland River and the visitor center. Turn right and circle around the loop at the end of the paved road to a sign where the Donelson Trail enters the woods.

The trail descends into a rich hollow of enormous tulip poplar, oak, sugar maple, shagbark hickory, beech, and sycamore rising above steep, fern-covered slopes. Spring wildflowers include phlox, crested dwarf iris, violet wood sorrel, giant chickweed, toadshade, spring beauty, slender toothwort, buttercups, and blue and yellow violets. After going down the opposite side of the hollow, the broad, easy trail climbs steeply out of it, crosses an old road next to a field, and descends into a nearly identical hollow. It runs down the hollow before climbing to a trail junction at 1.6 miles. (The trail leading left combines with the Donelson Trail to form the 1.9-mile River Circle Trail.)

Go right. You will immediately enter the fields above the river where the Confederate river batteries were located. There is no defined trail through here. After you have inspected the lower water battery, make your way down to the riverbank and go right, heading upstream.

It was here that General Grant hoped to repeat the easy naval assault that had helped capture Fort Henry on the Tennessee River. On February 14, he directed Foote to steam his boats up the river and attack Fort Donelson. The green Confederate gunners proved up to the task, though. In a fierce 90-minute battle, they repulsed the Union gunboats, sending them retreating down the river. If the Confederates at Fort Donelson were to be defeated, it would have to be by land, not by water.

The lower water battery is a good place to stop and enjoy the abundance of birds along the Cumberland. You're likely to see Tennessee's largest nesting bird, the great blue heron, wading in the shallows. You'll probably also encounter a flock of killdeer, a breed of plover that's a year-round resident. The land and water across the river is part of the Barkley Wildlife Management Area, owned by the Corps of Engineers but managed by the Tennessee Wildlife Resources Agency.

From the lower water battery, follow some steps from near the river up to the site of the upper water battery. A marker notes that the guns were manned by the Maury Artillery, a unit from the Columbia area.

The path leading away from the marker forks. Take the left fork up to the top of the bluff. The trail through here is an undefined route that crosses the road above the picnic area, passes a huge, lone sweet gum and an even larger oak, and circles below the wall of Fort Donelson to a sign.

Though the struggle here is known as the Battle of Fort Donelson, the fort actually took up only this immediate area. The fortifications you walked along earlier were part of the earthworks the Confederates built after the fall of Fort Henry. Fort Donelson was named for Confederate general Daniel Smith Donelson, grandson of pioneer leader Daniel Smith and nephew of Andrew Jackson. Donelson's splendid plantation home, Hazel Path, still stands in Hendersonville in an office park of the same name.

Follow the route down the hill through a meadow. When you reach the bottom, look up the ravine to see replicas of the log huts that housed Fort Donelson's small garrison.

Keep a lookout for red-tailed hawks. This is excellent habitat for these big birds, as they can work the edge between the woods and the open field. You might see red-headed woodpeckers, too. They prefer areas near swamps and river bottoms.

The trail curves, passes a pine plantation, and reenters the hardwoods. Finding the route through the nearly pure stands of oak can be tricky when the leaves are down. At 2.4 miles, the trail drops to meet an old road, which it follows left for 600 feet. The trail then takes off to the right and enters an aromatic thicket of pine and cedar, where the walking is easy on a carpet of moss.

At 2.7 miles, on a ridge above the highway, you'll come to a spur trail that leads 1.3 miles to the national cemetery. Whether you walk to it or drive to it, the cemetery is worth a visit. Located on high land back from the river where the Federals built a fort in 1863, it was designated a national cemetery in 1867. Of the 655 Union soldiers reinterred after the Civil War, 504 are unknown. One interesting feature of the cemetery is the 1877 Second Empire–style house that is now used as staff quarters.

The Donelson Trail goes to the right through an understory of dogwood and past a colonnade of large oak trees before it drops into a deep hollow. It then climbs out on some switchbacks and emerges into the field at the visitor center at 3.4 miles.

LAND BETWEEN THE LAKES

Outdoor opportunities are virtually unlimited at this 170,000-acre TVA-managed national recreation area that Middle Tennessee shares with western Kentucky. At Land Between the Lakes (LBL), you can enjoy relaxed walking on hundreds of miles of roads and trails. On the Tennessee side, the best walking is on the southern end of the 65-mile North-South Trail, which runs the length of LBL, and on the Fort Henry Trails, a 25-mile interconnecting network that follows the route Union troops took from Fort Henry to Fort Donelson during the Civil War. (For details of the campaign, see the chapter on Fort Donelson National Battlefield, pages 129–38.)

Other popular activities at LBL are hunting, fishing, horseback riding, bicycling, and bird-watching. The recreation area offers historic interpretations and a host of environmental education programs for organized groups and casual visitors alike. "Homeplace 1850" is a reconstructed farm that includes 16 log structures from the LBL region; staff members dressed in period clothing do a variety of seasonal chores for the farm and home.

LBL gets its name from two huge man-make lakes: Kentucky Lake on the Tennessee River and Lake Barkley on the Cumberland. Together, they provide LBL with more than 300 miles of shoreline. The two rivers come within a few miles of each other, creating an inland peninsula of gentle ridges that was once called "Between the Rivers." It became "Land Between the Lakes" in the 1960s, when Lake Barkley flooded the Cumberland River. The Tennessee River was already flooded by the huge Kentucky Dam the TVA completed in 1944.

The TVA came up with the idea for the recreation area in 1959, when the Corps of Engineers started building Barkley Dam, named for Alben W. Barkley, United States senator from Kentucky and vice president under Harry Truman. The concept for LBL was similar to the one implemented two decades earlier by the National Park Service at places like Fall Creek Falls and Montgomery Bell State Parks: take a place with limited potential for sustained agricultural or industrial development and turn it into a recreation area.

Because of its remoteness and the protection provided by the lakes, LBL has proven an excellent place to reintroduce animals that once flourished in Middle Tennessee.

Nesting bald eagles disappeared from this area in the 1950s, and wintering eagles hit a low point in the late 1960s and early 1970s. Bald eagles like areas around large bodies of water where there are plenty of fish to eat and trees in which to nest and roost. What better place to try to restore the population than LBL? An aggressive 10-year hacking program that started in 1980 was quite successful. Hacking involves gathering eight-week-old birds from their nests, bringing them to LBL, and placing them on caged platforms. The cages are opened at 12 weeks with the hope that the young eagles will return to the area in a few years to establish their own nests and reproduce.

Buffalo, or woodland bison—a species different from the plains bison—once lived in Middle Tennessee. They have been reintroduced in a protected area at LBL, as have red wolves. The

Tennessee Wildlife Resources Agency, its Kentucky counterpart, and the TVA are also considering introducing elk at LBL. Elk had just about disappeared from Tennessee by the Civil War. The last one was spotted near Reelfoot Lake in Obion County in 1865.

The United Nations has designated LBL as an International Biosphere Reserve. It's an excellent place to study the natural environment and the impact humans have on it.

LBL cooperates with the Center for Field Biology at nearby Austin Peay State University. The center publishes several fine books, as well as technical publications. Books can be purchased at the South Welcome Station or from the Center for Field Biology, Austin Peay State University, Clarksville, TN 37044.

PICKET LOOP

Highlights
Civil War earthworks, dogwood-filled hardwood forest, Kentucky Lake shore

Length
4.5-mile loop

Maps
LBL trail guide; USGS: Hamlin

Use
The trail is designated for hiking only. A permit is required for back-country camping.

Trailhead
The Fort Henry Trails parking area is located off Fort Henry Road. Turn off Fort Henry Road 4.6 miles north of its junction with US 79 or 6 miles west of the South Welcome Station.

Hike Description

This easy trail through an oak-hickory forest visits the site of Fort Henry's picket line and offers nice views of Panther Bay on Kentucky Lake. It's part of the 25-mile Fort Henry Trails network, constructed as a cooperative effort by the TVA, the National Park Service, historians, college students, and Boy Scout troops from Dover and Clarksville.

Enter the woods from the parking area and walk a few feet to the trail sign. The blue-blazed Picket Loop goes right. (Disregard the signs telling you that the Blue-Gray Trail is closed.)

Fort Henry is underwater today, covered by Kentucky Lake. It was flooded during the Civil War, too. That's one reason it fell so quickly to the Union navy. There were better sites downriver on higher ground, but Tennessee's secessionist governor, Isham G. Harris, didn't want to violate Kentucky's declared neutrality and push the Bluegrass State into the Union camp, so he ordered the fort built just inside Tennessee.

As 15,000 Federal troops steamed up the Tennessee River in February 1862, the 2,800 Confederates at Fort Henry found themselves poorly armed with shotguns and old muskets left over from the War of 1812. Much of their powder was wet from the flooding and therefore useless. And many soldiers were sick.

At the appearance of Federal gunboats, the Confederate commander, Brigadier General Lloyd Tilghman, sent most of his troops to Fort Donelson on the Cumberland. The only real resistance was offered by the guns in the fort. Ulysses S. Grant's soldiers landed downstream and started their march on the fort, only to have it surrender to the navy before they arrived.

The quick fall of Fort Henry opened the Tennessee River to the Union. Just to show how open the river was, a small Federal gunboat fleet steamed up the river 150 miles, all the way to Muscle Shoals, Alabama, and back.

The Picket Loop goes to the right, then turns left on an old road. Where the road reaches a bottom lined with matchstick-straight tulip poplar, the trail turns right and follows the bottom through beds of ferns. At 0.4 mile, it crosses the paved road to Boswell Landing.

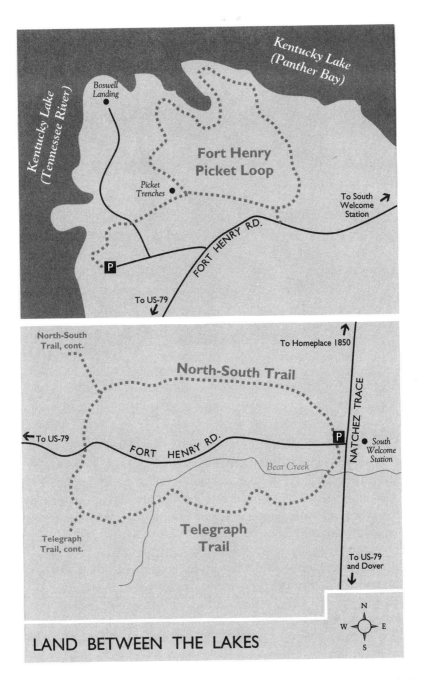

LAND BETWEEN THE LAKES

Panther Bay on the Picket Loop

TENNESSEE DEPARTMENT OF ENVIRONMENT AND CONSERVATION

The trail continues up the moist, fertile bottom through a forest dominated by large oak before climbing to a ridge where the shallow soil produces noticeably smaller trees. The understory of dogwood puts on a showy display of white in the spring. The trail crests the ridge and passes Civil War picket trenches at a trail junction at 0.8 mile.

During the Civil War, it was customary to station pickets outside fortifications—sort of an advance guard to slow down an attacking enemy. The Confederate pickets stationed here skirmished with Grant's Federals as they crept toward the fort.

At the junction, you'll see the first of the numbered markers placed along the Fort Henry Trails by the TVA. This junction is number 23. The loop begins here; turn left to hike it clockwise.

Middle Tennessee on Foot

Follow the trail along an old road that runs parallel to the picket trenches. Before long, it leaves the forest of old hardwoods and curves among cedar thickets, open glades, and scrub. After reentering deep woods, it reaches marker 24, where a yellow-blazed connector path leads left 0.4 mile to Boswell Landing.

Continue along the blue-blazed trail, where Kentucky Lake will come into view. The TVA started constructing Kentucky Dam in 1938 but didn't complete it until 1944. At the time it was built, the resulting man-made lake was the world's largest. It backs up the Tennessee River across the width of the Volunteer State almost to the Alabama border.

The trail circles a cove, alternating between the ridge and the bottom. In the quiet mud flats at the head of the cove, keep an eye out for turtles sunning themselves. At the same time a man-made lake destroys one environment, it creates another. The mud flats are a new environment created by the lowering of the reservoir in summer and fall. The flats are colonized by plants adapted to intermittent inundation and saturated soil and by species capable of completing a life cycle between the drawdown and the first frost.

After a swing to the right, the trail climbs the ridge above Panther Bay, the embayment created by Panther Creek.

It's not uncommon to find the name *Panther* in Middle Tennessee, though it's uncommon indeed to find an actual panther. As settlement moved westward, the panther, or Eastern cougar, disappeared. Every now and then, there are reported panther sightings, but none has been verified. Deer make up most of the panther's diet. With the restoration of Tennessee's deer herd, panthers may have a chance to reestablish themselves in the Volunteer State.

The trail follows an old road along the ridge through an understory of sugar maple. The walking is pleasant in this splendid forest overlooking Panther Bay. After reaching higher ground, the trail swings to the right—away from the lake—and follows an old road along the curving ridge through a disturbed area.

The TVA harvests timber at LBL. The idea is to create an

uneven-aged forest that's beneficial to certain wildlife species. Timber harvesting at LBL is controversial, though. Some critics say the agency should just leave the woods alone. The TVA's logging at LBL pays for itself, unlike other timber harvesting on federal lands, where trees are sold at a loss to the taxpayers.

After making a wide arc to the right, the trail straightens out and heads toward the paved Fort Henry Road. You will reach marker 26 just short of the road. Turn right, staying on the blue-blazed Picket Loop. (The yellow-blazed connector crosses the road to meet the Telegraph Trail, providing an alternate route to the trailhead that is slightly longer than the return on the Picket Loop.)

The Picket Loop briefly parallels the paved road before swinging to the right and running along the shallow trench dug by Fort Henry's Confederate pickets. In an open oak grove, it passes a deep sink on the right, then arrives at marker 23 at 3.7 miles. Turn left and retrace your route to the trailhead.

NORTH-SOUTH AND TELEGRAPH TRAILS

Highlights
Magnificent old forest, open fields, historic Civil War road

Length
6.3-mile loop

Maps
LBL trail guide; USGS: Tharpe

Use
Hiking is permitted, as is horse and vehicle use in some areas.
A permit is required for back-country camping.

Trailhead

The parking area is at the junction of The Trace and Fort Henry Road, across from the South Welcome Center.

Hike Description

This hike combines the southern tip of the North-South Trail with the historic Telegraph Trail, used by General Grant's soldiers to get from Fort Henry to Fort Donelson. Much of the hike goes through a magnificent old forest.

The white-blazed North-South Trail—which at first runs east to west—climbs away from the parking area through a stand of beech trees, swings left, and follows a gentle grade up a broad ridge through an understory of sugar maple that sets the late-October woods ablaze in yellow and orange. The trail stays on the ridge as it narrows between two deep sinks, then descends to a road at 0.9 mile.

Turn left and follow the road as it passes several pine thickets on the left. Except for a stand of shortleaf pines on nearby Devils Backbone, pines are not native to the LBL area. These were planted to control erosion and to provide cover for wildlife.

In the fall, when the floor of the oak-hickory forest is crisp with newly fallen leaves, you'll hear the constant rustle of gray squirrels scampering about as they prepare for winter. They're collecting hickory nuts and other hard-shelled nuts to bury. This not only provides the squirrels a source of food during cold weather but also helps regenerate the forest—gray squirrels don't have the greatest memories as to where they've buried their nuts. Look up into the trees after the leaves have fallen and you'll see squirrels' nests. They're made of leaves and twigs mounted in the forks of limbs. Squirrels also nest in tree cavities made by woodpeckers.

Other squirrels in Middle Tennessee are the fox squirrel and the Southern flying squirrel. Flying squirrels are active only at night, so you're not likely to see one. They get their name from the way they launch themselves from a limb and catch the air in folds of skin between their front and back legs. Using their tails as both rudder and brake, they can glide as far as 200 feet.

The trail passes through a cleared field, one of many the TVA keeps open to provide the edge habitat deer and other animals like so much. You will come to a junction at 2 miles. Veer left off the North-South Trail onto the road marked with a yellow blaze. This connector path follows the divide between the Tennessee and Cumberland Rivers. It goes through a cornfield before crossing Fort Henry Road at 2.8 miles. The TVA keeps such fields producing grain as yet another way of preserving the complex mosaic necessary for a diverse wildlife population. The land is leased to local farmers.

After you cross the road, take time to examine the small pond wedged between the paved and dirt roads.

Follow the dirt road. After a short distance, you'll pass a field on the right that's returning to forest. Reenter the woods. At 3.5 miles, you'll reach the Telegraph Trail at marker 10. Turn left on the red-blazed trail.

You won't see a telegraph line here now, but there was one during the Civil War. When the Confederates built Fort Donelson and Fort Henry, they cut a road between the rivers and strung a telegraph line. The trail follows that route.

Telegraph Road was one of two roads Union troops followed on February 11, 1862, to get from Fort Henry to Fort Donelson. The Southern weather was sure to be agreeable—or so thought many green Northerners as they discarded their heavy coats and blankets. Just two days later—when the temperature dropped to near 10 degrees, when the soldiers were not allowed to build fires, when sleet and snow fell on their blue backs—they longed for those coats and blankets littering this road.

The trail is covered in places with spongy moss and grass, making for comfortable walking. It descends through a stand of oak with an understory of beech, dogwood, and sugar maple, passes through a rough area covered with large cedar, and curves around a huge scarlet oak to the edge of a cornfield painted with the blooms of redbud and dogwood in April. It goes around the cornfield, turns left, and follows the bird-rich thicket between the woods and the field.

The trail then swings into the woods to run along the head-waters of Bear Creek. The fertile, moist soil here produces an incredible stand of huge tulip poplar, shagbark hickory, sugar maple, beech, and sycamore. The American sycamore is a common large tree in Middle Tennessee. More often than not, it's found along a stream, as here. It's recognizable by its bark, which is mottled white and light brown and often peels in irregular patches. To the pioneers who settled the region, the presence of sycamores meant rich soil.

You'll find all kinds of flowers blooming here in the spring—toadshade, giant chickweed, phlox, spring beauty, butterweed, rue anemone, violet wood sorrel, crested dwarf iris. But it's the Virginia bluebells that catch your attention. In April, they turn these rich Western Highland Rim bottoms almost solid blue.

After drifting again along the edge of the cornfield, the trail parallels the creek before reaching marker 11 at 4.1 miles. The trail to the right connects with the other route used by Grant's troops, known then as Ridge Road.

The Telegraph Trail follows the rough bank downstream, fords the creek, and follows the opposite bank past a long, deep pool before curving to the right and heading up a hollow. It passes one of the old-style Fort Henry Trails signs—number 12—then passes the remains of a log house in a grove of large sugar maple, then climbs the ridge to the right of the hollow.

From here to the end of the hike, the trail passes through a magnificent forest that has hardly seen an ax, a forest so special that it's a registered state natural area. This feels like virgin timber. As you climb the ridge, look into the hollow at the tall, straight tulip poplars and the stately beeches. Smooth-bark beeches keep their copper-colored fall foliage well into winter, providing splashes of color. Bear Creek State Natural Area contains a rare example of a mixed mesophytic forest, a forest type more often found on the Cumberland Plateau far to the east.

Near the crest of the ridge at marker 13, the trail veers left—away from historic Telegraph Road—and stays close to the edge of the beautiful hollow.

Wild turkeys love open forests where the trees grow far apart, so don't be surprised if you come upon a flock of them. By 1952, Tennessee's once-plentiful turkeys were reduced to 1,000 birds in only 18 of the state's 95 counties. The restocking program has been highly successful. Wildlife biologists now estimate there are well over 75,000 wild turkeys in Tennessee. Hunters kill in excess of 11,000 of the big birds annually. Indeed, hunting for wild turkeys is one of the most popular activities at LBL. The wild turkey is Tennessee's heaviest bird, weighing up to 20 pounds.

Soon, the giant poplars and beeches of the hollow give way to smaller oaks on top of the ridge as the trail follows the undulating crest through a quintessential oak-hickory forest. Where the trail crosses a moss-covered razorback between steep hollows, note the subtle differences between the forests on the north-facing slope, to your left, and the south-facing slope, to your right.

The trail dips and rises through some saddles and levels off briefly on a small, maple-covered plateau before making a rocky descent through patches of May apple to Bear Creek. Like the bottom you passed through earlier, this one is covered with wildflowers in spring.

The trail crosses the sycamore-lined creek without benefit of a bridge, passes a huge sweet gum on the opposite bank, and makes a beeline for the trailhead along the flower-dotted edge of the field. Various kinds of violets are among the flowers that flourish in the mowed fields here. You can recognize the Confederate violet by its whitish gray color.

JOHNSONVILLE STATE HISTORIC AREA

*I*t was one of the most bizarre fights of the Civil War—a battle between the cavalry and the navy. It took place on November 4, 1864, on the Tennessee River at the fortified Federal supply depot of Johnsonville. The town is gone now, but the fortifications can still be seen at Johnsonville State Historic Area, where nearly 5 miles of well-maintained trails penetrate a patch of river-bottom forest and upland woods.

To understand why the Johnsonville supply depot was so important, you have to look far to the southeast, to Atlanta, the transportation and manufacturing hub that fell to William Tecumseh Sherman's troops in September 1864. The capture of Atlanta boosted President Abraham Lincoln's chance for reelection in the war-weary North and stiffened resolve to win a military victory instead of negotiating a truce.

The Confederates hoped to reverse their declining fortunes by retaking Atlanta. But they couldn't do it militarily. Sherman's men had already whipped the Army of Tennessee under General John Bell Hood. The Confederates' best hope was to cut the supply line that fed Sherman's men in Georgia, which would force them to withdraw just to keep from starving.

The supplies Sherman's troops needed came by rail from occupied Nashville. From the North, those supplies were shipped via the Ohio River, then up the Tennessee River to Johnsonville, then by rail to the Tennessee capital. In fact, the Union army built the railroad to Johnsonville just for this purpose. Johnsonville was thus an inviting target.

Nathan Bedford Forrest was the right man to lead an attack, though he had only 3,000 cavalrymen and 12 artillery pieces. Regardless of one's opinion of the controversial Confederate general with no prewar soldiering experience, it cannot be denied that he was a daring and imaginative officer—a military genius, even.

Forrest led his men from Corinth, Mississippi, to near Paris Landing, located downstream from (north of) the Johnsonville depot. There, the Confederates captured two Federal boats, manned them, and launched them upstream. This impromptu navy—a collection of "horse marines," Forrest called it—was accompanied on land by the rest of Forrest's troops.

Johnsonville—named for Tennessee's military governor, Andrew Johnson—was lined with wharves bulging with food, clothes, blankets, whiskey, and munitions awaiting rail transport to Nashville.

Forrest placed artillery at Pilot Knob, on the heights across the river. Though his amateur sailors were outmanned by their professional opponents, Forrest's land-based guns sank or immobilized most of the Federal fleet. Forrest then turned his attention to Johnsonville itself. By nightfall, the town and its supplies were in flames. Forrest reported that he had captured or destroyed four gunboats, 14 transports, 20 barges, 26 artillery pieces, and $6.7 million worth of supplies. Some estimates place the Federal loss as high as $20 million.

But it was too late to force Sherman to retreat from Atlanta. If there was another general in the Civil War as bold as Forrest, it was Sherman, who had decided to abandon his vulnerable supply line and strike off on his famous March to the Sea, during which his men lived off the land.

Though Sherman had some choice words for "that devil

Forrest," as he called the Memphis native, the destruction of Johnsonville was immaterial to the welfare of the Union men. And it was immaterial to the outcome of the Civil War. Slightly more than five months later, in a field in Virginia, the curtain fell on this most tragic chapter in our nation's history.

JOHNSONVILLE REDOUBTS TRAIL

Highlights
Civil War fortifications, views of Kentucky Lake, varied forest

Length
1.7-mile loop

Maps
JSHA trails map; USGS: Johnsonville

Use
Hiking and day use only

Trailhead
The trailhead is at the museum parking lot. From US 70 at New Johnsonville, west of Waverly, turn onto Nell Beard Road and go to Old Johnsonville Road. Turn left into the park and follow the signs toward the picnic area and the museum. Just before the picnic area, take the dirt road to the right, then turn left up the steep paved drive. Note that trail maps are available at a display in the picnic area.

Hike Description
This trail descends to skirt the shore of Kentucky Lake and penetrate a rich, wooded bottom before circling back over the forested ridge and the remains of the Federal fortifications.

Before you start your walk, visit the earthworks next to the museum. This was the lower redoubt the Union army built to protect the depot at Johnsonville. The fortifications boasted 22 guns manned by the First Kansas Battery, but they were no match for Forrest's artillery, strategically placed along the opposite shore. And the guns on the Union boats proved ineffective, for they could not be raised enough to aim at the Confederate positions on the high land.

Inside the earthworks is a small graveyard, Winfrey Cemetery. The museum is open on weekends during the fall and spring and daily in the summer.

From the parking lot and the trail sign, walk toward the river a short distance to another sign at a junction. Go to the right through the oaks and shrubs. The bright red, orange, and yellow of the understory of sugar maple will greet you if you visit on the anniversary of the battle.

The trail drops steeply to curve around a big oak and meet an old road along Kentucky Lake. Turn left and follow the road through patches of April-blooming spring beauty and dwarf larkspur. The road comes to an inlet bordered by an often-muddy bottom filled with oak and sweet gum. The grassy point between the inlet and the main lake holds some bald cypress and is a nice place to enjoy expansive lake views. If the water is low, look for turtles on rocks in the lake.

To the right across the lake, you can see Pilot Knob, from which Forrest's cannoneers fired the shots that kept Federal naval reinforcements from reaching Johnsonville. (Pilot Knob is in 2,587-acre Nathan Bedford Forrest State Park, where visitors can day-hike or backpack on 20 miles of trail and visit the Tennessee River Folklife Center.)

Bald cypress trees like those here are common on the coastal plain of the Deep South, but you hardly ever see them growing naturally in Middle Tennessee. They tend to be found in swamps and flood plains and can even grow in standing water. If you visit Reelfoot Lake in West Tennessee, you'll see plenty of them. Because the wood is resistant to decay, it's prized for use in the construction of boats and docks. Though it looks like an ever-

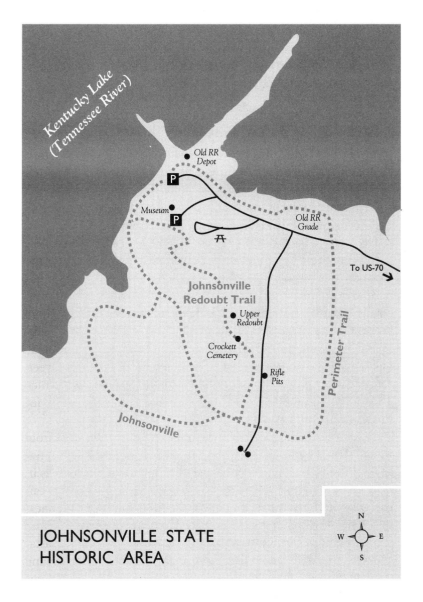

Kentucky Lake
(Tennessee River)

Old RR
Depot

P

Museum

P

🛉

Old RR
Grade

To US-70 →

**Johnsonville
Redoubt Trail**

Upper
Redoubt

Crockett
Cemetery

Rifle
Pits

Perimeter Trail

Johnsonville

JOHNSONVILLE STATE
HISTORIC AREA

N
W · E
S

green, the bald cypress is a deciduous tree that sheds its needles
in the fall.

From the point, follow the trail away from the lake, where

high water often deposits unsightly debris in this otherwise interesting bottom. You will arrive at a trail junction at 0.4 mile. Take the left fork. (The next hike follows the right fork.)

As you head for the uplands, you're likely to spot some of the deer that browse this rich bottom. Foxes and coyotes are occasionally seen here, too.

After some zigzags, the trail climbs steeply up the side of a hill under straight, tall oaks and hickories and next to azaleas that display their white and pink flowers in April. It levels off among spicebush and deerberry and follows a ridge spur to a junction. Take the left fork.

The trail abruptly leaves the woods at the end of a paved road at 0.8 mile. Go left above the flower-dotted bank before turning left and walking along the road. (The next hike follows the trail that crosses the road here.) The road penetrates Federal rifle pits manned in November 1864 by raw recruits from the 43rd Wisconsin Infantry and men of the 12th, 13th, and 100th United States Colored Infantry.

After passing an overlook that offers views across Kentucky Lake, you'll come to Crockett Cemetery. Turn left through the gap in the fence. A monument here honors the families that the TVA forced off their land when it dammed the Tennessee River in the 1940s.

After walking through the peaceful graveyard, return to the woods. You'll come to a sign after a few feet. Go right and walk around the top of the Federals' upper redoubt; children particularly enjoy walking on this snakelike enclosure. You'll then pass the grassy field that was the site of the Union army's horse corral. A small detachment from the 11th Tennessee (Union) Cavalry was part of the Johnsonville garrison.

Return to the trail and go right. You'll pass more azaleas and some mountain laurel that blooms around the first of May, then descend to a rocky gap and climb out of this tiny desert. After walking under a power line, you'll come to a junction at a good-size black cherry tree near some out-of-place bald cypress. Take the left fork.

The trail makes a hairpin turn around a broad plateau lined with rifle pits, then runs briefly along the power-line cut—a haven for songbirds—before curving to the junction near the parking lot where the hike started.

JOHNSONVILLE PERIMETER TRAIL

Highlights
Johnsonville town site, lakeshore walking, varied forest

Length
2.5-mile loop

Maps
JSHA trails map; USGS: Johnsonville

Use
Hiking and day use only

Trailhead
The trailhead is at the end of the dirt road below the museum. Follow the directions for the preceding hike, but instead of turning up to the museum, follow the dirt road to its end.

Hike Description
This hike visits the upland forest, the lakeshore, and the remains of Johnsonville. It's on a trail with no official name. The trail follows the park boundary for much of its length—thus the name *Johnsonville Perimeter Trail* used in this book.

Start the hike by walking along the gated road that curves below the lower redoubt. The old road runs along the shore of Kentucky Lake; your footsteps will be accompanied by the sound of the huge lake sloshing onto the rocky shore.

The route of the preceding hike soon comes in from the left, and the two hikes run conjunctively to the bald cypress–covered point and the bottom filled with oak and sweet gum. They separate at the trail junction at 0.5 mile. Go right and pick your way through the rich, often muddy flat to rejoin the old road south of the inlet. Follow it left a short distance, then turn left off it. To the sound of woodpeckers hammering away at the trees above, you'll walk under oak and hickory rising above an understory of sugar maple. After a right turn, the trail goes up a hill and tops out at a comfortable bench, a welcome sight after the steep climb. If the leaves are off the trees, you can sit here and look across Kentucky Lake.

This hike rejoins the previous one at 1.3 miles, then separates from it to cross the paved road. The walk down the dry, south-facing slope is steep but becomes more gentle as the trail enters Meredith Hollow. In the spring, violet wood sorrel, spring beauty, bluets, and violets flourish here.

After some level walking near a creek beneath a stand of straight, tall tulip poplar, the trail climbs over a rise and reaches the road at the park entrance at 2 miles. It crosses the road into an area that floods occasionally, then climbs to an old railroad grade along the Trace Creek arm of Kentucky Lake. Go left.

You're now walking on the bed of a Civil War railroad built for the Union army by Irish and German immigrants and recently freed slaves. Extended across the river after the war, this became the main line from Nashville to Memphis. The railroad was relocated from here when the lake was impounded.

The trail swings left off the bed and heads to the dirt road. Turn right and walk to the trailhead.

Started during the Civil War, Johnsonville remained a town for 100 years after the conflict. Look around and you'll see building foundations and the platform of the railroad station next to the roadbed. Much of the town, though, was buried by the waters of Kentucky Lake. New Johnsonville was born where the relocated railroad and US 70 cross the Tennessee River.

This ends the hike. If you like, you can follow the railroad bed as it juts into Kentucky Lake.

LADY FINGER BLUFF
SMALL WILD AREA

There are two good reasons to make your way to this remote spot on the Tennessee River: the enormous variety of spring wildflowers and the bluff's sensational views, which in fall and winter feature thousands of ducks and geese.

Lady Finger Bluff is one of several natural areas on TVA land that the agency has designated "small wild areas." It was originally called Ladies Bluff, supposedly because steamboat captains called their lady passengers on deck to admire the cliffs, which rise 200 feet above the river. The river here was quite narrow before being impounded as Kentucky Lake, which accounts for why the place was called The Narrows back in steamboat days. Even today, it's one of the thinnest stretches on Kentucky Lake's main channel.

The flowers along the trail tend to grow in species-specific communities—wildflower apartheid, in a manner of speaking. You'll see batches of false garlic, shooting star, toadshade, phlox, yellow wood sorrel, dwarf larkspur, and cut-leaf toothwort. Blue and yellow violets seem to be about the only species that don't mind mixing with the others.

LADY FINGER BLUFF TRAIL

Highlights
Bluff overlooking the Tennessee River and the wildlife refuge,
enormous variety of spring wildflowers

Length
2.7-mile loop

Maps
LFBSWA brochure; USGS: Jeannette

Use
Hiking and day use only

Trailhead
The parking area is off Lick Creek Road in Perry County. From Exit 143 off
I-40, take TN 13 south, turn west onto TN 50 between Lobelville and
Linden, and follow it for 12 miles to a junction. Take the right fork and
follow the paved road 5 miles to another fork. Follow the left fork for 0.1
mile, turn left on a dirt road, and proceed to the parking area. If you're
coming from Linden, turn right off US 412 onto Lick Creek Road just west
of town and follow the signs.

Hike Description
This short but dramatic trail is well worth the effort it takes to get
to the trailhead.

The trail leaves the parking lot, curves around a Kentucky Lake
backwater that sometimes floods during winter, and picks its way
along the steep, boulder-strewn hillside above the Lick Creek
embayment and then above the Tennessee River. (Mousetail Landing State Park and its Eagle Point Trail are just across the embayment.)
Keep an eye out for great blue herons wading in the shallows. If you
startle one, you'll know it from its loud squawking.

The trail soon curves around a lake inlet to cross a creek be-

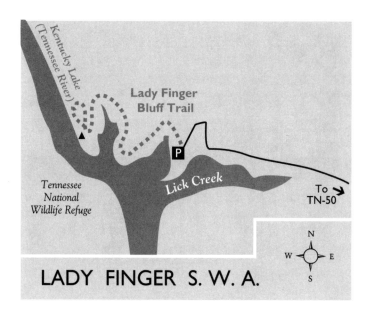

Lady Finger
Bluff Trail

Lick Creek

Tennessee
National
Wildlife Refuge

To →
TN-50

N
W ◆ E
S

LADY FINGER S. W. A.

neath some tulip poplar and beech trees; don't be surprised to see the white tails of deer hurtling away from you. The trail continues around the hill, then climbs to a sign. Go straight, as the sign instructs. A sensational view up and down the Tennessee River will open in front of you.

From your position next to gnarled cedars growing out over the sheer drop, you can look across to a unit of the Tennessee National Wildlife Refuge. The refuge was established in 1945, when Kentucky Lake was impounded. It is made up of 25,000 acres of water, 19,000 acres of woodland, and 5,000 acres of farmland and pasture in three units stretching 80 miles along the Tennessee River. Starting in October and extending through the winter, more than 150,000 ducks and 75,000 geese call at the refuge. At times, the water is covered with them.

There are two general kinds of ducks: diving ducks and dabbling ducks. The latter make up three-fourths of the refuge's population. Mallards are by far the most numerous of the 23 duck species, followed by widgeon, black ducks, and blue-winged teal.

Lady Finger Bluff Small Wild Area

Lady Finger Bluff overlooks the Tennessee National Wildlife Refuge

TENNESSEE VALLEY AUTHORITY

Wood ducks are the only ducks that nest here. They prefer holes in trees, just as woodpeckers do. But due to a loss of habitat, artificial nesting boxes must be used throughout the refuge. Among the geese seen here are the snow goose, the greater white-fronted goose, and the Canada goose. There are usually plenty of coots, too.

Since food for the ducks and geese is scarce, acreage is planted in corn, milo, soybeans, and winter wheat. Some fields are flooded, which creates a moist-soil environment that supports various natural aquatic plant foods.

You won't want to leave this lofty spot. But you must. From the bluff, the trail goes back into the woods, passes a deep lime-stone crevice, then climbs to an even higher bluff. The view from here is good, though not as expansive as that from the first bluff, due to the greater number of trees.

The unmarked route that loops back down the hill is difficult to follow; you may prefer to retrace your steps via the first bluff. If you do find the faint loop trail, follow it down to the intersection with the main trail, then walk back to the parking area.

MOUSETAIL LANDING STATE PARK

Mousetail is a key link in the chain of parks and preserves stretching along the Tennessee River and Kentucky Lake. The state park's 1,249 acres protect a mature hardwood forest, barren, rocky glades, meadows, and cedar-capped bluffs overlooking Tennessee National Wildlife Refuge. On Mousetail's two well-built trails, you're sure to see deer, wild turkeys, hawks, great blue herons, and a host of other wildlife, as well as colorful wildflowers in the spring and brilliant foliage in the fall.

The Tennessee River has been an important path of commerce since prehistoric times. During the 1800s, there was a river port at the site of today's state park. Leather tanning was a key industry in these parts. Hides were shipped by river to two competing tanneries, one at Rat Tail Landing and the other at Mousetail Landing. Supposedly, a fire at the larger tannery caused rats to flee their nests, an event that gave the place its name. The other tannery was smaller, so it was named Mousetail.

EAGLE POINT TRAIL

Highlights
Bluffs above the Tennessee River, varied forest,
abundant wildlife

Length
8.2-mile loop

Maps
MLSP trail map; USGS: Jeannette

Use
The trail is for hiking only. Camping at the two
back-country shelters is allowed by permit.

Trailhead
The trailhead is to the right of the main park road just
below the park office. To reach the park, turn off US 412 onto
TN 50 west of Linden. If you're coming from Lady Finger
Bluff, follow TN 50 southwest.

Hike Description
This hike passes through several forest types to a bluff overlooking the Tennessee River and a national wildlife refuge teem-
ing with ducks and geese in winter. It offers a display of spring
wildflowers, too. You'll see phlox, toadshade, May apple, and violets throughout the hike. And at select places, you'll come across
fire pink, false garlic, butterweed, spring beauty, rue anemone,
Virginia spiderwort, crested dwarf iris, pussy-toes, red buckeye,
hound's-tongue, and doll's eyes. The blue-and-orange trail blazes
are faint in places, so watch closely.

The trail wanders up the side of Kelly Hollow through a second-growth forest of oak, tulip poplar, and beech. It then drops
to a mowed field, crosses it, and reenters the woods on the other
side. The field is a good place to observe wildlife. Deer usually

browse here in early morning and late afternoon. Just about anytime, you're sure to see—and probably hear—a hawk high above the field scouting for an unsuspecting rodent.

After a short stretch next to a branch and the first of its many encounters with old roads, the moss-covered trail starts a long, gentle climb up Sparks Ridge, weaving into and out of the ribs connected to the ridge's narrow spine. Huge colonies of May apple and several kinds of ferns line the trail as it climbs beneath the oak and dogwood. Where the trail hugs the park boundary, look downhill and you'll see three massive beech trees shading the entire hollow.

The trail briefly teeters along the narrow ridge before dropping down a narrow rib between two steep hollows. It descends, then descends some more before reaching the bottom, where some ash trees grow next to a cleared field. It runs up this moist, flower- and fern-covered bottom before turning left to cross a sturdy bridge spanning the usually dry Parrish Branch. After skirting the edge of a field lined with cedar, redbud, and dogwood—another good place to spot deer—the trail enters a dry, young wooded area filled with cedar and maple.

Then the environment suddenly changes. The soft footing you've been enjoying turns to rocks as the trail enters a barren glade dotted with tall cedar trees. Several types of flowers take to this barren minidesert, including hoary puccoon and blue-eyed grass.

Watch where you step. Snakes love these dry, rocky places. In fact, this glade is home to at least one big timber rattlesnake. Of the 20 or so snake species in the Midstate, only four are venomous: the timber rattlesnake, the pygmy rattlesnake, the copperhead, and the cottonmouth. They can be distinguished from nonvenomous snakes by their triangular heads and, of course, in the case of rattlesnakes, by their rattles. Snakes are fairly common on the ridges along Kentucky Lake, but most are harmless. Even so, it's best to observe them at a distance.

The trail returns to the oaks and hickories, crosses a stream that's no more than a trickle, and reaches the beginning of the

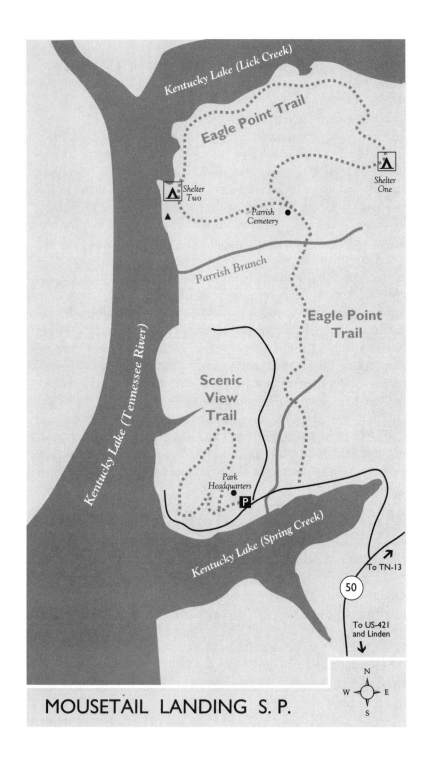

Kentucky Lake (Lick Creek)

Eagle Point Trail

Shelter One

Shelter Two

Parish Cemetery

Parrish Branch

Eagle Point Trail

Scenic View Trail

Park Headquarters

Kentucky Lake (Tennessee River)

Kentucky Lake (Spring Creek)

To TN-13

50

To US-421 and Linden

N
W E
S

MOUSETAIL LANDING S. P.

loop at 2 miles. Go right to hike it counterclockwise.

The trail climbs a dry, south-facing slope, levels off on a shallow-soil plateau, climbs, levels off again, then climbs to reach the ridge crest. After going over the edge, it picks up an old road and follows it into a saddle.

At 2.7 miles, the road splits. Go straight, following the faint blue blazes on the trees. Just beyond the saddle, the trail veers right off the old road to run beneath some tall cedars. After re-entering the older oak-hickory forest, it follows the curving ridge before swinging left over the crest and reaching the first of two back-country shelters at 3.1 miles. The shelters are sturdy, well-maintained, screened-in structures that can sleep up to eight people. There is no water, so if you camp here, you'll have to pack it in.

From the shelter, the trail follows the narrow ridge crest for 200 feet before angling left down the hill. (Don't be deceived by the path that stays on the crest and quickly leaves the park.) Where some blowdowns have covered the trail with a messy tangle of limbs and vines, the trail may be difficult to find. But once you're past this small jungle, the route becomes obvious.

The trail zigzags down a long hill and passes some tall, summer-blooming columbo. You're sure to see and hear lots of birds that are attracted to this mixture of cedars and hardwoods. (Note that the park trail map is misleading, for it shows the trail as being nearly straight here, rather than curving as it does.)

At the bottom of the hill, the trail picks up the remnant of an old road and plays tag with it for quite a ways. The trail cuts left off the road into the woods next to a stand of sweet gum and goes up and down through a rough area of small ravines, where it may be difficult to distinguish between the man-made trail and the natural trails made by water flowing off the ridge.

When you enter a quiet, soft, mossy cedar thicket, you'll know you're on the right trail. You'll then pass another cedar glade, where you'll find some June-blooming prickly pear cactus. Before long, you'll pick up the old road again and follow it into a broad bottom next to the Lick Creek embayment of Kentucky Lake.

The trail climbs gradually out of the bottom and circles some fern-lined gullies; in the spring, you'll see lots of blue and yellow violets here. The trail then reunites with the old road to cross a low saddle. If you're making this hike after a heavy rain, you'll have to tiptoe over impromptu creeks crashing off a ridge that rises 250 feet above the lake. As you enter an old forest of big trees, views of the lake will open up to the right. (The trailhead for the Lady Finger Bluff Trail, the preceding hike, is just across the embayment.)

The trail now runs along the bluff above the lake before it turns left with the road to make a short, steep climb. The road and trail part company again as the trail goes right and follows a fern-covered hillside. It then wanders down to meet the lakeshore at the head of a tiny cove near the mouth of Lick Creek. After cresting a cedar-covered rise, it passes a slightly deeper cove. This bottom is prone to flooding, so pay careful attention. The route can also be difficult to follow. You'll then make a long climb. If you look to the right to the break in the trees, you'll suspect that things are about to change. Sure enough, you'll soon find yourself on a tall bluff overlooking the Tennessee River, impounded as Kentucky Lake.

Some geologists consider the Western Valley of the Tennessee River to be a distinct physiographic region. It isn't much wider than the river itself, yet few places are endowed with as much public recreational land. Starting with Land Between the Lakes on the north and ending upstream with Pickwick Landing State Park on the south, a multitude of state and federal parks and preserves—everything from wildlife refuges to Civil War battlefields—is offered.

After this first peek at the river, the trail swings away from the bluff. At 5.6 miles, in a stand of big cedars, it reaches a path that leads to the right to the second shelter.

It's difficult to imagine a more interesting place to camp. The shelter sits near the edge of the bluff and its expansive views of the narrow valley. The river and the ponds of the wildlife refuge are covered with ducks and geese in winter. You might spot a bald eagle, too. In spring, you can enjoy a showy display of wild-flowers that includes false garlic and violet wood sorrel. Look left—upstream—and you'll see the Alvin C. York Bridge, which carries US 412 to West Tennessee. Mousetail Landing is just down the bluff to the left.

Alvin C. York was America's most decorated World War I hero. In the Argonne Forest, the young Tennessean single-handedly killed 25 German soldiers, then captured a major whom he talked into persuading 131 other Germans to surrender. York has been honored countless times, as he was here in Perry County, where the original bridge spanning the Tennessee River was named for him.

You'll probably see a towboat churning along the river with its load of sand, gravel, or some other bulk commodity. Kentucky Lake provides a year-round navigation channel where more than 45 million tons of cargo pass each year. The Tennessee is the fifth-largest river system in the nation, with a watershed covering 41,000 square miles. It's home to 241 species of fish and 100 species of freshwater mussels.

From the junction with the path to the shelter, the trail curves around a sinkhole, passes an enormous oak, and makes its way down through some cedars. It twice crosses the old road and runs through dry, boulder-strewn woods before coming to Parrish Cemetery at 6.2 miles. This graveyard is a peaceful, green spot watched over by tall cedars.

A few hundred feet past the cemetery, you will complete the loop at the trail junction. Retrace your steps to the trailhead.

SCENIC VIEW TRAIL

Highlights
Mature forest, tree-identification program,
mountainlike environment

Length
3-mile loop

Maps
MLSP trails map; USGS: Jeannette

Use
Hiking and day use only

Trailhead
The trailhead is behind the park office. To reach the office,
see the directions for the preceding hike.

Hike Description
This trail offers some of the Midstate's most delightful walking
on carpets of thick, green moss in an environment that looks more
like the southern Appalachians than the western edge of Middle
Tennessee. Your visit will likely be enhanced by the tree-identification program developed by several state agencies and private timber companies. The numbers on the trees correspond to those on a
brochure available outside the attractive, log park office.

Sparks Ridge throws off two spurs before it gives out near the
Tennessee River. The trail runs along the spurs and through the
hollow between them.

Climb to the eastern spur behind the office and walk through
its handsome forest to reach the start of the loop. Go left to hike
the loop clockwise.

At the end of the ridge above Kentucky Lake's Spring Creek
embayment, the trail curves down to an oak grove and crosses a
stream that's usually dry. It then runs along the side of the western spur and comes to an open field above the picnic pavilion.
Turn right just short of the field and climb the ridge.

If you're here in the spring, you'll think from the splashes of red
ahead that some inconsiderate slob has littered the ground. But as
you get closer, you'll discover a big field of fire pink, one of the
region's few bright red wildflowers. Fire pink is easily recognized
by its five-petaled, starlike shape.

A variety of oaks and lots of dogwoods cover the woods where the trail crests the ridge. It follows the ups and downs of the ridge top on a carpet of green moss so thick it looks as if someone has installed high-grade carpet.

You'll come to a junction with the short trail to the campground. Go right, following the crest of Sparks Ridge's eastern spur.

After walking a bit, stop, close your eyes for a moment, then open them. If you suddenly found yourself here in April, where would you think you were? The Blue Ridge Mountains, most likely. Mountain laurel dots the woods. Azaleas, both pink and white, bloom on the side of the ridge. Spicebush is everywhere. The narrow ridge crest is covered with the delicate flowers of silver bell. Chestnut oak is in the forest canopy. And of course, moss covers the ground.

Continue through this mountainlike environment to the start of the loop. Turn left and return to the park office.

HIKES

ON

THE

EASTERN HIGHLAND RIM

OLD STONE FORT
STATE ARCHAEOLOGICAL AREA

This prehistoric site is located in a dramatic setting where two forks of the Duck River cascade off the Highland Rim on their way to the Central Basin. A 2,000-year-old earthen wall is the main attraction, but the area's rugged beauty and diverse topography make it special for its natural setting alone.

The excellent trail network that winds through the archaeological site and above the tumbling streams offers some of the finest walking in Middle Tennessee. There's an easy walk of 1.25 miles around the wall, but it misses some of the most spectacular scenery. The hike described below combines part of the wall walk with more remote trails. The park's location within the city of Manchester makes its dogwood-lined roads popular with walkers, too.

Between the forks of the Duck and Little Duck Rivers is a plain lined in places by an earthen wall. If this wall were continuous, it would measure 4,600 feet in length and enclose more than 40 acres.

Until the state acquired the site in 1966 and asked anthropologists from the University of Tennessee to investigate it, no one knew the origin of the wall. There were several preposterous theories: De Soto's Spanish explorers built it in 1540; Vikings built it on a pre-Columbian expedition; Modac, the Welsh prince, built it in 1170. The most prevalent theory—and the one that made the most sense—was that this was an early Native American fortification. Hence the name Old Stone Fort.

That theory proved wrong, too. There is higher ground outside the enclosure that would have rendered the walls useless against attack. And there likely wouldn't have been enough people to defend such a large enclosure. More important, the excavations didn't reveal much in the way of pottery or other artifacts used in daily living. The conclusion: the walls set aside a place of spiritual significance.

Radiocarbon dating of charcoal samples established that the oldest section of the wall was built around 30 A.D. and the latest section around 430 A.D., which means that the site was used for at least 400 years. The dates place its construction during the Woodland Period, which began about 3,000 years ago and ended about 1,100 years ago. It was during this period that Native Americans shifted from being nomadic hunters and gatherers toward establishing an agricultural society that used pottery for storage. Most likely, the people who built and used the site lived downstream on more fertile land.

The core of the wall is made of limestone rocks about the size one person could carry. The rocks are covered with chert—a compact quartzite rock—and earth fill. There are breaks in the wall where the bluffs above the streams provide natural barriers.

The tastefully built stone museum on the bluff overlooking the Duck River is the place to start your visit to Old Stone Fort. It offers displays and programs about the site, about archaeology in general, and about Native American culture.

WALL, LITTLE DUCK RIVER, AND FORKS OF THE RIVER TRAILS

Highlights
Ancient rock-and-earthen wall, waterfalls,
old forest, rugged scenery

Length
3-mile loop

Maps
OSFSAA interpretative path guide; USGS: Manchester

Use
Hiking and day use only

Trailhead
The trailhead is outside the museum at the end of the
road leading into the park from US 41.

Hike Description
Even without the archaeological site, this hike on the edge of
Manchester would rank as one of the best in Middle Tennessee.
It passes through an impressive old forest along bluffs overlooking the cascading forks of the Duck River.

The trail starts in a grove of large oak at the end of the paved
walk outside the museum. Follow it among walls, ditches, and
mounds into the enclosure. Stay on the trail as it bears left. You'll
soon reach one of several points where you'll have the option of
walking inside or outside the wall. Walk outside it whenever
possible, so you can catch views of the many waterfalls and cascades in the two gorges.

Turn left on the stile and walk outside the wall. Several side
paths lead to overlooks far above the cascades and falls on the
Little Duck River. The river was once called Bark Camp Fork. It

glides over bedrock innocently enough, then all of a sudden starts a tumultuous drop into the ever-deepening gorge. Its first drop is straight down.

Next, you'll pass high above Little Falls, which is actually the biggest waterfall on the Little Duck. It's a tiered affair that falls off a curved layer of bedrock and drops 20 feet over ledges.

The riverside hosts a wildflower display. Here and at other places at Old Stone Fort, you'll see two-flowered Cynthia, fire pink, bluets, squawroot, phlox, lousewort, May apple, violets, toadshade, giant chickweed, daisies, purple phacelia, bluets, and Carolina vetch. Blooming shrubs include mountain laurel, spice-bush, azaleas, and deerberry. Flowering trees include redbud, red maple, dogwood, and tulip poplar.

After returning inside the enclosure via another stile, you'll reach a place where the wall ends. Here, the cliffs serve the same purpose as the wall: separating the enclosure from its surroundings.

The wall resumes at 0.5 mile, where the trail makes a sharp right turn at a marker noting the 1966 excavation. The deep ravine to the left is called "The Moat," which suggests that some-one believed it to be a large, man-made ditch used to protect the "fort." In truth, this ravine was once the path of the Duck River. Thousands of years of erosion caused the river to take a different course even before the Woodland people built the wall.

Continue along the trail as it returns inside the enclosure and curves right on a boardwalk before reaching a junction at 0.8 mile. Turn left. This short access trail leads to three longer trails: the yellow-blazed Forks of the River Trail, the red-blazed Little Duck River Trail, and the green-blazed Moat Trail.

The trail makes a short, rocky descent to another junction. Go straight a short distance to another fork; bear right. (The left fork follows The Moat through a stand of even-aged tulip poplar and rejoins the Wall Trail at the 1966 marker.) You'll soon come to yet another junction. Take the left fork, the red-blazed Little Duck River Trail.

The trail climbs steeply to the craggy, narrow backbone sepa-rating The Moat from the Duck River. This fascinating stretch

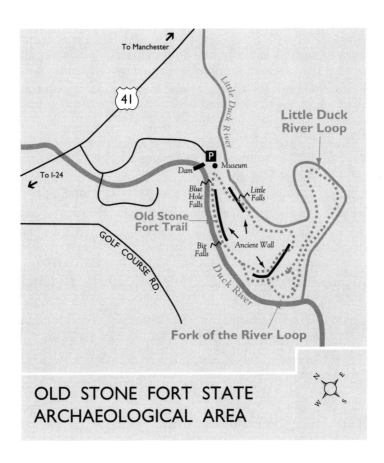

To Manchester

41

To I-24

Little Duck River

Little Duck
River Loop

Dam

P

Museum

Blue
Hole
Falls

Little
Falls

Old Stone
Fort Trail

GOLF COURSE RD.

Big
Falls

Ancient Wall

Duck River

Fork of the River Loop

OLD STONE FORT STATE
ARCHAEOLOGICAL AREA

through mountain laurel and deep green moss is reminiscent of the southern Appalachian Mountains. In places, the backbone is barely wide enough to hold the trail. If you're here in the fall before the first killing frost, expect to see lots of purple aster blooming.

The Little Duck River Trail emerges into the oak forest just before the ridge widens into a small plateau. After a steep descent, the trail reaches an old road at 1.5 miles; turn left. Just short of the Little Duck River, turn right to follow the river downstream.

After some rocky hiking on the flood plain, you'll enjoy easy walking for quite a ways. Then the hike's character changes again as the trail scrambles over rocks and roots below the backbone. The walking gets easier before the junction at 2.2 miles. Take the left fork onto the yellow-blazed Forks of the River Trail, which leads to the confluence of the Little Duck and Duck Rivers. The meeting of the waters is a lovely spot to stop, linger, and perhaps enjoy a picnic.

The rest of the hike goes upstream along the part of the Duck River once known as Barren Fork. Continue on the yellow-blazed trail to one of the junctions you passed earlier. Go left and retrace your route up the short access trail to the Wall Trail at 2.5 miles. Bear left and continue along the Wall Trail as it traverses the bluff high above the cascading river.

You'll soon hear the roar of the biggest of the Duck River falls, appropriately named Big Falls. Here, the 90-foot-wide river drops seven feet, then plunges 30 feet over a bedrock overhang into a big, deep pool.

Again, take the outside-the-wall options. The trail hugs the rim of the gorge before reaching a building foundation of cut limestone. You'll pass beds of crested dwarf iris and dwarf larkspur if you're here in April. The ground is blue with phlox, too.

As the marker points out, this was once the site of a paper mill. Back in the days when falling water was the main source of industrial energy, this was an obvious place for mills. Several were located here at one time or another—a gunpowder mill, a sawmill, a gristmill, a rope factory. Local people had high hopes of making this a major industrial center, as is reflected in the name they chose in 1836. Manchester, the Coffee County seat, is named for the English industrial city.

At 2.8 miles, the path leads left to an overlook above impressive Blue Hole Falls. Here, the river bounces down 35 feet over shelves of jagged rock that slice 200 feet diagonally across the gorge.

After continuing along the bluff, the trail reaches the museum.

EDGAR EVINS STATE PARK

Most people go to Center Hill to enjoy one of America's most beautiful man-made lakes. Here, the clear waters of the Caney Fork River are backed up into countless coves in the rugged knobs of the Eastern Highland Rim escarpment.

Edgar Evins State Park provides an opportunity to enjoy 6,000 acres of shoreline, steep hills, and deep hollows. Its rich second-growth forest is a good place to look for spring and summer wildflowers and to enjoy brilliant fall foliage. There is only one hiking trail at Edgar Evins, but more are planned.

The late Joe L. Evins from nearby Smithville represented the Upper Cumberland in Congress from 1946 to 1976. Incidentally, he was preceded by Albert Gore and succeeded by Albert Gore, Jr., both of whom have homes on the Caney Fork downstream from Center Hill Dam. Evins used his position as chairman of the House Appropriations Subcommittee on Public Works to get the Corps of Engineers to set aside land for the park, which opened in the 1970s. It's named for his father.

HIGHLAND RIM TRAIL

Highlights
Rich, old forest, wildflowers, striking fall colors, views of
Center Hill Dam and Lake

Length
1.5-mile loop

Maps
EESP brochure; USGS: Center Hill Dam

Use
Hiking and day use only

Trailhead
Begin the trail from the parking lot in front of the park
office. The park entrance is on TN 96 between I-40's
Exit 268 and Center Hill Dam.

Center Hill Dam creates the lake at Edgar Evins State Park.

Hike Description

This trail gives you a chance to hike on the knobby Eastern Highland Rim escarpment and sample the beauty of the transitional forest where the dissected rim starts to give way to the lower Central Basin. The trail circles the ridge down to Center Hill Lake and back.

Descend the white-blazed trail into a moist, north-facing hollow that shelters some big trees—tulip poplar, beech, white ash, buckeye—rising above the steep, green hillside covered with ferns, among them Christmas fern, ebony spleenwort, and maidenhair fern. If you take this easy walk around the first of April, you'll be treated to an unforgettable wildflower show. You'll find flowers blooming everywhere—purple phacelia, toadshade, prairie trillium,

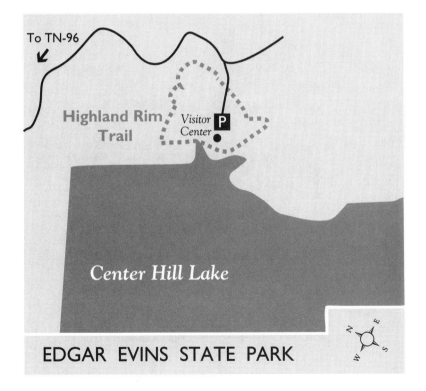

dwarf larkspur, doll's eyes, rue anemone, false rue anemone, jack-in-the-pulpit, May apple, giant chickweed, and waterleaf, just to name a few.

The grade becomes more gentle as the trail follows an old road down the hollow to a soggy flat where the trees are covered with bright green moss. After crossing a wet-weather stream at 0.4 mile, the trail makes a level curve around the side of the ridge. Here, you can enjoy views of the lake and dam.

Soon, the mossy limestone outcrops and tall cedars give the feel of a Central Basin cedar forest—quite a contrast to the Highland Rim hardwoods you just left. The trail follows a cove and passes the jumbled remains of a house that stood before the lake

Highland Rim Trail starts at an overlook above Center Hill Lake.

was created. Just past the head of the cove, it starts its climb back up the escarpment, passes a canebrake, and enters a south-facing oak-hickory forest. As the trail continues to climb, it seems like the environment changes with every foot of elevation.

Before long, you'll round the same hill you traversed in the opposite direction in the cedars below. You'll then return to the wetter northern slope and the forest dominated by beech and tulip poplar. On this stretch in winter, the absence of foliage allows nearly continuous views of the clear, blue lake and the dam that creates it.

At 1.2 miles, you'll take a sharp right turn up some rock steps and then come to another switchback in front of a huge, old sugar maple. Notice the holes around the maple. They're in such neat rows that you might think a carpenter made them. But it's actually a species of woodpecker—the yellow-bellied sapsucker—that pecks row after row of these holes, sometimes around an entire tree, to get to the soft inner bark and sap it feeds on.

Contrary to what many people think, woodpeckers do not harm trees. They often peck holes to get to wood-boring beetles and their larvae, thus removing pests from the trees. The nesting cavities woodpeckers make in trees do not harm them either, because the birds choose the soft, dead wood of trees that have been damaged by insects, disease, fire, or storm. And of course, their cavities are used as nests by a host of other forest critters.

Yellow-bellied sapsuckers are migratory birds that come south to Tennessee in August and stay until May. There are five common year-round woodpeckers in this area: the downy, the hairy, the red-bellied, the flicker, and the pileated.

The trail makes another switchback near a big maple, then crests the ridge. The walking now becomes easy as the level trail passes black cherry, beech, oak, sassafras, and shagbark hickory. In pioneer times, sassafras root bark was thought to have medicinal properties. The roots are still used for tea and root beer. They're used to perfume soap as well.

Along here in the fall, the sharp contrast between the northern and southern slopes might remind you of another fall spectacle: the Tennessee-Alabama football game. The orange of the sugar maple lights up one side of the hill, while a tide of crimson red maple brightens the other.

You'll reach the park office at 1.5 miles.

STANDING STONE STATE PARK

Standing Stone State Park and the surrounding state forest cover 11,000 acres of uncommonly rugged terrain on the Eastern Highland Rim. The park's focal point is a 69-acre lake nestled in the rugged hills. Though hiking opportunities are limited, those who take to the park's trail in March and April will be rewarded with one of the region's grandest wildflower displays. Fall colors are brilliant, too, as the forest of maple, hickory, and dogwood turns orange, yellow, and red.

The park and forest began as a New Deal "land use area" in the 1930s. With help from the Resettlement Administration, and with workers provided by the Works Progress Administration, the United States Forest Service acquired abused land, checked erosion, and began a reforestation program. The beautiful stone dam and recreational facilities were built during this period. In 1939, the state took over the management of Standing Stone. In 1955, it became the owner of the park and forest.

The "Standing Stone" was a large rock along the Walton Road, the important east-west route William Walton cut over the Cumberland Plateau in 1802. The road linked Kingston on the

Clinch River with Carthage on the Cumberland, following an Indian path. I-40 follows roughly the same route.

Said to resemble a big, gray dog, the stone supposedly marked the boundary between lands claimed by two groups of Indians. After the rock broke, a remnant of it was mounted in a park in Monterey. No one seems to know how this park came to be named for the Standing Stone.

If you visit Standing Stone State Park in August, you can see the National Rolley Hole Marbles Championship. "Rolley hole" marbles are popular in a small area in Tennessee and neighboring Kentucky. The game is played on a "marble yard," a rectangle of compacted, level soil 25 feet by 40 feet. The marbles are shot with tremendous speed, so ordinary glass marbles won't do. Shooters often pay as much as $50 for a good marble made of flint.

LAKE TRAIL

Highlights
Rich second-growth forest, scenic lake, remarkable spring wildflowers, fall colors

Length
4.6-mile loop

Maps
SSSP brochure; USGS: Hilham

Use
Hiking and day use only

Trailhead
The trailhead is at the picnic area below the dam on the main park road, TN 136. The park is off TN 52 between Livingston and Celina.

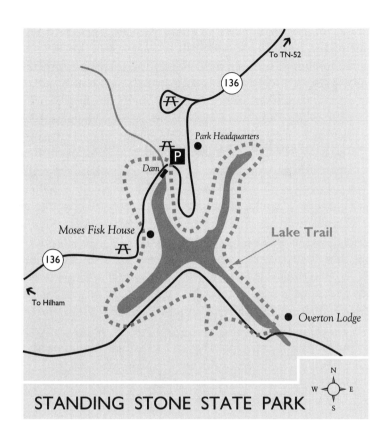

STANDING STONE STATE PARK

Hike Description

This white-blazed trail goes around the lake from the shore to the heights above it. Old maps call parts of the trail by different names, but it now seems to be uniformly known as the Lake Trail.

Begin by crossing the swinging bridge over Mill Creek. You'll climb on a series of switchbacks—some with steps—to the top of the ridge. Take care not to be misled by any of the side paths.

If you're here in early spring, you'll quickly discover why so many people come to Standing Stone to see the wildflowers. Going up the steep hill, you're nearly eye level with phlox, fire pink, crested dwarf iris, toadshade, violets, shooting star, May apple, giant chickweed, and prairie trillium.

After the steep climb, the trail levels off in a forest dominated by oak and hickory. You'll also note tulip poplar, beech, sugar maple, basswood, ash, and dogwood, so plentiful on the Eastern Highland Rim. The trail climbs through some tall, whispering pines and some equally tall cedars before coming to a bluff over the lake. Here, you can see that the lake takes the shape of an **X** as it spreads into four hollows. You'll also see more flowers—bluets and pussy-toes—in the mossy areas along the trail.

The trail curves around the head of a ravine in a second-growth forest of sizable trees and comes to the road at the restored home of Moses Fisk at 0.6 mile.

Massachusetts native Moses Fisk was one of the men responsible for the settlement of the Upper Cumberland after the Third Tellico Treaty made it legal in 1805. Following Fisk's graduation from Dartmouth College in 1796, the college's president persuaded him to travel to Tennessee to study the feasibility of a mission among the Cherokees. Fisk liked what he saw. After reporting back to Dartmouth, the gifted mathematician came to the Upper Cumberland frontier to work as a surveyor.

Fisk helped establish three Tennessee counties, but education was his first love. In 1806, he founded Fisk Female Academy at Hilham, just south of today's park. He later started a similar school for boys. One of the region's largest landowners, Fisk is said to have owned more than 30,000 acres when he died in 1843. The nearby town of Celina is named for his oldest daughter.

The trail passes the Fisk house in a grove of tall beech trees, then makes a hairpin turn through a steep hollow that is home to a seasonal stream that cascades down the hill after a good rain. If you're here in April, you'll see wild geraniums, large-flowered trillium, Indian strawberry, and Carolina vetch, in addition to a fair number of the flowers you've already noted on this hike.

As the trail descends, it curves through another steep hollow. Here, you'll see more new flowers, among them rue anemone and foamflower. The trail passes another seasonal cascade, then comes to a paved road in the lush bottom along Bryan Fork at

Lake Trail passes a Depression-era dam built by the WPA.

1.2 miles. You can now add purple phacelia to your spring wild-flower list.

Go left across the bridge. Follow the trail off the road as it bears to the right through a beech forest along the ridge. Add dwarf larkspur to your list. You'll then pass a tall, tiered, seasonal waterfall as the easy walking continues past beds of crested dwarf iris. The trail curves gently up the hill, tops out above the lake, then starts down. It drops on switchbacks to the road at the edge of the lake at 2.2 miles.

Go right on the road beneath a row of incredibly tall pines planted in the 1930s. This unusually scenic course also features cedar, sycamore, redbud, and dogwood.

Cross the bridge over Morgan Creek and head for Overton Lodge. Standing Stone State Park is in Overton County, named for Nashville's John Overton. (For information about Overton, see the chapter on Radnor Lake State Natural Area, pages 21–34.) Bear left around the lodge; don't be surprised if you're serenaded by croaking frogs among the cattails.

Behind the lodge, you'll return to the woods and reach a junction with the Cooper Mountain Trail. You won't find this trail on the park map. That's because it's in the state forest, and state forests are managed by a different department of state government. The Cooper Mountain Trail is an 8-mile loop that runs to the top of a 1,400-foot mountain and passes Standing Stone Sink, an unusual mountaintop depression.

The Lake Trail climbs through a layer of shale, swings through a ravine cleared for a power line, curves around the center of the blue-green lake, and runs up another of the lake's four prongs. Under a mossy, rocky bluff here, you'll find just about every kind of flower you've already seen on this walk.

After another swing through a ravine, the trail resumes its course along the lake. As you approach the head of a cove, you'll encounter a fourth species of trillium—wake-robin or red trillium—to add to the three you've already seen—large-flowered trillium, toadshade, and prairie trillium.

Where the lake ends at a low stone dam, go left under the sycamores and across the bridge over Mill Creek; you'll reach a second junction with the Cooper Mountain Trail just as you get on the bridge. Past the bridge, the trail makes a hairpin turn beneath some beeches, crosses a trickling tributary, and heads down its opposite bank. You'll then cross the butt of a ridge spine and walk along the bottom next to the lake. Don't be surprised to see a water snake slithering off the bank.

The flower show picks up once again. You can now add lyre-leaved sage, bright blue Virginia spiderwort, two-flowered Cynthia, and stonecrop to your list. Lyre-leaved sage gets its name from its leaves, which supposedly resemble the harplike musical instrument. Stonecrop was imported from Europe, where it was used on the skin to remove ulcers and warts.

You'll then come to a junction. The trail leading right goes up the flower-filled hollow to the recreation building. (If you like, you can use this as an alternate route to the trailhead; go along the road from the recreation building to the steep path that leads down to the dam.)

Bear left at the junction and continue walking around the lake. The trail passes a boathouse and bends around a rocky bluff beneath some cedars. You'll pass through a ravine holding some small stone dams the WPA men built, then pass another boathouse. The path stays along the lake on a dry, rocky slope where flowers finally become scarce. At the third boathouse, rental boats are available in season. Fishing here is for largemouth bass, bluegill, catfish, and trout.

Go to the top of the dam and walk down the road to the picnic area, where the hike started. The alternate route over the ridge comes steeply down from the right.

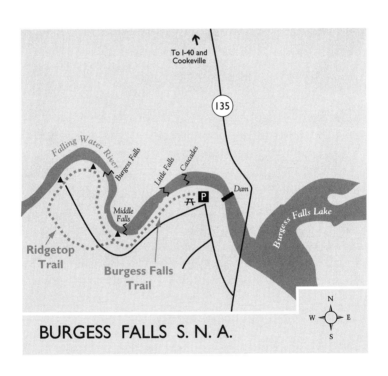

To I-40 and
Cookeville

135

Falling Water River

Burgess Falls

Little Falls

Cascades

Dam

P

*Middle
Falls*

Burgess Falls Lake

Ridgetop
Trail

Burgess Falls
Trail

BURGESS FALLS S. N. A.

N
W E
S

BURGESS FALLS
STATE NATURAL AREA

The walk to Burgess Falls is short on distance but long on rewards. The 130-foot waterfall is arguably the most beautiful in a region blessed with many lovely falls. A trail of less than a mile takes you along the rim of the Falling Water River Gorge, past two other major falls and countless small ones. The hike offers a show of spring wildflowers. You may also elect to see the remains of an early hydroelectric project.

Like so many Middle Tennessee settlers, Tom Burgess settled on a grant given for his Revolutionary War service. This spot, located where the narrow gorge squeezes the river, was ideal for a mill. The Burgess family started both a sawmill and a gristmill in the early 1800s.

In 1924, the city of Cookeville built a dam on the river to generate electricity. A flood washed it away in 1928. It was replaced by the concrete-and-steel dam you see today. The arrival of TVA electricity in the 1940s rendered the dam obsolete, but the people of Cookeville had the wisdom to preserve the area for outdoor recreation and wildlife conservation. A cooperative-management arrangement with the state led to the recognition of Burgess Falls as a state natural area in 1980.

BURGESS FALLS AND RIDGETOP TRAILS

Highlights
Three major waterfalls, scenic gorge, wildflowers

Length
1.5-mile loop

Maps
BFSNA brochure; USGS: Burgess Falls

Use
Hiking and day use only

Trailhead
Begin the hike at the lower parking area, located just inside the park. You can reach Burgess Falls via TN 135 south of I-40's Exit 286 at Cookeville.

Hike Description
This is one of Tennessee's most dramatic trails. It follows the rim of the Falling Water River Gorge past a series of waterfalls before reaching gigantic Burgess Falls.

The roar can be deafening as the trail descends on some steps next to Falling Water Cascades, where the river bounces 10 feet over ledges. The trail then turns left to follow the river downstream.

As the river drops through its gorge, the trail stays fairly level at first. This is a beautiful spot any time of the year but is especially appealing in April, when the bright blooms of redbud frame the white foam of the turbulent water.

The concrete foundations you'll pass once held the wooden flume that ran from the dam to the hydroelectric plant at the foot of Burgess Falls. The pillars and cables that look like an abandoned footbridge carried the flume to the tunnel still visible across the river.

The forest on this cool, moist, north-facing slope looks more like the Cumberland Plateau—located a few miles east—than the Highland Rim. Hemlock trees line the gorge. You'll also see ironwood, birch, and bigleaf magnolia, distinguished by its huge "elephant ear" leaves.

You'll soon hear the roar of the first big waterfall, called Little Falls only because it's smaller than the next two. Here, the river bounces 30 feet downward over layers of bedrock.

Take a close look at the rock overhangs you're walking beneath. You'll see some grayish white nodules within the limestone. These quartz deposits contain silica, which makes them resistant to erosion. This explains why these rock are still here, though the river has worn through other types of rock.

You might be startled by a huge, slate-gray bird flying up the creek. It's a great blue heron. North America's largest heron is often seen here wading in shallow water, looking for an unsuspecting fish or frog to eat. Tennessee's largest nesting bird, the great blue heron has an average height of four feet and an average wingspan of seven feet.

The trail leaves the hemlocks, enters an upland forest of tulip poplar and beech, and crosses a wet-weather stream that bounces over layer after layer of moss-covered rock. In the spring, you'll see crested dwarf iris, large-flowered trillium, jack-in-the-pulpit, phlox, shooting star, spring beauty, and the fiddleheads of Christmas fern.

After climbing some steep steps, the trail levels off high above the river and passes through mountain laurel that marks the boundary between the hemlocks on the right and the poplars and beeches on the left.

At the Middle Falls overlook, you'll be treated to spectacular sounds and sights. The falls roar with energy, and the view is framed by graceful boughs of hemlock. Some 150 feet below, the river widens to 200 feet and slides 50 feet down rock layers into a big pool.

From the Middle Falls overlook, it's a short walk to the Burgess Falls overlook and one of Tennessee's most beautiful sights. Here, the river narrows, rounds a bend, and drops 130 feet.

Look across the gorge and you'll see flat sedimentary-rock strata laid down over millions of years. The waterfall was created when the river, which had gradually eroded the gorge, hit beds of siliceous limestone resistant to erosion. As you'll notice, it's not a straight drop. Instead, the water bounces off a series of ledges. Color is added to the falls by the differing hues among the rock strata and the bright green aquatic plants that have taken hold among the wet rocks.

The trail descends steeply to the lip of the falls. If you choose, you can continue down some steps on the sheer canyon wall to a rough manway that threads its way among slick boulders to the base of the falls. The constant mist creates its own environment here. Grass grows in pockets of soil in the jumble of rocks. It's an impressive sight at the base, altogether different from the view from the overlook.

If you want to see the remains of the hydroelectric plant, take the manway downstream a few hundred feet. Center Hill Lake backs up here much of the year, so you may have to take to higher ground.

Return to the Burgess Falls overlook if you've elected to make the descent to the base of the falls and the hydroelectric plant. Veer right to begin the Ridgetop Trail.

After a steep climb, the trail crosses the end of the gravel access road and follows the bluff 300 feet above the Falling Water River as it rushes into Center Hill Lake. You'll soon reach an overlook dotted with cedar, beech, hemlock, and mountain laurel. Follow the trail as it hugs the rim of the gorge. The roar of Burgess Falls will become fainter as the trail swings away from the gorge through the oak-hickory forest.

When you come to the gravel road, go right, then left between two large cedars onto an unmarked path that leads to the Middle Falls overlook. (The map on the park brochure incorrectly shows the trail continuing straight across the gravel road.)

Return to the trailhead the way you came. Heading upstream, it's easy to see how the Falling Water River got its name—you'll find yourself facing one white-foam fall after another. On its route through the gorge, the river drops 300 feet in less than a mile.

ROCK ISLAND STATE PARK

At Rock Island, the swift Caney Fork River crashes through a 200-foot-deep gorge as it drops off the Eastern Highland Rim into Center Hill Lake. The park is home to the Caney Fork's Great Falls, the deep Blue Hole below it, a natural-sand swimming beach at Badger Flat, and a wooded, wildflower-covered peninsula between the Caney Fork and Collins Rivers. The park's historic sites include a century-old textile mill and one of the region's earliest hydroelectric dams.

The merging of three rivers provides the setting. Having completed its wild ride off the Cumberland Plateau, the Caney Fork flows gently along the Eastern Highland Rim to where the Rocky River empties into it upstream from the state park. The island where these two rivers meet gives the park its name. A little farther downstream, the Collins River snakes around a bluff and gives its waters to the Caney Fork. Actually, since the Tennessee

Electric Power Company built Great Falls Dam in 1917, it's the other way around. When the water is high, the Caney Fork flows up the Collins, where it is diverted into a tunnel that drops 150 feet into the gorge downstream from Great Falls, turning the turbines to generate electricity.

This oddity—a river flowing upstream—has created another oddity. Water backed up on the Collins River flows through caves and crevices in the narrow backbone between the rivers and emerges above the gorge in a series of spectacular, 80-foot waterfalls. You can see them 0.25 mile downstream from the overlook at the Great Falls picnic area.

Wherever water drops off the Eastern Highland Rim, you can count on finding the remains of early industry, as falling water was an efficient means of generating energy in days gone by. McMinnville textile magnate Asa Faulkner recognized the power of Great Falls, but he died before he realized his dream of a mill here. His son, Clay Faulkner, took up where Asa left off. With two partners, he built the Great Falls Cotton Mill in 1892. It's the brick building in the gorge wedged between the river and the road. A whole company town, Fall City, grew around it. The wettest day on record in Tennessee came on March 28, 1902, when 11 inches of rain fell in this area. The flood destroyed the mill wheel, and the owners decided it was not feasible to rebuild it. The town then faded from existence.

There's an intriguing structure called "the Witch's Castle" or "Spring Castle" in the damp, mossy cove across the road from the mill. No one knows for sure who built the structure or why it was built, but the masonry resembles that used by the power company that constructed the dam in 1917.

Rock Island's history goes back well before the construction of the dam and the mill. The Chickamauga Path was a trail used by the Lower Cherokees, or Chickamaugas, to travel from their towns along the Tennessee River into the game-rich Cumberland country. After 1779, they and their allies the Creeks used it for raids against the fledgling Cumberland settlements. The Chickamauga Path crossed the Caney Fork at Rock Island. After a raid in November 1793, Lieutenant William Snoddy was dispatched with a company of militia to pursue the raiders. The soldiers caught up with the Indians at the Rock Island crossing. The ensuing battle was one of the last engagements between settlers and Indians in Middle Tennessee.

The crossing became a focal point when settlers started filling the Caney Fork region. Rock Island was the county seat from the time White County was established in 1806 until the seat was moved to Sparta in 1810. The Drover's Road—also called the Kentucky Road—was the route by which stock was taken to market; it crossed the Caney Fork at Rock Island. Later, the Nashville-Knoxville stage route crossed here, too.

The community of Rock Island shifted downstream in 1881, when the railroad came through between McMinnville and Sparta. You can still see the charming Victorian-era depot in the village.

Great Falls Cotton Mill stands on the bank of the Caney Fork River.

In the 1920s, the accessibility provided by the railroad and the recreation offered by the lake led to Rock Island's reincarnation as a summer retreat for wealthy Nashvillians. Their "camps" still stand along the Collins River arm of Great Falls Lake. Many are owned by descendants of the original owners.

The TVA later took over Great Falls Dam. In the 1940s, the Corps of Engineers acquired land for Center Hill Lake. These public lands were made available to the state in the 1960s, when the decision was made to include Rock Island in the state-park system. The park opened in 1969.

COLLINS RIVER TRAIL

Highlights
Views of the Collins River stem of Great Falls Lake, diverse forest

Length
2.8-mile loop

Maps
RISP brochure; USGS: Campaign, Doyle

Use
Hiking and day use only

Trailhead
The trailhead is on TN 287 across from the TVA office, which is located between Great Falls Dam and the state-park office. To get to the dam and the park from TN 136 (Old US 70S) between McMinnville and Sparta, turn onto TN 287 in the village of Rock Island.

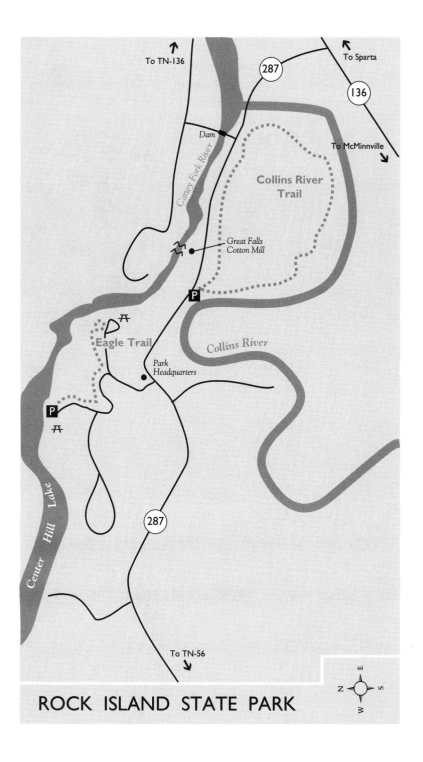

To TN-136

287

To Sparta

136

Dam

To McMinnville

Caney Fork River

Collins River Trail

Great Falls
Cotton Mill

P

Eagle Trail

Collins River

Park
Headquarters

P

287

Center Hill Lake

To TN-56

N
E
S
W

ROCK ISLAND STATE PARK

Hike Description

This is a pleasant, easy walk around the peninsula created by the Caney Fork and Collins Rivers.

Hike the loop counterclockwise. After walking through a power-line cut, you'll notice that the environment changes dramatically as you step onto the bluff above the impounded Collins River. The trail follows the bluff through mountain laurel beneath a canopy of oak, tulip poplar, and hickory with an understory of dogwood, beech, and maple. It then veers away from the bluff and picks up the old road it follows for most of its course.

You may be wondering about the big black birds soaring above you and roosting in the trees and on the transmission-line towers. They're black vultures. These birds are slightly smaller than the familiar turkey vultures, or buzzards, which are distinguished by their naked red heads. Rock Island has one of Tennessee's largest concentrations of black vultures.

The trail follows the ridge crest parallel to the bluff through an area dotted with red maples. It then swings left away from the bluff in a stand of tall, whispering pines.

As you pass a dead oak standing on the right, you're sure to see and hear pileated woodpeckers, easily recognized by their red crowns. Woodpeckers excavate holes in snags like these. The holes are then used as homes by a variety of wildlife, including 28 cavity-nesting birds ranging in size from turkey vultures to chickadees.

Before long, the trail passes beds of Spanish bayonet, a type of yucca more common in the rocky cedar forests of the Central Basin than here. Spanish bayonet is often planted as an ornamental—you can see it around the park office. It was probably started here before the TVA took over this land in the 1930s.

The trail descends through a mixed forest of pines and hardwoods, zigzags through a power-line cut, and enters a forest of old trees before finally descending to the lakeshore. This is a good place to spot deer and wild turkey. The trail then turns left and parallels the lake across from the summer homes built in the

1920s. The cabins the state constructed at the park in the mid-1990s were tastefully designed to resemble these old camps.

After a long level stretch, the trail reaches a promontory above the confluence of the Collins and the Caney Fork. The old iron bridge that runs parallel to the new one is a historic structure. Part of it was built in 1887 as the Bordeaux Bridge in Nashville. It was moved here in 1924.

At 1.7 miles, the trail swings left and parallels the Caney Fork. It then leaves the old road and passes the end of the dam. It runs through areas invaded by ivy and privet and through groves of straight, even-aged tulip poplar. The trail crosses the old road, winds through an ivy-covered disturbed area, and comes to a rutted road under a utility line at 2 miles. Turn right on the road, then left into the woods. As you climb the ridge away from the Caney Fork, you'll pass the grave of John Cunningham, a veteran of the War of 1812. Cunningham was born in 1781 and died in 1858.

The trail's course through the oak forest may be hard to find, as it's been rerouted around a jungle of downed trees; pay attention to the white blazes. After climbing gently among oak, hickory, and tulip poplar, it dips through an open area next to the road before climbing again to arrive at the mowed field where the hike started. Walk past some cedars and a black walnut tree to reach the trailhead. Black walnut trees are valued both for their nuts and their wood, used in cabinets, furniture, and gunstocks. The pioneers used the black husks for dye.

EAGLE TRAIL

Highlights
Gorge of the Caney Fork River, Blue Hole

Length
1.3 miles out and back

Maps

RISP brochure; USGS: Campaign

Use

Hiking and day use only

Trailhead

The trailhead is at the Badger Flat picnic area, located near the end of the main park road, which turns off TN 287. See the previous hike for directions to the park.

Hike Description

This is a short but interesting walk along the bluff above the cascading Caney Fork River on its short dash for freedom between Great Falls and Center Hill Lakes.

The hike takes off from the picnic area, where a sign notes that the trail was built in 1987 under the supervision of an Eagle Scout. After running through a diverse bluff-top wooded area of hemlock, tulip poplar, beech, oak, and sugar maple, the trail turns right and goes up a narrow, steep gorge.

April wildflowers are abundant here. If you get confused about the different types of trillium, this might be the place to educate yourself. Whichever variety your specimen is, it will have three of everything—leaves, petals, sepals, and stigmas. Thus the name *trillium*. You'll see lots of large-flowered trillium, which has big white petals that turn a lovely shade of pink as they age. Toadshade, or sessile trillium, has purple petals and blotchy leaves. Prairie trillium looks similar but has solid green leaves and drooping sepals, the little leaves growing outside the petals. Wake-robin, or red trillium, looks like the previous two except that its petals are elevated on a stalk above the leaves. Wake-robin gets its name because it's said to wake up the robins in spring, its blooming season. The flower of the yellow trillium is erect, which makes it look as if it's closed.

If all this seems confusing, you can take consolation in knowing that even some experts use the common names interchangeably. Just forget about the distinctions and enjoy the beauty of these common residents of Tennessee's woods.

The trail turns to climb a hollow and cross a sturdy bridge. As you circle around to the opposite ridge, you'll start to hear the river ahead. The ugly yellow paint splashed on the trees along here lets you know that the land downhill is owned by the Corps of Engineers. The Corps leases it to the state for inclusion in the park.

The Eagle Trail stays high on the bluff and ends at the Blue Hole picnic area at 0.6 mile. If you care to take an optional side trip down to the Blue Hole, walk through the parking lot and turn left down the steps. When you come to a fork, go right. The trail descends the multicolored, lichen- and moss-covered bluff on steps, then becomes a rough manway as it drops toward the river. The water seeping out of the bluffs comes from the Collins River, backed up by Great Falls Dam. The river has migrated through the razorback ridge in underground passages. Twin Falls, the larger waterfalls created by this phenomenon, are just upstream.

The manway eventually gives out in a rock garden on the last bluff above the Blue Hole. You can scramble down to the river if you like, or you can pick your way upstream to Twin Falls. This area is rich with all kinds of shrubs, vines, and flowers. Among the spring flowers are foamflower, phlox, rue anemone, purple phacelia, giant chickweed, violets, May apple, little brown jug, sweet shrub, golden alexanders, slender toothwort, hepatica, dwarf larkspur, and stonecrop. Poison ivy is one of the vines on the bluff.

When you've finished your explorations, return up the steps to the Blue Hole picnic area. Retrace your route on the Eagle Trail or, if you prefer, walk back to Badger Flat on the paved road. Even if you're an experienced hiker, don't be snooty about walking on roads in Tennessee's parks. Road walking offers the opportunity to view the forest from an opening. It can be particularly rewarding in the fall, when there are splashes of color in the understory. This road is lined with redbud and dogwood. In April, the latter turns the Eastern Highland Rim's forests into clouds of white.

CARDWELL MOUNTAIN

Cardwell Mountain is a detached piece of the Cumberland Plateau that rises 1,000 feet above the scenic Collins River near McMinnville. It is named for Francis Cardwell, who settled in the area in 1806. There are two trails here. One climbs to the massive bluffs and boulders on top of the mountain, and the other meanders along the riverbank. Cherokee Indians came through here in 1838 on their forced removal from their homeland, which accounts for why Cardwell Mountain's trails are sometimes called the "Trail of Tears."

It's not the awesome mountain scenery that draws most people to Cardwell's steep, wooded slopes. It's what's under the mountain. Cumberland Caverns is the largest cave network in Tennessee and the eighth largest in the nation. The caverns' biggest room, Hall of the Mountain King, is one of America's largest cave rooms. The regular tours offered from May through October range from visits that last an hour and a half to stays during which you actually spend the night in the cave.

Both trails start near the caverns' visitor center. They're on private property, so be sure to stay on the trail. Maps are available at the visitor center.

CARDWELL MOUNTAIN TRAIL

Highlights
Boulder-covered mountaintop, historic cave entrance

Length
5.5-mile loop

Maps
Trail of Tears–Cardwell Mountain map;
USGS: Cardwell Mountain

Use
Hiking and day use only

Trailhead
Take TN 8 southeast from McMinnville and follow the signs to the Cumberland Caverns visitor center.

Hike Description
This trail climbs to the massive bluffs and boulders atop Cardwell Mountain, passing the gated, historic entrance to Cumberland Caverns along the way.

The white-blazed trail leaves the dogwood-fringed field below the visitor center and goes quietly through a clump of pines before entering the oak-hickory forest and crossing a fern-covered ravine. Spring is a good season to hike this trail. You'll see why as you climb out of the ravine: bluets, violets, phlox, butterweed, spring beauty, yellow trillium. Farther along, you'll find violet wood sorrel, shooting star, hound's-tongue, dwarf larkspur, star grass, and jack-in-the-pulpit. The rough, odd-looking, cornlike, brown plant poking up from the forest floor is squawroot, a parasite whose roots penetrate the roots of oak trees to draw food. This accounts for its alternate name, cancerroot.

Fall is a good time to visit Cardwell Mountain, too. The orange, yellow, and red leaves of maple, hickory, dogwood, and sourwood make for an unforgettable color show.

After threading its way through a limestone rock garden, the trail comes to the first of many junctions with old roads. Go right on an easy, level stretch that follows the route of the Chickamauga Path, the Indian road that ran from the Cherokees' Lower Towns near present-day Chattanooga into what is now Middle Tennessee. The path crossed the Caney Fork River at nearby Rock Island. (For more information, see the chapter on Rock Island State Park, pages 199–208.)

Aaron Higgenbotham walked this path in 1810 and almost didn't live to tell about it. Shortly after the Third Tellico Treaty legalized settlement of the Upper Cumberland in 1805, Higgenbotham migrated from Virginia to settle around Cardwell Mountain. One day when he was walking along the Chickamauga Path and surveying his land, a rush of cool air caught his attention. He found its source, a small crevice in the limestone just off the trail. Higgenbotham made himself a torch from a nearby pine tree, left his knapsack and gear on the path, and lowered himself into the slit in the rock. To his amazement, he found a huge room covered with crystals that reflected the flicker of his torch.

Higgenbotham's curiosity got the best of him: he went deeper into the cave. Suddenly, the torch slipped from his hands and fell far below. Surrounded by total darkness, he decided to stay put, lest he fall just as his torch had. All he could do was hope someone would figure out where he was and come looking for him. A day passed and no one came. Another day passed. At the end of the third day, his friends found his gear near the entrance, lowered themselves 25 feet into the cave, and found Higgenbotham alive. The cave has been known as Higgenbotham Cave ever since.

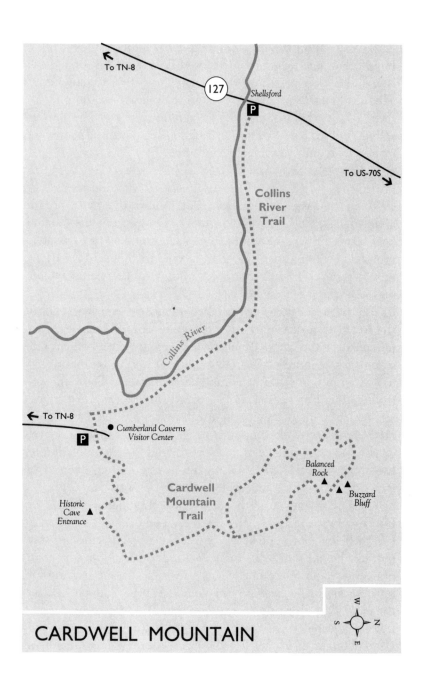

CARDWELL MOUNTAIN

At 0.7 mile, you'll come to the slit in the limestone Higgenbotham entered. Just beyond it is another entrance at the bottom of a sink. If red is your favorite color, you'll love the bluff above the sink. It boasts an exceptional growth of fire pink in the spring. And in the fall, the poison ivy you see everywhere turns deep red.

Henshaw Cave is the other major cave at Cumberland Caverns. No one seems to know how it got its name. A passage connecting Higgenbotham and Henshaw Caves was discovered in 1953. A few years later, the name Cumberland Caverns was adopted, and the commercial use of the caves began. Visitors pass through an enlarged entrance to Henshaw Cave. The entrances to Higgenbotham Cave are blocked by gates, as you'll note.

Past the historic cave entrance, the trail swings left off the Chickamauga Path and follows the ups and downs of ridge spurs through pine thickets before coming to another old road in some fern beds. Walk left up the road through a dry, rocky, shallow-soil area covered with small trees and vines. Just after the old road crosses a marked property line watched over by big oaks, the trail angles right onto a steep hillside. It then crosses a stream at a tumble-down footbridge. This stream is no more than a trickle most of the year. But when it fills up with water in winter and early spring, it creates a small waterfall that drops off a ledge below the trail crossing.

After a short, almost level stretch, the trail crosses another old road and climbs to the beginning of the loop at 1.5 miles. Go right to hike the loop counterclockwise.

As the trail negotiates a boulder field and comes once again to a road, the landscape starts to feel more like that of a mountain. Climb left up the rocky road. The trail levels off, dips to cross a small branch, and reaches a fork. Go to the right up the hill. The oak forest grows increasingly open as the climbing gets more serious.

At 2.3 miles, the trail once again leaves the road. Go right. You're about to embark on the strenuous part of the hike and enter one of the most dramatic settings in Middle Tennessee.

The trail runs into and out of a jumble of house-size boulders, then passes some even bigger boulders. Next, it curves to run under the towering rocks of Buzzard Bluff. Pay careful attention to the blazes for the next 1.5 miles, as the trail is nothing more than a faint route through rocks and woods.

After passing under an enormous rock—appropriately named Balanced Rock—precariously balanced above you, the trail curves among huge boulders before heading back in the opposite direction. You'll see one flat-topped boulder covered with the bright blue flowers of Virginia spiderwort and a sprinkling of violet wood sorrel.

You may notice shadows darting past you on the ground. Look up at the big birds casting them and you'll see why this is called Buzzard Bluff. If you're here late in the day, you may be serenaded by the low hooting of a great horned owl.

You'll then descend through a crevice, scramble over some rocks, and pick your way beneath boulders several stories high. Oak trees—huge ones—seem to grow out of solid rock. The boulders then get smaller and the footing easier.

Continuing on the marked trail, you'll soon pass a rock formation that looks like a toadstool. After that, the trail makes a hairpin curve, passes a big, deformed oak, and makes a long, steady descent to some sandstone. You'll walk through rock gardens before closing the loop at the sign at 4 miles. Return to the Cumberland Caverns visitor center the way you came.

COLLINS RIVER TRAIL

Highlights
Scenic river, wildlife, spring wildflowers

Length
2 miles one-way

Maps
Trail of Tears–Cardwell Mountain map;
USGS: Cardwell Mountain

Use
Hiking and day use only

Trailhead
Same as previous hike

Hike Description
This easy, level walk follows the bank of the scenic Collins River. It's rich in wildlife and abundant in wildflowers.

From the road below the visitor center, the trail descends through oak, hickory, sassafras, and dogwood enlivened by beds of spring-blooming yellow trillium and bright green, summer-blooming columbo. Where an old road comes in, go right. Follow the road past a field brightened in winter by the low sun shining through tan broomsedge.

Soon, the road comes to the Collins River, which bends slowly around the base of Cardwell Mountain. Of the three major streams that come together in Savage Gulf State Natural Area (see pages 239–48), the Collins is the one that gets to keep its name. It tumbles out of the mountains into one of the Midstate's most scenic valleys, then meanders to its confluence with the Caney Fork at Rock Island.

From here to the Shellsford canoe access area, the trail and the old road run together intermittently. Keep alert for the white blazes when the two separate. The trail hugs the river, so whenever the road seems to leave it, you'll likely see the blazes veering left.

This walk has just the right mixture of water, old fields, and woods to keep it alive with wildlife. On the river, you'll see coots, wood ducks, and belted kingfishers. Kingfishers are fun to watch. They patrol rivers and streams, occasionally diving into the water and coming up with fish in their beaks. Blue jays and crows carry on along the bank, and songbirds flutter about the briers, shrubs, and small trees. Turtles, lizards, chipmunks, squirrels, and other small animals are common, as are deer.

The riverbank and the woods are covered with spring wild-flowers. In addition to the yellow trillium you saw near the trailhead, you'll find prairie trillium, large-flowered bellwort, fire pink, phlox, butterweed, toothwort, golden alexanders, lyre-leaved sage, Southern dewberry, false garlic, Solomon's-seal, and lots of dogwood. Summer bloomers include Spanish bayonet and columbo.

The river straightens out and picks up speed as you walk along the cool, green bottom past bluffs on the opposite bank. You'll cross a bridge over a tributary next to a shallow rapids, then continue downstream as the bottom widens. Swing right to climb the steps to the parking area. Unless you've arranged a shuttle, you'll need to walk back to Cumberland Caverns.

The old ford here was called Shellsford in honor of James Shell, an early settler who ran a gristmill. Shellsford was a stop on the Trail of Tears. The thousands of Cherokees the army rounded up in the hot summer of 1838 were kept in crowded camps in the Chattanooga area while awaiting transportation to present-day Oklahoma. The plan was to send most of them by river, but low water on the Tennessee and a shortage of boats prevented that, so many were marched overland on two routes. The route the Cherokees knew as the "Trail Where They Cried" passed through here, then on to McMinnville and past Nashville. The Indians traveled in groups of about 1,000. Each of the groups that stopped at Shellsford remained for several days.

It's estimated that as many as 4,000 Cherokees died during the removal. Several are buried in the graveyard next to Shellsford Baptist Church, located across the river.

HIKES
ON
THE

CUMBERLAND PLATEAU

VIRGIN FALLS POCKET WILDERNESS STATE NATURAL AREA

At Virgin Falls, a creek flows from a cave, makes a thunderous 110-foot drop, then disappears into a deep limestone sink. And that's only one of the natural features here. On the all-day hike, you'll pass lovely Big Branch Falls, massive Big Laurel Falls, and the cascades at Sheep Cave. You'll stop on the rim of the Cumberland Plateau to take in sweeping views of the wild headwaters of the Caney Fork River. And if you're here in early spring, you'll enjoy one of Middle Tennessee's finest wildflower shows.

Virgin Falls is one of several places of unusual scenic beauty that the Bowater Southern Paper Corporation has set aside on its vast Cumberland Plateau timberlands, which supply its huge mill in East Tennessee. The company built and maintains hiking trails on lands designated state natural areas under Tennessee's Natural Areas Preservation Act of 1971.

Bowater started buying Cumberland Plateau timberland in the early 1950s and owns close to 100,000 acres. The corporation has converted about two-thirds of its holdings to the growing of loblolly pines, which are harvested by clear-cutting in 15- to 20-year cycles. No one knows the long-term ecological effects of this conversion, but Bowater earns high marks for its stewardship of the land. It routinely keeps a 50-foot buffer on either side of streams and maintains its roads in ways that reduce the threat of erosion and stream sedimentation.

Unfortunately, only a small part of the trail's route is in the pocket wilderness. The trail also passes through Scott's Gulf, part of the 15,000 acres owned by Bridgestone/Firestone, the tire manufacturer. From time to time, the company floats proposals to sell its acreage. A proposed sale in the mid-1990s energized a preservation effort. In 1997, the Tennessee General Assembly authorized the Tennessee Wildlife Resources Agency to acquire the property. Only time will tell whether this vast tract of near-wilderness is to be preserved for the public's enjoyment.

VIRGIN FALLS TRAIL

Highlights
Waterfalls, cascading creek, bluff-top overlook

Length
7.7-mile loop

Maps
Bowater Trails map; USGS: Lonewood

Use
This trail is for hiking only. Camping is allowed at the designated campsite.

Trailhead
From DeRossett, located 11 miles east of Sparta on US 70, turn south

at the store onto the paved road. Go 5.9 miles to Scotts Gulf Road. Turn right and drive 2 miles to the trailhead.

Hike Description

This rugged, all-day hike is without question one of Tennessee's finest. It drops into the narrow valley of the Caney Fork River to visit waterfalls so unusual that they must be seen to be believed.

The walking is easy at first as the trail wanders through a strip of second-growth hardwoods surrounded by pine plantations. Before long, you'll come to Big Branch—which isn't very big— and follow its often muddy course through stands of mountain laurel, holly, and hemlock. The moist soil offers a nice display of ferns and spring wildflowers.

On the Cumberland Plateau, a thickening growth of evergreen shrubs and trees signals that you're nearing the edge of a gorge. Sure enough, the trail and creek start to descend. At 0.8 mile, you'll come to a rough spur leading left to the first waterfall, Big Branch Falls. Though not as spectacular as the others on this

A Tennessee Trails Association member at Virgin Falls

PHOTO BY PATTI LATTA

Virgin Falls Pocket Wilderness

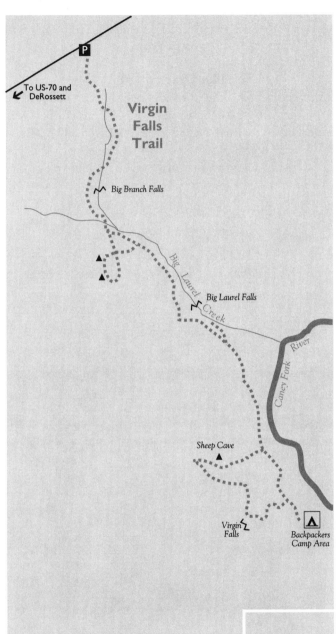

P

To US-70 and
DeRossett

Virgin
Falls
Trail

Big Branch Falls

Big Laurel Creek

Big Laurel Falls

Caney Fork River

Sheep Cave

Virgin
Falls

Backpackers
Camp Area

VIRGIN FALLS
POCKET WILDERNESS

N
E
S
W

hike, it may be the most beautiful. It's a lovely, fan-shaped fall created by the creek's 20-foot stairstep tumble off the first line of bluffs.

From the spur leading to the waterfall, the main trail descends on switchbacks to cross Big Laurel Creek without the benefit of a bridge. When the water is low, getting across is no problem, but when it's up—and that's when most people want to take this hike—crossing can be tricky. Use caution.

On the other side of the creek, the trail struggles over roots and rocks before reaching a junction at 1.5 miles. Swing right to take in the bluff-top overlooks. The trail curves around the mountain and enters a collection of boulders that have broken off the bluff. Take the blue-blazed overlook trail to the right.

After a climb, you'll come to a caged ladder that will take you up to the sandstone bluff. There are two overlooks, one where you first reach the bluff top and another farther down. Both are good places to enjoy a view of the narrow valley of the upper Caney Fork River and Scotts Gulf. The view is particularly rewarding in mid- to late April, when redbud, dogwood, and the pastel green of new growth brighten the woods. The multihued bluffs are interesting, too, especially where the twisted pines seem to grow out of sheer rock.

From the second overlook, the trail makes its way down via another ladder. Walk beneath the bluff back to where the overlook spur started and turn right. Follow the trail's rocky and sometimes steep course down toward Big Laurel Creek, where you'll reunite with the main trail, which follows the creek. Go right, still picking your way through fields of rocks.

Before long, you'll catch your first glimpse of Big Laurel Falls to the left. The farther you walk, the more intriguing the view becomes. After making a steep descent through an area offering a nice spring wildflower show, turn left and circle to the base of the falls. The creek makes a thunderous 40-foot drop. But instead of flowing on toward the Caney Fork, it flows backwards into a huge, shallow cave, then disappears into the ground. You can walk into the cave and look out through the water as it crashes in front of you.

Virgin Falls Pocket Wilderness

Sierra Club hikers at thunderous Virgin Falls

From the waterfall, follow the dry streambed a short distance, then veer right onto the side of the mountain. The next mile is fairly easy walking, as the level trail curves out of Scotts Gulf and parallels the river, alternating between deep woods and typical Cumberland Plateau rock gardens.

You'll come to a junction in a grove of shagbark hickory at 3 miles. This is the beginning of the loop that leads to Virgin Falls itself. Go right. After a short climb up a small gorge, you'll come to yet another spectacular fall at Sheep Cave. The trail crosses a narrow spine of land between the gorge and a huge sink. Ahead, you'll see and hear the creek cascading down in a series of falls. It flows from the cave, drops, disappears, emerges, falls again, disappears, then falls into the huge sink far below. In all, the creek falls about 100 feet.

A steep spur runs up the left side of the sink to the mouth of the cave. From the point where the spur takes off, the trail climbs into the gorge of Little Laurel Creek, follows it a short way, crosses the usually dry creek, and runs along the opposite side of the gorge. As the trail curves around the mountainside, the loud roar up ahead lets you know you're about to reach your destination, Virgin Falls.

And it is truly a magnificent sight. After emerging from a cave, the stream plunges 110 feet into a big, deep sink and goes underground. If you're here during high water, you'll find its power awesome. The spray rising from the waterfall has created its own microclimate, which you'll note from the vegetation.

It's possible to circle the sink and visit the cave from which the water flows. But if you take this side trip, be sure to stay away from the lip of the falls. It's slick and quite dangerous.

When it's time to pull yourself away from this spot, follow the steep ravine down to near the river. You'll come to an old road. The designated back-country campsite is to the right. Hike left, following the Caney Fork upstream. After picking your way among some rocks, you'll come to the junction where you began the Virgin Falls loop.

Retrace your route to Big Laurel Falls and the junction with the trail coming from the overlook. Go straight, following the main trail as it hugs the bluff right next to cascading Big Laurel Creek. When you reach the junction with the trail that took you to the overlook, go straight and walk back to the trailhead.

FALL CREEK FALLS STATE PARK

Awesome scenery, a wide variety of activities, and superb accommodations combine to make this Cumberland Plateau park one of America's premier state-managed recreation areas. Though a portion of the park is developed, two-thirds of its 19,000 acres are a state natural area.

The deep gorges slicing through the plateau create ideal places for streams to fall off the rim. Fall Creek Falls is the best known of the park's six major waterfalls. A sheer drop of 256 feet earns Fall Creek Falls the distinction of being the tallest continuous fall east of the Rockies. Other falls are Piney Creek, Cane Creek, Cane Creek Cascades, Rockhouse, and Coon Creek. The last two tend to go dry in the late summer and fall, but the rest flow year-round. The hikes in this chapter visit all but Piney Creek Falls.

Every season offers something at the park. Winter's frozen waterfalls and cascades and its trees coated with frozen mist from the falls can be dazzling. Spring brings a display of wildflowers that rivals that of the Great Smokies; well over 200 species bloom at Fall Creek Falls. In summer, the forest stretches like carpet from overlooks above Cane Creek Gorge. And in the fall, an understory of maple, hickory, dogwood, and sourwood creates brilliant colors.

Hiking is available on 35 miles of trails that range in length from 0.2 mile to 13 miles. The two longest trails—the Upper and Lower Cane Creek Loops—are designed primarily for overnight use, and a permit is required. Unfortunately, heavy use and lack of maintenance have turned some of the park's trails into muddy gullies. If the state doesn't commit the resources to keep up these once-fine trails, they'll continue to deteriorate.

There is excellent walking, too, on the 3-mile paved path along the lakeshore from the inn to Fall Creek Falls. And visitors can enjoy an exciting walk on the one-way scenic drive leading from Fall Creek Falls along the rim of Cane Creek Gorge; the views from the overlooks are as dramatic as any in the eastern United States.

The establishment of Fall Creek Falls as a state park grew out of the state-park movement launched at a 1921 conference convened by National Park Service director Stephen Mather. Like most states, Tennessee had no state parks then. Following the conference, the Tennessee legislature established the State Park and Forestry Commission, which was given the authority to acquire land for parks and forests.

James O. "Hap" Hazard held a Ph.D. in forestry from Yale and served as state forester under the commission. He was interested in acquiring land for state parks and forests. While prowling the Cumberland Plateau in the early 1930s looking for tax-delinquent land, he heard a tremendous roar in the woods and followed the noise to its source. He could hardly believe what he saw—a waterfall higher than Niagara. It was only a matter of time before Fall Creek Falls would be included in a state park.

Though Tennessee made progress toward establishing state parks before 1936, most parks came about as a result of New Deal public-works and land-reclamation projects. The three agencies most responsible for Tennessee's parks are the Tennessee Valley Authority, the National Park Service, and the United States Forest Service.

During the first 100 days of the administration of President Franklin D. Roosevelt, Congress created the TVA as an integrated, interdisciplinary agency dedicated to resource conservation and development. Most TVA-sponsored parks are in East Tennessee on TVA lakes, but the federal agency's influence on park development was felt statewide. In 1937, following the TVA's recommendation, the Tennessee legislature replaced the park and forestry commission with the Tennessee Department of Conservation, now part of the Department of Environment and Conservation. This became the management agency for Tennessee's state parks.

Fall Creek Falls, the highest waterfall east of the Rockies

Fall Creek Falls State Park

The National Park Service and the United States Forest Service sought to achieve similar goals by different means.

Fall Creek Falls and Montgomery Bell State Parks were developed by the National Park Service as "recreation demonstration areas" to promote the advantages of the recreational use of submarginal agricultural land. The National Park Service deeded these parks to the state in 1944.

The United States Forest Service acquired worn-out farms as "land use areas" primarily for erosion control and reforestation. Recreational use was seen as a by-product of resource conservation. Cedars of Lebanon and Standing Stone State Parks were developed as land-use areas. Management of these combination parks/forests was transferred to the state in 1939, and outright ownership was transferred in 1955.

It's ironic, then, that the long-term abuse of land and one of the darkest periods in American history—the Great Depression—are the two factors that led to the preservation of areas treasured today.

James R. Taft, a local preacher, teacher, and businessman, is credited with interesting the National Park Service in developing a recreation demonstration area in this remote part of the Cumberland Plateau. The original plan called for acquiring the entire watersheds of Cane Creek and Fall Creek, but less than half that area was purchased. That decision has consequences even to this day, as the watersheds outside the park are threatened by strip mining.

The land the government acquired was so badly eroded and unproductive that the average price per acre was less than seven dollars. At first, the plan was to strictly limit development. But the potential of Fall Creek Falls as a vacation destination was soon realized, and the National Park Service revised its plan in 1940 to include cabins, a lodge, and other amenities. By the time World War II ended work on the project, only a few miles of road and some trails, picnic areas, and scenic overlooks had been completed. The area was reforested and restocked with native birds, mammals, and fish.

Interest in making Fall Creek Falls a vacation destination revived after the war, and the state started constructing more facilities. Finally, in the 1970s, the conversion of the park into a major resort was completed. Today, visitors enjoy hiking, golf on a nationally recognized course, tennis, boating, fishing, bicycling, swimming, horseback riding, and sightseeing. An inn overlooks the lake, and there are cabins both on the lake and in the woods. Some 227 campsites are offered as well.

The development of the resort might have ruined the area's natural features if not for careful planning. Accommodations at the park are in demand. For example, weekend cabin rentals usually need to be arranged a year in advance. So if you're going to stay overnight, be sure to plan ahead.

GORGE OVERLOOK AND WOODLAND TRAILS

Highlights
Waterfalls, overlooks above Cane Creek Gorge

Length
2-mile loop with an optional 1-mile side trip

Maps
FCFSP day-use trail guide, FCFSP trail map; USGS: Sampson

Use
Hiking and day use only

Trailhead
The trailhead is at the Betty Dunn Nature Center on TN 284 near the park's northern entrance, which is located off TN 30.

Hike Description

This easy walk leads to the most spectacular scenery in the park, including 85-foot Cane Creek Falls, 256-foot Fall Creek Falls, and overlooks above virgin timber deep in Cane Creek Gorge. You won't find many hikes this short that offer such dramatic rewards.

To reach the trailhead, make your way to the Betty Dunn Nature Center, named for the wife of Winfield Dunn, governor of Tennessee from 1971 to 1975. Many of Tennessee's natural areas were preserved during Dunn's administration. Take time to enjoy the center's exhibits on the natural and cultural history of the region and to visit the spectacular overlooks around the center.

Begin the hike on the sandstone sidewalk behind the nature center. You'll bounce across Cane Creek on a swinging bridge just upstream from the Cane Creek Cascades, the first waterfall on this hike. Here, the park's major stream tumbles 45 feet down stairstep layers of sandstone. During high water, the roar is deafening. The Cane Creek Cascades are also lovely during the low water of summer and fall, when the creek splashes down in one delicate mini-waterfall after another.

After crossing the bridge, you'll climb steps out of the craggy gorge to a trail junction. Go to the right up the hill to reach the junction of the Gorge Overlook and Woodland Trails. Bear right on the red-blazed Gorge Overlook Trail. (This trail runs conjunctively with the Lower Cane Creek Loop, which accounts for the white blazes.)

The well-worn trail levels off in the pines on the edge of Cane Creek Gorge, then descends to a short spur leading to the Cane Creek Falls overlook. Turn right on the spur. As you pick your way down the rocky path, you can look through the boughs of a Virginia pine and across the gorge to Rockhouse Falls, where Rockhouse Creek shoots off the edge and falls 125 feet into a pool.

As you walk closer to the rim, Cane Creek Falls will come into view—though you've known it's there all along, thanks to the everlasting roar. This is a spectacular sight, particularly in

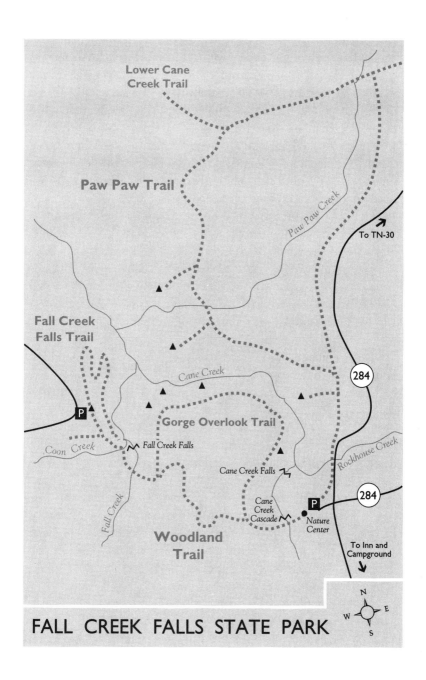

Lower Cane
Creek Trail

Paw Paw Trail

Paw Paw Creek

To TN-30

Fall Creek
Falls Trail

Cane Creek

284

P

Coon Creek

Fall Creek Falls

Gorge Overlook Trail

Rockhouse Creek

Cane Creek Falls

284

P

Fall Creek

Cane
Creek
Cascade

Nature
Center

Woodland
Trail

To Inn and
Campground

FALL CREEK FALLS STATE PARK

N
W   E
S

winter and spring, when both Rockhouse and Cane Creek Falls are at their fullest. When the water is low, the delicate beauty of Cane Creek Falls is unsurpassed. Cane Creek is 50 feet wide where it drops 85 feet into the deep, green pool.

Return to the main trail and follow it as it dips through a hemlock grove next to some impressive oaks. You'll soon reach a spur leading to a rocky outcrop overlooking the wild Cane Creek Gorge. From the spur junction, the broad, heavily used Gorge Overlook Trail drifts lazily along the edge of the gorge as it alternates among stands of oak, pine, and hemlock.

Soon, the trail reaches two overlook spurs. The first leads to Rocky Point, a knifelike promontory separating Cane Creek Gorge from the smaller Fall Creek Gorge. The other spur leads through mountain laurel to a rock above Fall Creek Gorge. If you look left from this rock, you can get your first look at Fall Creek Falls, as the overlook is just above its lip; to the right, you can see into Cane Creek Gorge.

Back on the main trail, you'll descend to join the Woodland Trail at 0.9 mile and cross Fall Creek in a tunnel of rhododendron. You'll notice that the creek's bedrock has an unnatural orange color, and you may detect a faint odor of sulphur. The unfortunate discoloration and smell have resulted from man's attempt to manipulate nature. The excavation of a 345-acre lake on Fall Creek cut into a coal seam. Water then removed iron and sulphur from the coal and carried it downstream, where it was deposited on the normally grayish brown sandstone.

The trail climbs over a laurel-covered rise, then descends beneath a rhododendron canopy to cross Coon Creek just above its dramatic drop into the gorge. The trail makes a steep, curving climb to an overlook that offers magnificent views of the upper part of Fall Creek Falls, Rocky Point, and the bluffs lining Cane Creek Gorge.

At an unmarked junction just past the overlook, the Lower Cane Creek Loop leaves the Woodland Trail. Veer right up through the rocks to the principal Fall Creek Falls overlook. You'll hardly believe your eyes as Fall Creek makes its drop in front of you. During wet weather, Coon Creek Falls—only six feet shorter than Fall Creek Falls—is even more spectacular. No man-made dam impedes its rush off the rim. Both creeks drop into a nearly circular amphitheater. Rocky Point juts into the gorge against the backdrop of the rugged, colorful, pine-covered bluffs of Cane Creek Gorge.

The mowed area around the overlook is one of the many edge environments at Fall Creek Falls. You're likely to spot deer here, particularly around dawn and dusk. By the time the Great Depression hit, deer and other game had just about disappeared from this part of the Cumberland Plateau, victims of overhunting and habitat destruction. Wildlife restoration was an important part of the New Deal project. White-tailed deer were trapped in the Northeast and brought to Fall Creek Falls for restocking. When a truckload came through the nearby town of Spencer, people reportedly came out to look, since most of them had never seen a deer.

Wild turkey restoration has not been as successful. After some initial progress, the population started to decline when Fall Creek Falls began its transformation from a primitive wilderness to a resort park. There is speculation that road construction—particularly the construction of the scenic drive along the gorge that begins here at the overlook—disrupted the turkeys' habitat so much that they left.

From the overlook, you can make an optional side trip, a strenuous descent to and return from the base of the falls. The hike is 0.5 mile each way. Down in the gorge, you'll be in the midst of one of the few patches of virgin forest remaining on the Cumberland Plateau. And you'll get a wholly different perspective of the falls.

From the overlook, retrace your steps to the junction of the Woodland and Gorge Overlook Trails. Turn right and follow the Woodland Trail back to the nature center. Or if you want to revisit the overlooks, return on the slightly longer Gorge Overlook Trail. Whichever way you go, your ears will tell you when you're getting close to Cane Creek Falls and Cascades.

PAW PAW TRAIL

Highlights
Waterfall and gorge overlooks, easy walking in a mixed forest

Length
5-mile loop

Maps
FCFSP day-use trail guide, FCFSP trail map; USGS: Sampson

Use
Hiking and day use only

Trailhead
Same as previous hike

Hike Description

This pleasant trail wanders through a plateau oak-pine forest to overlooks offering dramatic views of Cane Creek Falls, Fall Creek Falls, and Cane Creek Gorge.

The walk starts on the side of the road that leads to the nature center. The orange-blazed trail makes a quick, rocky descent into the rhododendron-lined gorge of Rockhouse Creek.

Rhododendron is a member of the heath family, which includes mountain laurel and flame azalea. Mountain laurel is common on the Cumberland Plateau, particularly along the rims of gorges, where its glossy leaves provide a year-round green border. It produces large clusters of white-to-pink flowers, usually in May. Azaleas are less common and tend to grow in shallow soil in open woods. They bloom about the same time as mountain laurel. Azalea flowers range from pinkish white to bright orange.

The rhododendron that grows along stream banks on the plateau is rosebay rhododendron. Its blooms are white-to-pink, in contrast to the purple of Catawba rhododendron, which grows on outcrops of the Great Smokies and the Blue Ridge. Rhododendron blooms in summer. If you see it in very cold weather, notice how the leaves protect themselves against the cold by rolling into tight coils and bending downward.

After a rough stretch, the trail climbs to the road and crosses Rockhouse Creek. The Paw Paw Trail then reenters the woods and makes a rocky climb before leveling off in the oak-pine forest. (The white blazes reflect that the Paw Paw Trail and the Lower Cane Creek Loop run conjunctively here.)

At 0.4 mile, go left on the spur to an overlook that offers good views of Cane Creek and Rockhouse Falls. Return to the main trail and follow it to a junction. The Paw Paw Trail loop starts here. Go left.

The easy trail follows the gentle ups and downs of the plateau through oak and pine with an abundant understory of holly. You'll soon come to a spur leading left; follow it through mountain laurel to a bare rock ledge above a bend in Cane Creek.

Before the 1880s, the Cumberland Plateau was a land of virgin timber. Then the timber companies came. By 1930, the original forest was gone, except for a few pockets of old growth in remote gorges. You're looking at one them. This stand and the one in nearby Savage Gulf (see pages 239–48) are the only two sizable tracts of virgin timber on the plateau in Tennessee.

Large-scale logging came to Cane Creek Gorge only once, in 1922. The portions of Fall Creek Gorge and Cane Creek Gorge between this overlook and Cane Creek Falls were largely spared, and what logging there was involved selective cutting, as opposed to clear-cutting. In the intervening years, the logged part of the forest has returned to near its original state.

Another remarkable feature of the Cane Creek Gorge forest is its diversity. There are no fewer than six distinct plant communities, each dominated by a particular species or two of trees. Among them are a hemlock–yellow birch community, a chestnut oak community, and an oak-hickory community. This incredible variety in such a small area is caused by extreme variations in soil, microclimate, and exposure.

Return to the spur junction and resume your original course.

The trail curves through a shallow hollow and crosses Paw Paw Creek. Pawpaw is an uncommon shrub or small tree found in moist areas. It's brownish maroon flowers appear in April.

You'll reach yet another spur trail, this one a little longer than the others. It leads left to distant views of Fall Creek and Coon Creek Falls. The overlook is across Cane Creek Gorge from where Fall Creek Gorge empties into it. When the trees shed their leaves, you can see the colorful bluffs to the right.

Back on the Paw Paw Trail, you'll dip to cross a wet-weather stream about to take a plunge off the bluff. The trail then runs along the rim of Cane Creek Gorge before curving inward above a narrowing hollow.

In these deep woods, you stand a chance of seeing a ruffed grouse. You'll know it, for this large, chickenlike bird is likely to spring out of nowhere and startle you with its flapping wings. The ruffed grouse's range in Tennessee is limited mostly to the mountains of the Cumberland Plateau and the state's eastern border. If you camp on the plateau in spring, you may hear the nighttime drumming of the male courtship ritual.

After passing some signs, the trail turns sharply right and comes to where the Lower Cane Creek Loop leaves the Paw Paw Trail at 2.5 miles. The lower loop is better suited for backpacking than for day-hiking. You won't miss much scenery by not walking the loop, as you'll see just about all its great sights where the loop runs conjunctively with the Gorge Overlook and Paw Paw Trails or on the scenic drive along the rim. The one exception is where the loop descends to cross the bottom of the gorge in a dark grove of virgin hemlock.

Just after recrossing Paw Paw Creek, you'll come to another junction. Go right. The trail passes through a fertile bottom that has produced straight, tall tulip poplar and oak, then passes through an extensive stand of tall pine with an understory of beech above a ground cover of partridgeberry. It then returns to the hardwoods, crests a rise, and descends to the first trail junction at 4.5 miles. Retrace your steps to the nature center.

SAVAGE GULF STATE NATURAL AREA

It's the wildest, most untamed place in Middle Tennessee, 11,500 acres of rugged Cumberland Plateau gorges, or "gulfs." The gorges of Savage and Big Creeks and the Collins River are often likened to the imprint of a giant bird's foot. Three 800-foot-deep, 5-mile-long canyons snake below the plateau's rim. More than 50 miles of trail lead to dramatic bluff-top overlooks, along the floors of boulder-strewn canyons, and to several impressive waterfalls.

The lush Appalachian landscape is home to more than 680 species of plants, a total that represents nearly 30 percent of the plant species in Tennessee. The 500-acre virgin stand in the gulf of Savage Creek is the largest and best remnant of the mixed mesophytic forest that once covered two-thirds of the eastern United States. (*Mixed mesophytic* means a type of forest that cannot be named for two or three dominant species.) Nearly every mammal common to eastern America is found here.

Savage Gulf State Natural Area is the largest of several units combined under common management as South Cumberland State Recreation Area. Other areas described in this book are Grundy Forest State Natural Area (Fiery Gizzard) and Carter State Natural Area. South Cumberland State Recreation Area has a visitor center and recreational facilities on US 41 between Monteagle and Tracy City.

The name *Savage* certainly suits this wilderness, but it actually comes from the John Savage family, who owned land here in pioneer days. Sam Werner, one of the Swiss colonists who settled Grundy County in 1869, later came to own the acreage that includes the virgin forest in Savage Gulf. Sam Werner III encouraged the state to acquire Savage Gulf in the mid-1960s. Before long, a preservation effort was under way, led first by the Middle Tennessee Conservancy Council and later by the McMinnville-based Savage Gulf Preservation League.

The vehicle for preserving the area was the Natural Areas Preservation Act of 1971, a product of the intense conservation movement of the 1960 and 1970s, which also brought about the Tennessee Scenic Rivers Act, the Tennessee Scenic Trails Systems Act, and a variety of important national legislation including the 1964 Wilderness Act. The still-vibrant conservation groups formed during this era include the Tennessee Scenic Rivers Association (TSRA), Tennessee Citizens for Wilderness Planning (TCWP), the Tennessee Trails Association, and the Sierra Club's Tennessee chapter.

Tennessee's Natural Areas Preservation Act grew from the realization that many threatened areas worthy of preservation could not qualify as traditional state parks. State Representative Victor Ashe—later Knoxville's mayor—and Memphis senator Bill Bruce navigated the law through the rough waters of the general assembly. Much credit also goes to the TSRA's Bob Miller, a geologist for the state; TCWP founders Lee and Bill Russell, two Oak Ridge scientists; and the indefatigable Mack Prichard of the Tennessee Department of Conservation.

The state acquired the 3,700-acre Werner Tract in 1974 to

form the nucleus of the natural area. Additional purchases through 1986 brought it to its current size. More land desperately needs to be included in the park, especially on the rims of Collins and Big Creek Gulfs.

The entrances into Savage Gulf State Natural Area at the Savage and Stone Door Ranger Stations are on opposite ends of the park, quite a distance apart by highway. The demanding hike described here is from the Stone Door Ranger Station, the entrance accessible from Nashville and Middle Tennessee. You can read about the rest of the natural area's trails in *Tennessee's South Cumberland*, by Russ Manning and Sondra Jamieson.

STONE DOOR, BIG CREEK GULF, AND BIG CREEK RIM TRAILS

Highlights
Dramatic bluff-top overlooks, the Great Stone Door, waterfalls, rich forest

Length
9-mile loop with optional 1-mile and 3-mile side trips

Maps
SCSRA Savage Gulf and Stone Door trails system; USGS: Altamont

Use
The trails are for hiking only. A permit is required for camping at the designated campsites.

Trailhead
The trailhead is at the Stone Door Ranger Station, located off TN 56 at Beersheba Springs.

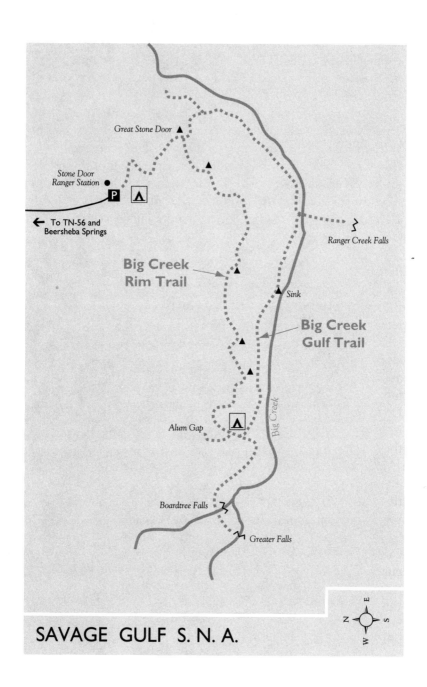

Great Stone Door ▲

Stone Door
Ranger Station ●

P

To TN-56 and
Beersheba Springs

**Big Creek
Rim Trail**

Ranger Creek Falls

Sink

**Big Creek
Gulf Trail**

Big Creek

Alum Gap

Boardtree Falls

Greater Falls

SAVAGE GULF S. N. A.

N E S W

Hike Description

This hike has just about everything Savage Gulf State Natural Area offers: sweeping bluff-top views, cascading creeks, waterfalls, and what is nearly a year-round growth of wildflowers. It goes through the Great Stone Door, a 100-foot-long, five-foot-wide crevice in the bluff that provides access to the gorge below.

This is one of the most strenuous hikes in this book, but it's also one of the most rewarding. It passes through the deep, rocky gorge of Big Creek, returns along the rim, and offers side trails to several impressive waterfalls. It's suitable for a long day-hike or an overnight trip; back-country camping is permitted at Alum Gap and near the ranger station.

Start on the easy, 0.9-mile Stone Door Trail, which leads away from the ranger station. The thickets of mountain laurel and stands of Virginia pine tell you that you're on the rim of a gorge. Before long, you'll come to the end of the pavement at the Laurel Gulf overlook.

If you don't go anyplace else in the natural area, this stop alone will make the trip worthwhile. As you stand on a platform above the gorge of Laurel Creek, much of the park opens up in front of you. On the right, beneath the bluffs at the Great Stone Door, Big Creek Gulf comes in from the right. You can see where it meets Collins River Gulf. Beyond that are the bluffs above the lower end of Savage Gulf.

From the overlook, the sandy trail follows the gorge rim like a giant snake. On the right, you'll see an oddly misshapen pine that has two trunks that merge into one. If you're here in May, you'll catch mountain laurel and flame azalea in bloom.

You'll pass a sign telling you that the Nature Conservancy contributed to the acquisition of Savage Gulf. The conservancy purchased 4,138 acres from the J. M. Huber Corporation and transferred ownership to the state in 1978. The Nature Conservancy is an international, nonprofit organization dedicated to protecting plants, animals, and natural communities by preserving the lands they need to survive. It's been successful in protecting more than 55,000 acres in Tennessee, including part of Radnor Lake State Natural Area and several of the cedar glades unique to Middle Tennessee.

At 0.9 mile, you'll reach a junction with the trail leading to the Great Stone Door. The Big Creek Rim Trail—the trail you'll use for the return—takes off to the right. This hike follows the Big Creek Gulf Trail down through the Stone Door.

But first, take time to visit the bluff overlook to the left, which offers the most expansive view in the whole natural area. You'll walk over a huge crevice to the bluff, located above the confluence of Laurel and Big Creeks. The pines here seem to grow out of solid rock, and the sound of the wind whispering through them competes with the roar of the cascading creeks far below. Look to the right and you'll see the gorge you'll soon be walking through.

Return to the trail junction. Just as you start to descend through the Stone Door, take the wooden bridge leading to another overlook. This is a popular place for rock climbers. After enjoying the view, descend through the Great Stone Door past an ancient, misshapen hemlock. You'll emerge into a different world—a Cumberland Plateau gorge. Instead of an oak forest with sandy soil, you'll find a forest of incredible diversity. There's oak, of course—several different kinds—but there's also tulip poplar, maple, hemlock, ash, buckeye, hickory, sycamore, sassafras, persimmon, sourwood, sweet gum, redbud, cherry, magnolia, beech, ironwood. The list goes on and on. Just about every kind of wildflower in Middle Tennessee grows in this gorge.

From the Stone Door to the "bench" about a third of the way down the 800-foot drop in elevation, the trail is merely a marked route among fields of boulders that have broken off the rim. When you get to the bench—the local term for a mini-plateau on the side of the escarpment—the walking gets easier. Look up. If you're here when there's no foliage, you'll see hues of orange, yellow, and gray on the bluff.

The trail makes its way downward in a series of long switchbacks. The roar of Big Creek rushing through the gorge

The view from Stone Door takes in much of the
Savage Gulf Natural Area.

gets louder with each step. After passing the junction with the
Connector Trail—which leads into the heart of the natural area
and to the other two gorges—the trail passes an interesting boulder field that's home to all sorts of flowers and other plants.

At 2.1 miles, you'll reach an old logging road. The trail turns
right on the road and follows it off and on for the next 3 miles.

Except in the wettest weather, Big Creek does what many
streams do in Cumberland Plateau gorges—it goes underground.

Savage Gulf State Natural Area

If you walk down the old logging road to the left a short distance, you'll come to the spring where Big Creek emerges from its underground passage.

To continue the trail, walk to the right, heading upstream on the road. You'll quickly come to an overlook under a tall hemlock. From here, you can see down into either a dry creek bed or a raging torrent, depending on the season.

Walking on the road is a nice respite after the rocky descent from the Stone Door. But the respite doesn't last long. The trail swings right to pick its way up the side of the gorge, first through a jumble of rocks, then through a stand of even-aged tulip poplar, then through a nearly pure stand of white oak. After cresting on a bench that offers good views of the massive bluffs towering above the creek, the trail drops through beds of ferns to rejoin the old road.

The walking gets easy again on the old road, which is lined with hemlocks. But soon, the trail leaves the road for a detour through some rocks. After rejoining the road, you'll come to a trail junction at 2.9 miles. The blue-blazed side trail leads to Ranger Falls, where Ranger Creek drops off a 20-foot ledge and disappears into a sink. It's well worth the round trip of about 1 mile, but you can't do it when Big Creek is up, as there's no safe way to get across it.

The Big Creek Gulf Trail follows the old road as it makes a steep, rocky climb among huge boulders. It then swings left off the road to drop to the creek. At 3.5 miles, it reaches an unmarked path leading a short distance to the sink where Big Creek goes underground. The sink is in a beautiful setting beneath the limestone bluff under a canopy of sweet gum, tulip poplar, and beech. The view here varies considerably depending on the water level. When it's low, you can see where the creek flows into a cave and disappears. If you're here when it's up, you'd never know there's a sink, but you'll be able to enjoy a magnificent wet-weather waterfall plunging into the gorge.

From the path to the sink, the trail rejoins the old road above a whitewater cascade where the creek squeezes through the narrow gorge. After a steep, rocky climb, the trail levels off for some easy walking beneath the tall bluffs, past huge hemlocks, and next to wet-weather waterfalls crashing down from the right. You'll make another detour off the old road, followed by a steep climb back to it.

The old road leads up out of the gorge, then runs along a notch in the bluff called Alum Gap. The reappearance of pine and mountain laurel tells you that your long climb is about to end. During wet weather, Alum Gap Branch makes a magnificent fall off the plateau in a big bridal-veil cascade and several sheer drops.

After leaving the gorge, you'll level off on the plateau. You'll then come to a four-way trail junction at 4.9 miles in an area covered with scarlet oak and holly. The trail to the left passes Boardtree Falls and goes to Greeter Falls. If you have the time and energy, it's a worthwhile 3-mile round trip to Greeter Falls and back. Hemlock-lined Firescald Creek funnels around a tight curve and drops 15 feet, then another 50 feet into a deep, green pool at the bottom of a big amphitheater of layered limestone and sandstone. One of Middle Tennessee's most impressive waterfalls, Greeter Falls is named for a family that once owned the land. It can also be reached by a shorter trail from TN 56 between Beersheba Springs and Altamont.

From the four-way trail junction, follow the Big Creek Rim Trail past the Alum Gap back-country campsite. On this easy trail, you'll cross the small, wet-weather streams that provide the water for the falls you walked past earlier. You'll also go by four dramatic overlooks. The first one, at 5.4 miles, offers an opportunity to look down into the gorge and see where you just walked. You'll come to the Pine Rock overlook at 5.6 miles and the Sinks overlook at 6.5 miles. At the latter, you can look down to where Big Creek goes underground; when the water is up, you can see the waterfall next to the sink. At the Split Rock overlook at 7.8 miles, you can see the bluffs at the Great Stone Door.

You'll reach the junction with the trail to the Great Stone Door at 8.1 miles. Return to the ranger station on the Stone Door Trail.

GRUNDY FOREST STATE NATURAL AREA (FIERY GIZZARD)

You won't find many places that pack so much dramatic scenery into such a small area, not in Tennessee or elsewhere in the United States. Cascading mountain streams, waterfalls, pinnacles, ancient trees, wildflowers, dazzling winter ice formations, abundant wildlife—they're all here in this Cumberland Plateau preserve. And if that's not enough, you can follow trails out of the natural area down the wild gorge of Fiery Gizzard Creek to overlooks with sweeping vistas of the untamed South Cumberland wilderness.

Grundy Forest State Natural Area is the official name, but to most people, it's the Fiery Gizzard. There are several theories about how this place earned its unusual name. Russ Manning explains them in *The Historic Cumberland Plateau: An Explorer's Guide*. In the 1880s and 1890s, a furnace located here took locally mined coal and made coke for Birmingham's steel mills. Some say the name came from the way that furnace belched smoke and steam. Another theory is that Davy Crockett burned his tongue on a turkey gizzard while camped along the creek. Crockett did, in fact, live for a time in adjoining Franklin County. Others say the name was born during a meeting between Indians and whites, when an Indian ripped the gizzard from a turkey and threw it on a fire to get the whites' attention. Whatever the source, the name adds color and intrigue to this exceptional natural area.

If you look into how Grundy Forest and nearby Savage Gulf came to be preserved as state natural areas, you're sure to come across the name of Herman Baggenstoss. From the 1930s into the 1970s, Baggenstoss was the driving force behind South Cumberland preservation efforts. He was also a founder of the Tennessee Conservation League, one of the state's foremost conservation organizations.

Herman was the son of John and Louise Baggenstoss, two of the original members of the Grundy County Swiss settlement at Gruetli. It was this family who started the renowned Dutch Maid Bakery in Tracy City. (*Dutch* is a corruption of *Deutsche*, meaning German; the settlers were German-Swiss.) In 1934, while serving as superintendent of the local camp of the Civilian Conservation Corps, Herman Baggenstoss initiated a fund-raising drive to purchase what is now Grundy Forest State Natural Area. After the 211-acre site was purchased for $440 and deeded to the state in 1935, the CCC camp relocated here.

Decades later, Baggenstoss was a leader in the drive to establish Savage Gulf State Natural Area. He also worked to establish the Fiery Gizzard Trail, which opened in the late 1970s. Few have contributed as much as Herman Baggenstoss to the preservation of the Volunteer State's scenic resources.

The CCC was one of the first New Deal agencies created after President Franklin D. Roosevelt's 1933 inauguration. Single, jobless men between the ages of 18 and 25 were recruited into "Roosevelt's Tree Army" to work on a variety of conservation projects across the nation. In addition to the pay—"CCC boys" received $30 per month, all but $5 of which had to be sent home to their families—the young men received room, board, clothing, health care, and educational opportunities. More than 70,000 Tennesseans served in the CCC between 1933 and 1942. The CCC built the trails in Grundy Forest, the picnic shelter at the parking lot, and a variety of facilities found today in Tennessee's state parks. The quality of CCC trail construction in Great Smoky Mountains National Park is unsurpassed.

You'll notice a CCC monument near the trailhead, one of several erected by CCC alumni in Tennessee parks worked on by that organization.

The visitor center for South Cumberland State Recreation Area is just a few miles from Grundy Forest on US 41 between Monteagle and Tracy City. The center offers interesting displays about the region's natural and cultural history. And you can pick up a trail map and a schedule of the many ranger-led outings in the South Cumberland.

FIERY GIZZARD AND DOG HOLE TRAILS

Highlights
Cascading streams, waterfalls, unusual rock formations, wildflowers, mountain vistas

Length
9.7-mile loop

Maps
Fiery Gizzard and Buggytop trail maps; USGS: Burrow Cove, Monteagle, Tracy City, White City

Use
The trails are for hiking only. Camping is allowed by permit at the designated campsite.

To US-41

P

Black Canyon Cascade

Blue Hole Falls

Sycamore Falls

Dog Hole Trail

Fiery Gizzard Creek

Yellow Pine Falls

Fiery Gizzard Trail

▲ *Werner Point*

▲

⬛ *Arch*

▲ *Raven Point*

N
W ✦ E
S

GRUNDY FOREST S. N. A.

Trailhead

Grundy Forest State Natural Area is off US 41 just inside
Tracy City. From the South Cumberland visitor center,
located between Monteagle and Tracy City, take US 41 toward
Tracy City. Turn right onto Third Street after 2.3 miles. Follow
the signs a short distance to the parking area.

Hike Description

The Fiery Gizzard Trail is rated as one of the best hiking trails
in the United States. This hike combines parts of that trail with
the Dog Hole Trail to make a loop along the rim and in the
gorge of Fiery Gizzard Creek. It's the most difficult hike in this
book. No matter how fast you usually walk, the going will be
slow.

This is a magnificent hike any time of the year but is probably at its best in winter, when the gorge is a ribbon of green set
against the season's dull brown and gray. A forest canopy of giant hemlocks covers the understory of holly, mountain laurel,
and younger hemlocks. Mats of partridgeberry blanket the ground
in many places. Even the rocks and tree trunks are green, laden
with moss. Winter's wet weather produces too many seasonal
waterfalls and cascades to count. During really cold weather, they
freeze, treating hikers to a dazzling display of ice formations.

The creeks stay high in the spring, when warm weather and
long days bring out an abundance of wildflowers, among them
Solomon's-seal, sharp-lobed hepatica, crested dwarf iris, lady's-
slipper, and the several kinds of trillium common to Tennessee's
woods. The pastels of new spring foliage cover the hillsides visible from the spectacular bluff-top overlooks.

It can get hot in the gorge in summer, but that, too, has its
advantages—like a dip in a pool beneath a scenic waterfall. The
overlook views are great in summer, too, as the forest looks like
a massive green carpet covering the earth.

Fall colors at the Fiery Gizzard can be spectacular, particularly in places where the understory has an ample supply of sugar
maple.

Start the hike by entering the woods at the sign at the parking lot. For the first 0.7 mile, the Fiery Gizzard Trail runs conjunctively with the 2-mile Grundy Forest Day Loop, the next hike in this book.

After crossing the top of a bluff, you'll make a sharp right turn and descend the well-worn trail into a wild Cumberland Plateau gorge. The temperature is usually 10 degrees cooler than in the surrounding uplands, and it's always damp. A different world of plants exists here; over 636 species of vascular plants have been identified in this gorge. Common trees include hemlock, tulip poplar, beech, birch, buckeye, bigleaf magnolia, cucumber magnolia, and sycamore.

The huge bluff—or "rockhouse"—you'll walk under is the same one you just walked over. It's called Cave Spring Rockhouse, for the trickle of water flowing from it.

Winter on the Fiery Gizzard Trail

TENNESSEE DEPARTMENT OF ENVIRONMENT AND CONSERVATION

Little Fiery Gizzard Creek gets louder as you approach Blue Hole Falls, where the creek drops nine feet into a seven-foot-deep pool. The foundation of the CCC pump house next to the trail is a nice place to stop and enjoy the falls.

The trail continues down the creek beneath the bluffs, passes a lovely cascade, and reaches a trail junction and a bridge. Turn left and cross the bridge. (The Grundy Forest Day Loop goes straight.)

Just past the confluence of Big and Little Fiery Gizzard Creeks at 0.9 mile, the creek shoots through a narrow slit in the rock and descends into a stretch called the Black Canyon. Organic stains have turned the rocks deep green and black. The trail climbs over the bluff above a horseshoe bend. At 1.2 miles, it comes to Chimney Rocks, five isolated columns of layered rock rising almost to the treetops.

Just past Chimney Rocks, the trail and creek separate before the trail reaches the blue-blazed path to Sycamore Falls, the tallest waterfall on Fiery Gizzard Creek. Here, the creek shoots off the cap rock and plunges 12 feet into an inviting swimming hole. Just above the falls, a wet-weather cascade trickles down from the gorge rim.

From the Sycamore Falls spur, the trail crosses a hemlock and beech flat, then crosses a clearing for an underground pipeline, then makes a rocky climb to intersect the Dog Hole Trail at 1.5 miles. Turn left and climb the Dog Hole Trail as it threads its way through a jumble of rocks that have fallen from the bluff. (The Fiery Gizzard Trail continues down the gorge and reconnects with the Dog Hole Trail after another 2.8 miles.)

You'll soon reach the entrance to an abandoned dog-hole mine. These coal mines got their name from their narrow entrances, so low that only dogs could enter them standing upright.

From the mine entrance, the trail slices up the side of the gorge and leaves the lush, moist forest of old-growth hemlock for dry second growth of oak and pine. It curves around a notch in the bluff as it leaves state land and enters the property of the Werner family. Sam Werner was one of the area's original Swiss settlers, and his descendants graciously permit the state to run trails across their land. Be sure to stay on the trail. Long-range plans call for the state-owned land to take in the entire gorge and a significant chunk of uplands—a total of 10,000 acres—but it remains to be seen whether such plans will ever be carried out.

The walking is easy for the next several miles, as the trail drifts along the plateau. At 2.7 miles, you'll come to a short spur leading left to Yellow Pine Cascade, a lovely seasonal waterfall set in an alcove covered in pine, tulip poplar, and oak below the first row of bluffs.

Continuing along the Dog Hole Trail, you'll come to an abandoned car and pass the stone remains of an old Werner Farm outbuilding. At 3.1 miles, you'll pass a beautiful spot where chestnut oaks line a crevice between the bluff and some fern- and moss-covered boulders that have separated from it. But it's not the natural beauty of this spot that will catch your eye. It's the collection of 1950s cars that have been pushed over the bluff. These cars have given the place the incongruous name of Junk Bluff.

At 3.4 miles, take the short spur to Werner Point, a rock ledge jutting from the plateau rim high above Gizzard Cove. You can see down the gorge past a series of pine-covered points that include the hike's destination. You can also look upstream into the state natural area. The bluffs themselves are beautiful, too, as miniature Virginia pines grow out of crevices in rocks that are covered with moss and lichen of various colors.

The trail plays tag with several mountain laurel–enclosed overlooks before reaching a four-way trail junction at 4.3 miles. The Dog Hole Trail ends here at its second junction with the Fiery Gizzard Trail. The left fork leads to the back-country campsite. The fork straight ahead goes to Foster Falls, located on US 41 south of Tracy City. Take the right fork—the Fiery Gizzard Trail—which will carry you back to the trailhead.

You'll soon come to another junction. Go straight on the path to Raven Point. On the right just past this second junction is a lovely natural sandstone arch on the edge of the bluff. A

Raven Point above the gorge of Fiery Gizzard Creek

TENNESSEE DEPARTMENT OF ENVIRONMENT AND CONSERVATION

Grundy Forest State Natural Area

faint path leads to it. The arch spans 12 feet and has a six-foot clearance.

Continue on the trail. The plateau gets narrower and narrower until it reaches the rocks leading down to Raven Point. The view from here shares honors with those from the Great Stone Door at Savage Gulf and Green's View at Sewanee as the most dramatic in the South Cumberland. As you get nearer the edge, the panorama opens. By the time you get to where you can walk no farther, the view is nearly 360 degrees. You can see far down Gizzard Cove, which eventually opens into the valley of Battle Creek—the one I-24 passes through on the Chattanooga side of the mountain below Monteagle. You can see up a tributary gorge to your left. And you can look to your right up the gorge of Fiery Gizzard Creek.

As you sit on the rocks listening to the wind in the pines and the roar of the distant creek, you may hear a brief, high-pitched whistling sound. Look up and you'll see a red-tailed hawk above the Cumberland wilderness. Soaring turkey vultures are a common sight here, too.

After enjoying Raven Point, return to the last trail junction, turn left, and follow the Fiery Gizzard Trail as it crests the rim and begins a steep, rocky, difficult descent into the gorge. Below the natural arch, the trail makes some switchbacks before leveling off on a rock-covered bench. Between here and the first Dog Hole Trail junction, the route is not so much a trail as it is a marked course over millions of rocks. This is slow, difficult walking.

Where the trail reaches bottom, a wet-weather waterfall is visible up the bluff on the opposite bank when there's no foliage.

Though difficult, the next stretch of trail is also rewarding, as it travels along one of the most beautiful mountain streams anywhere. Take time to feel its soothing effect and enjoy the splendid forest.

The trail leaves the rocks briefly to run along an old road next to the creek. Where it rounds a bend in a magnificent flat, you can see across the creek to a waterfall emerging from a cave in the bluff. You'll then climb away from the creek, return to the rocks, and pass through an interesting rock-covered sink before making a steep descent to the creek. There's a cascade just downstream on the other side.

You'll then climb again and pass an unusual waterfall on the main creek. The water plunges over a layer of bedrock so straight that it looks like a street curb. Continue up the creek, which tends to flow underground during dry weather. At 7.4 miles, you'll pass beneath a strange-looking, honeycomb bluff on the right, a fairyland place where trees seem to grow out of solid rock.

The trail alternates between creek-side walking and bluff-top rock-hopping before returning to state property and coming to the Fruit Bowl, an area of massive boulders at 7.8 miles. Surrounded by moss-covered rocks, ferns, and giant hemlocks, you might swear you're in a rain forest in the Pacific Northwest.

You'll then climb out of the Fruit Bowl on some steps and walk through another rock field. This area has benefited from decades of public ownership. The hemlock trees have never been logged; many are more than 500 years old.

You'll enjoy some easy walking before ascending through another rocky area on the CCC-built trail. After passing through a quiet, pleasing area with a regal stand of tall hemlock and tulip poplar above a ground cover of partridgeberry, you'll return to the first Dog Hole Trail junction at 8.3 miles. Continue straight, retracing your steps past Sycamore Falls and Chimney Rocks, through the Black Canyon, up Little Fiery Gizzard Creek, past Blue Hole Falls, and under and over Cave Spring Rockhouse to the trailhead.

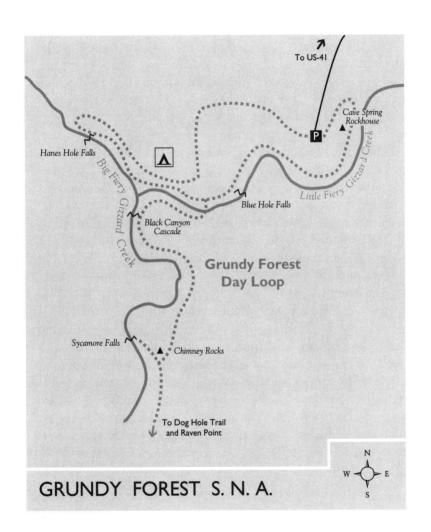

To US-41

Cave Spring
Rockhouse

Hanes Hole Falls

Big Fiery Gizzard Creek

Little Fiery Gizzard Creek

Blue Hole Falls

Black Canyon
Cascade

**Grundy Forest
Day Loop**

Sycamore Falls

Chimney Rocks

To Dog Hole Trail
and Raven Point

N
W E
S

GRUNDY FOREST S. N. A.

GRUNDY FOREST DAY LOOP

Highlights
Waterfalls, huge trees, intriguing rock formations

Length
2-mile loop with a recommended side trip of 1.2 miles

Maps
Fiery Gizzard and Buggytop trail maps; USGS: Burrow Cove,
Monteagle, Tracy City, White City

Use
This loop is for hiking only. Camping is allowed
by permit at the designated campsite.

Trailhead
Same as preceding hike

Hike Description
This CCC-built trail gives you a chance to sample the magnificent South Cumberland gorges without making the long, strenuous hike all the way to Raven Point on the Fiery Gizzard Trail.

Hike the loop counterclockwise. The trail enters the woods at the sign past the picnic shelter. You'll immediately encounter a gorge-rim environment of bare and moss-covered rock, mountain laurel, and Virginia pine. The trail crosses School Branch, which—when flowing—falls 20 feet off the bluff just to the left of the trail.

After skirting the edge of the park through tall pine and oak, the trail turns into the heart of the natural area and runs along the first line of bluffs. You'll hear the creeks playing on the rocks below as you arrive at the site of the CCC camp—now a designated back-country campsite—at 0.6 mile.

A short distance from the campsite, the trail drops into the green world of the gorge and reaches Big Fiery Gizzard Creek, which soon starts to tumble over one rock ledge after another. The trail goes under some huge hemlocks and passes Hanes Hole Falls at 1.1 miles. Here, Big Fiery Gizzard Creek shoots over some jagged rocks and drops nine feet into a pool.

Just past the falls, the trail drops to an overlook above the confluence of Big and Little Fiery Gizzard Creeks. Downstream, you can see the cascade where the merged creek slices through a crevice and enters the Black Canyon. The trail now leads upstream above Little Fiery Gizzard Creek. You'll come to a trail junction and a bridge at 1.3 miles.

From here, the Grundy Forest Day Loop runs conjunctively with the Fiery Gizzard Trail back to the trailhead. But a short side trip down the Fiery Gizzard Trail through the Black Canyon, past Chimney Rocks, and to Sycamore Falls—a round trip of 1.2 miles—is a must. (You can read about this side trip and the return to the trailhead in the description of the first part of the Fiery Gizzard Trail, page 255.)

From the bridge, it is a walk of 0.7 mile past Blue Hole Falls and Cave Spring Rockhouse to the trailhead.

CARTER STATE NATURAL AREA (BUGGYTOP CAVE)

The Buggytop entrance to Lost Cove Cave is one of the most dramatic spots in Tennessee. The opening is 100 feet wide and rises 80 feet beneath a towering 150-foot cliff.

Lost Cove gets its name from the way it's formed. It's completely surrounded by mountains. The creek flowing through it, Lost Creek, disappears into the cave at Big Sink. It flows underground through the saddle separating the isolated upper cove from the lower cove, then reappears at the Buggytop entrance as Crow Creek. It then cascades through a thin, steep-sided gorge.

A 2-mile trail leads from TN 56 to the cave. The original part of the property was donated in 1974 by the late Harry Lee Carter, for whom the natural area is named. Carter owned thousands of acres of South Cumberland timberland, including about 4,000 acres around Lost Cove Cave. The plan was for the state to acquire most of Carter's land east of TN 56, but that never came about. The trail from the highway to the state-owned land runs across private property.

BUGGYTOP TRAIL

Highlights
Dramatic cave entrance, cascading stream, wildflowers

Length
2 miles one-way

Maps
Fiery Gizzard and Buggytop trail maps; USGS: Sinking Cove

Use
Hiking and day use only

Trailhead
The trailhead is at the pull-off on TN 56 that is 6.7 miles
south of the TN 56/US 41A junction at Sewanee.

Hike Description
The trail climbs through a rocky wood featuring several kinds
of small oak, then crests The Spur, a long, thin ridge extending
from the main body of the Cumberland Plateau. After turning
left, it climbs gently up The Spur. Drainage is not good here, so
the trail may look more like a muddy rut during wet weather.

The trail climbs gradually through patches of cane, past sink-
holes on the right, and among cedars, then drops into a saddle at
0.7 mile. It veers to the right off the crest of The Spur and descends into lower Lost Cove in a series of sweeping curves. In
places, the trail picks its way among rock outcrops.

Wildflowers are usually abundant here in the spring and sum-
mer. One you might see is the rare Gattinger's rosinweed, or
Cumberland rosinweed, an eight-foot-tall plant that blooms in
August.

You'll start to hear the sound of Crow Creek tumbling down
the mountain as the rocky descent gets steeper. After curving
through a belt of rocks, the trail reaches the old road from

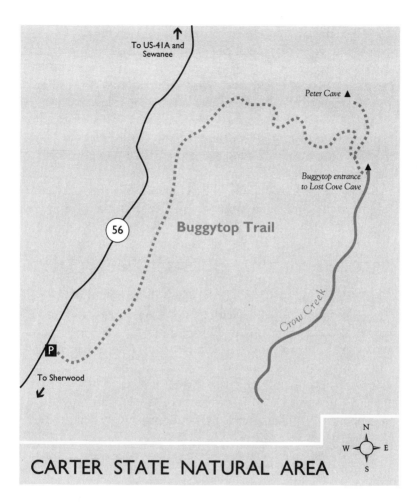

To US-41A and
Sewanee

Peter Cave ▲

Buggytop entrance
to Lost Cove Cave

56

Buggytop Trail

Crow Creek

P

To Sherwood

CARTER STATE NATURAL AREA

N
W ⬥ E
S

Sherwood into upper Lost Cove at 1.7 miles. This road runs near the top of the bluff above the cave entrance. People once used it for Sunday picnics. Perhaps that's how the Buggytop entrance got its name—from the buggies atop the entrance.

Cross the old road and walk onto the bluff. The sound of Crow Creek is now a roar. Take the right-hand fork along the curving bluff. You'll thread your way through a fascinating stretch of boulders supporting a growth of tiny ferns. The trail drops onto a ledge high above the creek, then circles to make a steep, rocky, difficult descent to the cave entrance. The view is overwhelming.

If you're an experienced caver, you can go through the cave and come out at the Peter Cave entrance upstream, except during high water. The sensitive cave environment is home to rare and endangered species of bats and salamanders, so don't disturb anything. If you're not an experienced caver but still want to explore the underground world, take one of the ranger-led outings from the South Cumberland State Recreation Area visitor center.

Scramble back to the top of the bluff and take the rocky path leading to the Peter Cave entrance. You'll pass a smaller entrance on the left in a beech grove before the path crosses a rocky, mostly dry streambed. You'll be able to hear the creek flowing through this entrance, which was created by a breakdown in the cave ceiling.

After crossing the dry branch, climb the saddle to the Peter Cave entrance, located beneath a huge, overhanging rockhouse. On cold, damp days, the air flowing from the cave feels warm and often condenses into fog. On hot days, it feels refreshingly cool. This entrance leads down into a chamber 200 feet wide and 300 feet long, the largest in the cave.

Caves like this were often sources of saltpeter, an ingredient in gunpowder, which probably explains how this entrance to Lost Cove Cave got its name.

From Peter Cave, retrace your steps to the trailhead.

DOMAIN OF THE UNIVERSITY OF THE SOUTH (SEWANEE)

The University of the South owns 10,000 acres of the South Cumberland Plateau. The "domain," as it's called, is home to classic plateau scenery: waterfalls, bluff-top overlooks, interesting rock formations. You can see it all on a network of carefully marked, student-maintained trails. The hikes described here travel parts of the 20-mile Perimeter Trail, which circles the mountaintop over a collection of existing trails and forest roads.

While you're at Sewanee, don't miss the chance to stroll the distinctive campus, which boasts Gothic architecture reminiscent of Oxford. You can combine a campus walk with the third hike included here, the one starting at Memorial Cross. And you'll want to walk through "Abbo's Alley," a natural botanical garden located in a moist, 0.5-mile-long ravine off South Carolina Avenue. Sewanee professor Abbott Cotten Martin developed it over the course of 25 years. When he found himself without student workers during World War II, he received the help of German prisoners from the POW camp at nearby Tullahoma.

The idea for an Episcopal university in the South came mainly from Leonidas Polk, a member of the influential Polk family of Maury County. Shortly after graduating from West Point, Polk abandoned his career as a soldier to become an Episcopal priest. He eventually became bishop of Louisiana, where he promoted the idea of a world-class university that would rival Oxford and Cambridge. In 1856, he met with other bishops to discuss the idea. It was agreed that the new school should be above the "malaria line"—away from the lowlands of the Deep South, which suffered from the twin plagues of malaria and yellow fever. A mountaintop would be ideal.

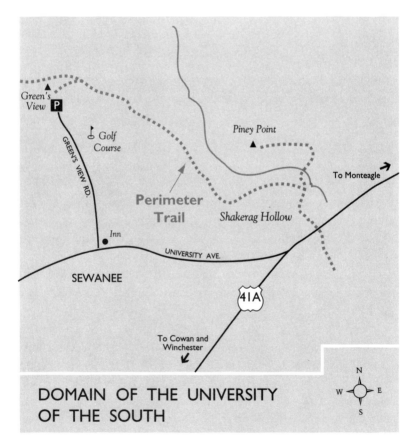

DOMAIN OF THE UNIVERSITY
OF THE SOUTH

It just so happened that the newly formed Sewanee Mining Company was looking to stimulate business for its rail line up the mountain. It agreed to donate land for the university. The huge tract became the "domain." The cornerstone of the first building was laid in 1860.

Then came the Civil War. Bishop Polk never lived to see his dream realized. While serving as a general in the Confederate army, he was killed near Atlanta in 1864.

The little school was destroyed during the conflict. Tennessee bishop Charles Todd Quintard took up the cause after the war and got the university off the ground, using funds he raised in England. The magnificent Gothic buildings were constructed between 1875 and 1915, though the most noted building, All Saints Chapel, was not completed until 1957.

PERIMETER TRAIL THROUGH SHAKERAG HOLLOW

Highlights
Dramatic bluff-top view, mature forest, incomparable spring wildflowers

Length
1.4 miles one-way

Maps
"The Perimeter Trail: Map and Information"; USGS: Sewanee

Use
Hiking and day use only

Trailhead

The trailhead is at the end of Green's View Road.
Coming from Monteagle, turn right off University Avenue
onto Green's View Road at the Sewanee Inn and go to the
end of the road.

Hike Description

This hike combines one of Middle Tennessee's most expansive mountaintop views with Shakerag Hollow and its stands of huge, old trees. The hollow offers one of the region's best spring wildflower shows. Winter and spring rains swell the creeks pouring off the mountain into dozens of waterfalls and cascades.

From Green's View, you'll gaze over a mountain cove and across a green, brown, and tan patchwork of rich Eastern Highland Rim farms. If the sky is clear, you can see all the way across the Highland Rim to the hills separating the rim from the lower Central Basin. To the right, the Cumberland escarpment runs straight north toward McMinnville, giving you a full view as it fades into the distance.

Take the white-blazed spur trail as it falls steeply through a crevice in the bluff line. If you take this hike in April to see the flowers, as hundreds do, you'll be struck immediately by the purple phacelia. It turns the whole mountainside blue.

Follow the spur to the right beneath the bluff to its junction with the blue-blazed Perimeter Trail. Go right. Now the real wildflower parade begins. To the hum of bumblebees gathering pollen from the phacelia, you'll come across crested dwarf iris, false rue anemone, violets, wild geraniums, giant chickweed, foamflower, bellwort—the list goes on and on. You'll encounter three varieties of trillium: large-flowered, yellow, and toadshade. For sheer coverage, the wildflower display here probably beats any other in Middle Tennessee.

The trail curves gently down the mountain beneath some enormous trees—oak, hickory, tulip poplar, ash, buckeye, sugar maple, basswood. They're all so big you'll swear you're in virgin timber. The walking is easy on this rich, moist, north-facing slope as the trail curves around the mountain into Shakerag Hollow. The

CCC company stationed at Grundy Forest near Tracy City put in this stretch of trail.

Shakerag Hollow gets its unusual name from the days when moonshine was made here. Customers descending into the hollow waved a rag over their heads to assure the clandestine distillers that they intended to make a purchase and meant no harm.

As the trail makes a few ups and downs, you'll start to hear the sound of a tumbling mountain stream. After crossing the double-pronged creek, the trail turns rocky and starts to climb steeply up the mountain. It turns left on an old road near the original Sewanee mine, then runs high above a mountain stream that is one small waterfall after another in wet weather.

After a long, curving climb, the trail reaches the bluff line at a tiered waterfall and comes to the spur trail that leads left for 0.7 mile to Piney Point, an open bluff that affords views into Shakerag Hollow and Roarks Cove far below.

At another spur just ahead, go to the right up the hill on the Perimeter Trail. You'll notice the absence of wildflowers and big trees as you walk through a dry, shallow-soil woods of young trees before reaching US 41A just inside the university gate.

If you haven't arranged a shuttle, you can walk back to Green's View the way you came or turn right on the road.

BRIDAL VEIL FALLS AND PERIMETER TRAILS

Highlights

Lovely waterfall, interesting geological features,
bluff-top views, spring wildflowers

Length

2.4-mile loop

Maps

"The Perimeter Trail: Map and Information"; USGS: Sewanee

Use

The trails are for day use only. Hiking and
horseback riding are permitted.

Trailhead

The trailhead is at the Lake Cheston parking area. If you're
arriving in Sewanee from Monteagle, turn right off
University Avenue onto Texas Avenue, which becomes
Breakfield Road. Turn left onto Crossly Drive at the baseball
field and go to the end of the road. The trail enters the
woods at a low gate marked with double white blazes.

Hike Description

This strenuous walk loops below the plateau rim to visit one
of the South Cumberland's finest waterfalls. It returns over several bluff-top overlooks.

The trail starts at the locked gate on the edge of the Lake
Cheston parking area and descends through an understory of
mountain laurel, azalea, spicebush, and holly beneath a canopy
of oak, hickory, tulip poplar, and buckeye.

You'll come to a paved road. Go left across Wiggins Creek,
then turn right to intersect the Perimeter Trail where the creek
starts its tumble down the mountain. Go right across the bridge,
then make an immediate left on the white-blazed Bridal Veil
Falls Trail. The creek and trail penetrate the bluff line together
but soon part company as the rocky trail swings right to run under the bluff.

If you take this walk in early spring, you'll be treated to a
wildflower display that includes phlox, rue anemone, wild geraniums, Carolina vetch, Southern dewberry, and blue-eyed grass.
If poison ivy bothers you, be sure to stay on the trail, as it's everywhere here.

After a brief level stretch, the trail descends sharply among
some massive boulders that have fallen from the cliffs. It then

levels off on one of the benches so common to the Cumberland Plateau's western escarpment. Before the first killing frost, the ground here and at other places on the trail is covered with green leafcup.

The trail leaves the boulders and runs along another bench. You'll start to hear the falls as you come to a four-way trail junction. Go straight a short distance to see a balanced rock, then return to the junction and go right, following the blazes. The sound of the falls will grow louder as you curve down steeply to a fork in the trail. Take the right fork. You'll descend to the narrow saddle in front of the falls.

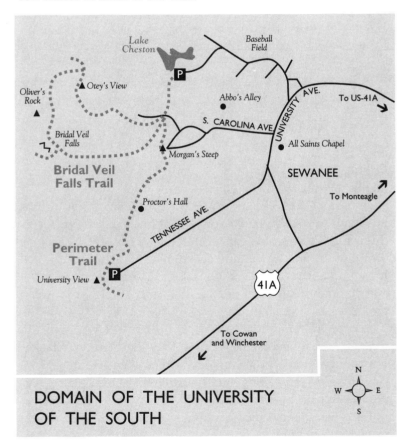

DOMAIN OF THE UNIVERSITY
OF THE SOUTH

Fifty-five-foot-high Bridal Veil Falls is not a sheer drop, which is one reason it's so pretty. Its cool, crystal-clear water flows from inside the mountain, drops over a rock ledge, then another ledge, then another, and so on until it makes its final 20-foot plunge and disappears into a sink. You'll notice that, except in high water, Bridal Veil is actually two falls side by side.

Take time to explore this geologically and botanically interesting place. You can wander down into the Peeples Cave sink below the saddle among some of the tallest trees in these parts. Or you can walk from the last fork in the trail out the narrow ridge to the flower-covered bluff, where a huge boulder sits precariously on the edge. Be careful when you come upon a huge crevice. This seemingly bottomless pit is actually an entrance to Kirby-Smith Cave, part of the large cave network under the mountain.

After satisfying your curiosity, return to the four-way junction above the falls. Go straight, following the white blazes. The trail curves around to another junction. Take a short side trip to the left to see Oliver's Rock, a huge monolith standing alone on the mountainside. If you walk beyond the rock, you'll soon come to Pickney Branch and another waterfall. Though this fall is much smaller than Bridal Veil, it also loses its water to a sink.

Return to the fork and continue on the blazed trail up the mountain as it makes a curving ascent back into the boulders through great stands of leafcup. A long stretch of level walking comes to an end as the trail makes a hairpin turn to a small stream and heads uphill. The reappearance of mountain laurel tells you that the plateau rim must be close. Sure enough, you'll soon come to a second junction with the Perimeter Trail.

Turn right. From here back to the first Bridal Veil Trail–Perimeter Trail junction, the route follows the bluffs. You'll pass Otey's View along the way. From here, you can see down into Hawkins Cove and along the Cumberland escarpment as it carries the Appalachian Mountains to their terminus in Alabama.

Like many natural features around Sewanee, Otey's View is named for a person instrumental in the development of the university. James H. Otey came to Middle Tennessee in 1821 at age 21 to become headmaster of Harpeth Academy in Franklin. After a few years, he returned to North Carolina, studied for the priesthood, and was ordained. He returned to Franklin in 1827 to organize St. Paul's, the first Episcopal congregation in Tennessee. He became the denomination's first bishop in Tennessee and was, with Bishop Leonidas Polk, one of the founders of the university.

The plateau's edge becomes less severe as the trail curves into and out of the laurel, skirts some houses, and returns to the first junction. Retrace your steps to Lake Cheston.

PERIMETER TRAIL FROM UNIVERSITY VIEW TO MORGAN'S STEEP

Highlights
Bluff-top views, waterfalls

Length
1 mile one-way

Maps
"The Perimeter Trail: Map and Information"; USGS: Sewanee

Use
Hiking and day use only

Trailhead
The trailhead is at University View. If you're coming from Monteagle, turn right off University Avenue onto Tennessee Avenue and go to the end of the road.

Sewanee's Perimeter Trail passes Memorial Cross.

Hike Description

This short but surprisingly difficult walk starts at University View and its Memorial Cross. It runs beneath the bluffs, past waterfalls, and to the road access at the bluff at Morgan's Steep.

Memorial Cross was built as a memorial to men from the University of the South killed in World War I. In 1982, memorials were added for Sewanee students and local citizens who served in World War II, Korea, and Vietnam. The spectacular vista from University View looks out over the forested mountain and the rich Highland Rim farms below.

You'll leave Memorial Cross on an easy, graded trail the CCC built in the 1930s. Where it dips to a creek and an abandoned road—the old Sewanee-Cowan Road—turn left to descend briefly on the rocky road before swinging to the right.

From this point, the trail travels beneath the first row of bluffs. You'll go under overhanging rocks that harbor a profusion of wild-flowers, including bright red round-leaved catchfly, which is similar in appearance to fire pink, its cousin. In places, it seems to grow out of solid rock.

The bluff becomes taller as the trail threads among boulders and patches of Virginia spiderwort, which blooms in late spring. As the trail curves around to a notch in the bluff, Proctor Falls will come into view. Here, a small creek shoots off the plateau rim and plunges 20 feet before tumbling down the mountain in a series of cascades.

Past the falls, the trail goes under a massive overhang and climbs to Proctor's Hall. The collapse of rocks from the bluff has created a chamber, a near-perfect rectangular passage through the rocks. A rough side path leads to the huge rock that is the ceiling of Proctor's Hall.

After passing through Proctor's Hall, you'll have to scramble down an often-slick rock ledge to resume your walk below the bluff. As you start to curve to the right into a cove, you'll hear the rush of a mountain stream ahead. You'll then climb to cross a small stream, weave under another overhanging bluff, and descend steeply to a large creek, where you'll see one small waterfall after another.

The trail follows the creek under a bluff colored various shades of red, green, and gray. It then passes through a thicket of mountain laurel, turns left to cross the creek on a bridge, and follows the opposite bank downstream. After some rough walking where you'll have to pick your way among some rocks, you'll pass a deep crevice in the second line of bluffs and reach the steps at Morgan's Steep. Climb them to the overlook, from which you'll be able to see down into Hawkins Cove. Part of this cove is a state natural area.

From Morgan's Steep, you can retrace your route to University View. Or you can walk a short distance on the Perimeter

Trail to the Bridal Veil Falls Trail, the preceding hike. Or you can make a pleasing return to University View by road, a 2-mile walk past Abbo's Alley and the main part of the Oxford-inspired campus. If you decide to take the road, follow the loop to South Carolina Avenue, turn right, walk to University Avenue, turn right again, and go to Tennessee Avenue, which will take you to University View and Memorial Cross.

PART II

WALKS ON COUNTRY ROADS

PART II: WALKS ON COUNTRY ROADS

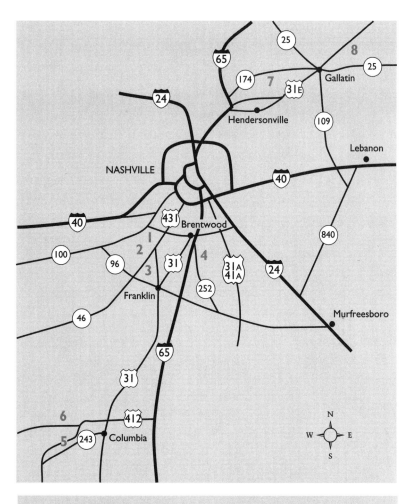

HARPETH BEND WALK

Moran Road and Old Natchez Trace Road

Highlights
Historic houses, prosperous horse farms

Length
2.3 miles

Starting Point
The starting point is at the edge of the Sneed Forest subdivision on Moran Road, 0.5 mile west of Hillsboro Road (US 431). Turn onto Moran Road 2.7 miles south of Old Hickory Boulevard between Nashville and Franklin.

Ending Point
Old Natchez Trace Road at the Harpeth River

Traffic Level
Moderate

This walk through rich, green pastures in bends of the Harpeth River passes several historic houses and some interesting modern ones as well.

Harpeth Side is the lovely house you'll see on your left after you leave the Sneed Forest subdivision. It's appropriately named, for it overlooks the Harpeth River. Though you cannot tell it today, it's actually a log house, as are so many of Middle Tennessee's old frame houses. Early settlers had an abundance of logs but hardly any milled lumber, so they built their houses out of hewn logs. Later, when there were sawmills, many log houses were covered with frame siding.

John Motheral was a Revolutionary War veteran from Pennsylvania who bought 500 acres along the Harpeth in 1800. With his wife, the former Jane Currie, he built this two-story log house around 1805. It passed to their daughter Mary, who married Dr. Joel Walker in 1830. In 1870, the Walkers added the double front porch, covered the logs with siding, and built a frame addition. The house has not been significantly altered since then and is immaculately maintained by its current owners.

Just past Harpeth Side, you'll cross the tree-lined Harpeth River. The winding Harpeth flows through one broad bend after another on its 125-mile journey through Rutherford, Williamson, Davidson, Cheatham, and Dickson Counties to the Cumberland River. Moran Road cuts across Sawyer and Bradley Bends, which together make a giant S-curve in the river.

There are actually four rivers named Harpeth: the Big (or just plain) Harpeth and three tributaries, the West Harpeth, the Little Harpeth, and the South Harpeth.

The name *Harpeth* is as pleasing to the ear as the river's beauty is to the eye. The origin of the name is a mystery. Some say it

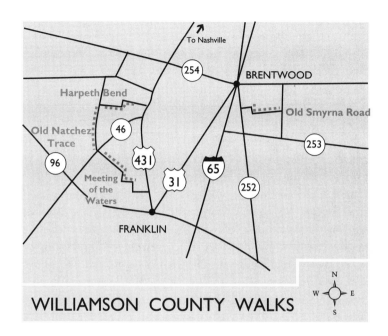

WILLIAMSON COUNTY WALKS

Map labels:
To Nashville
254
BRENTWOOD
Harpeth Bend
Old Smyrna Road
Old Natchez Trace
46
253
96
431
65
Meeting of the Waters
31
252
FRANKLIN

N
W · E
S

comes from the murderous Harpe brothers, two outlaws who preyed on travelers on the nearby Natchez Trace. But the river was called the Harpeth before the Harpe brothers started their lives of crime, so that theory doesn't hold water. Others say that the name is a corruption of *Harper*. In fact, the river was called the Harper in some early texts. But no one knows where the name Harper came from.

The most likely source of the name is *The Spectator*, the popular London periodical published by Joseph Addison. The August 23, 1714, edition contained a tale of two Oriental brothers, Harpath and Shalum, who became rivals for the affection of the beautiful Hilpa. When Harpath won her hand, Shalum cursed him. Harpath eventually drowned—so the legend goes—in a river that was forever to be called by his name. The earliest maps of Middle Tennessee call the river the Harpath, providing support for this theory.

The walk continues next to the river until Moran Road curves sharply left. Here, a drive leads up to another historic house, Locust Guard. Joseph Motheral, fifth son of the Motherals of Harpeth Side, and his wife, the former Anness Lea Williams, built Locust Guard in 1823. Today, this house is identified with the Ring family. Emaline Tennessee Motheral, daughter of Joseph and Anness Lea, married Hiram Eleazer Ring, a well-known teacher originally from Lancaster, Ohio. Emaline moved to her parents' house after Hiram's death in 1858, and the house has been in the Ring family ever since.

Past Locust Guard, the road makes a curving climb out of the Harpeth River's rich bottom and passes a huge contemporary house on the left. Look left at 0.9 mile and you'll see the rambling log house of Blue Spring Farm. Before 1810, this land was owned by General James Winchester, whose splendid home near Gallatin, Cragfont, is a state historic site. (For more about Cragfont, see the chapter on Bledsoe Creek State Park, pages 71–78.)

James Pearre bought the property from Winchester, a fellow Maryland native. James leased the land to his brother, Joshua, who, like Winchester, was a Revolutionary War veteran. In 1840, the property was purchased by James Clark Robertson of Nashville, whose home stood on the site of the old Maxwell House Hotel at what is now Fourth Avenue and Church Street.

Whether Robertson or the Pearre brothers built the house at Blue Spring Farm is uncertain, but it is known that Robertson moved here shortly after he bought the place. Several additions were made to the home, and the logs were covered with siding. The house stayed in the Robertson family until 1965, when it was purchased by Dr. and Mrs. Addison Scoville, Jr., whose remodeling removed the siding and exposed the ancient logs.

After some more curves, the road straightens between a stone fence on one side and a wooden fence on the other. Moran Road is reminiscent of an English country lane as it continues through the bright green pastures of prosperous horse farms until it ends at Old Natchez Trace Road.

Turn left and walk between Old Natchez Trace Road's stone fences. Where the road starts to make its steep descent to the river, a drive leads to the right to another historic house, Woodland. This home is not visible from the road. Its earliest section is a log cabin built by Winfield Knight in 1820. The place was bought in 1857 by Sam Houston Moran, whose descendants still own it.

As you walk down the steep hill, you might see a bicyclist struggling up the grade. The stretch from the Warner Parks to Franklin along Old Natchez Trace Road is the most popular cycling route in the Nashville area.

When you get to the riverbank, you've reached the end of this walk and the start of the next one.

OLD NATCHEZ TRACE WALK

Old Natchez Trace Road

Highlights
Scenic Harpeth River, route of the Natchez Trace, historic houses, prehistoric village

Length
2.6 miles

Starting Point
Where Old Natchez Trace Road meets the Harpeth River south of the junction of Old Natchez Trace Road and Moran Road

Ending Point
Old Natchez Trace Road at Old Hillsboro Road (TN 46)

Traffic Level
Moderate

This walk will let you encounter one of the region's most important prehistoric Native American villages, take you to three historic houses, and introduce you to the pioneer Perkins family, who owned most of the land around here in the first half of the 1800s.

Most important, it will let you enjoy one of Middle Tennessee's oldest roads. The route we now call the Natchez Trace evolved from a buffalo path to an Indian path to the Boatman's Trail to an official national road. (For more information, see the chapter on the Natchez Trace Parkway, pages 107–22.) In 1800, it was designated a post road for carrying mail from Nashville to faraway Natchez on the Mississippi River. The postmaster general persuaded President Thomas Jefferson to use the army to upgrade the primitive route, which was relocated off Backbone Ridge to this gentler course in the Harpeth Valley. So when you stroll down this peaceful lane next to the old stone fences, you're connected with our earliest history as a nation. You're walking a route personally approved by Thomas Jefferson.

But it's the natural beauty—not the history—that will first catch your attention. The walk starts where the previous one ends—where Old Natchez Trace Road meets the Harpeth River in Bradley Bend. You'll depart from a tree-shaded bottom right next to the river, a bottom dotted with colorful wildflowers much of the year. You can see from the ropes hanging from trees that this is a popular swimming hole. It's also a good place to launch a canoe for a springtime float.

Old Natchez Trace Road swings away from the river past the intersection with Temple Road and crosses a bridge. At 0.7 mile, it passes the stone gates guarding the drive to Fairmont, which dates to 1850. Fairmont is typical of plantation homes from the 1840s and 1850s. It's a two-story white frame house with Greek Revival detailing. The basic style, though, was around before the Greek Revival fad. Some call the style Georgian, some call it Federal, and others call it "glorified pioneer." Such houses have a central passage with one or two rooms on each side on both floors. They also have chimneys at each end.

Past Fairmont, Old Natchez Trace Road reunites with the river and enters one of the most historic spots in Middle Tennessee, an area that has been inhabited off and on for at least 1,000 years—and possibly 5,000 or even 10,000 years. Called Old Town, the site includes the remains of a prehistoric Native American village, the remnants of an 1801 bridge, and an 1846 plantation house.

As you cross Brown Creek, look to your right to see the stone abutments of the 1801 bridge. The abutment on the northern bank still stands, but the other one has crumbled in recent years.

It's often said that Andrew Jackson led his troops over this bridge on the way to fight the British at New Orleans during the War of 1812, the event that made him a national hero. But that story cannot be true, for Jackson was already on the Gulf coast before he went to New Orleans. It is probable, however, that he returned from his meeting with destiny on this route. The current bridge replaced the old one in 1913.

As you walk past the bridge, you'll see two mounds in the pasture. These are the remains of the prehistoric village for which Old Town is named. A highly developed Mississippian Period culture flourished in Middle Tennessee from around 1000 A.D. to 1700 A.D.; this is one of several important sites along the Harpeth River. Large mounds are the characteristic remnants of such villages. It was originally thought that these were burial mounds, but excavation at Old Town by Dr. Joseph Jones around 1868 revealed that they had a ceremonial function. Temples were erected on them. The deceased were buried in stone-lined graves, which accounts for why those who lived here are sometimes called the Stone Box People. (Their society is sometimes called the Middle Cumberland Culture.) Jones found 50 such graves at this site.

At Old Town, a 2,470-foot-long, crescent-shaped fortification enclosed a 12-acre village. The inhabitants had a sociopolitical system and practiced rather highly developed agriculture. Among their crops were beans, squash, and maize.

No one knows why the culture vanished or where its people went. But evidence of its existence—mounds, graves, cleared

Old Town sits next to the site of a prehistoric native village.

land—was here when the first Europeans arrived. In fact, early explorers and settlers referred to some areas as "old fields."

Less-developed civilizations existed here during the Paleo-Indian Period (10,000 to 14,000 years ago), the Early and Middle Archaic Periods (5,000 to 10,000 years ago), and the Late Archaic and Woodland Periods (1,100 to 5,000 years ago). A squash seed found along the Harpeth has been dated to 6,990 years ago. It is thus entirely possible that the Old Town site was inhabited before the Mississippian Period.

The house known as Old Town stands just beyond the temple mounds. Thomas Brown, its builder, was a Virginian who came to Tennessee in 1820. He married Nancy Allison in 1828. Two boys were born to the couple, but Nancy died young. She was buried with her parents along the South Harpeth River. Three weeks later, Brown married Nancy's cousin, Margaret Bennett Hunter, herself recently widowed. Such marriages were common, for widowers needed someone to care for their children and widows needed a place to live. Brown apparently never got over the loss of his first wife. Though he lived 32 years and had four children with Margaret, he requested that he be buried next to his first wife.

The graceful plantation house is in the Greek Revival style.

The main entrance and the door opening onto the upstairs portico are original, as is much of the interior. One of the log outbuildings is the original 1846 smokehouse.

Past Old Town, the road leaves the river and curves gently uphill. Where it straightens among some prosperous horse farms, look to the right for your first glimpse of Montpier, which sits beautifully on a hill. Nicholas Perkins built Montpier in the Federal, or "glorified pioneer," style around 1821. The Greek Revival portico is an 1850 addition.

If you've read any history of this part of Middle Tennessee, you're sure to have come across the name of Nicholas Perkins—and not just as it applies to the man who built Montpier. So many Perkins men were named Nicholas that it's hard to keep them straight.

Montpier's Nicholas Perkins was called "Bigbee," a nickname derived from his ownership of land along the Tombigbee River in what are now Alabama and Mississippi—the Mississippi Territory in those days. President Jefferson appointed Bigbee the register of lands for the territory, a position that thrust him into

Nicholas "Bigbee" Perkins' Montpier

one of the great dramas of American history, the treason trial of former vice president Aaron Burr. Suspected of plotting with the Spanish, Burr was a fugitive on the night of February 18, 1807, when Perkins participated in his capture. Perkins was then placed in charge of the detail that took Burr all the way to Virginia to stand trial.

Bigbee settled in Williamson County. While visiting his cousin and his brother-in-law—another Nicholas Perkins—he met and fell in love with Mary Perkins, another cousin. They were married in 1808. He was 29 and she was 14.

Bigbee went on to become one of the wealthiest and most influential men of his day. He owned 12,000 acres, served in the state legislature, and was a prominent lawyer. He and Mary— also known as "Pretty Polly"—had 11 children. One of them, William O'Neal Perkins, was the man who sold the Old Town property to Thomas Brown. Bigbee and Polly eventually moved into her late parents' home, Meeting of the Waters (visited on the next walk). Montpier then passed to their oldest daughter, Mary Elizabeth, and her husband, Leland J. Bradley.

Another splendid Perkins home, Eventide, stands to the south off Old Hillsboro Road. Originally called Walnut Hill, it was built by the former Sara Agatha Perkins and her husband, Nicholas Lafayette Marr.

The historic road continues next to a rock fence built by Montpier slaves and past a subdivision carved out of the estate. Where today's county road makes a sharp left turn, the Natchez Trace probably went straight and followed the general route of Old Hillsboro Road past Eventide and on to what is now the village of Leipers Fork, once called Hillsboro. This community was the source of the name *Hillsboro* applied to so many features in the Nashville-Franklin area. The village had to change its name when it got a post office, as there was already a Hillsboro, Tennessee.

The walk ends at Old Hillsboro Road in the Forest Home community. Forest Home was given its name by yet another Nicholas Perkins—Nicholas Edwin Perkins, a son of Bigbee and

Polly. The intriguing Queen Anne–style house on the northwestern corner was once the home of Squire Jamie Payne, a longtime county magistrate.

Notice the monument at the southwestern corner. It's one of many such monuments the Daughters of the American Revolution (DAR) erected along the route of the Natchez Trace beginning in 1909. The DAR markers played a major role in keeping the memory of the trace alive. This eventually led to the construction of the Natchez Trace Parkway.

The next walk starts where this one ends. Old Hillsboro Road leads left to Hillsboro Road (US 431) and right to Leipers Fork and a junction with the Natchez Trace Parkway.

MEETING OF THE WATERS WALK

Del Rio Pike

Highlights
Historic houses, meeting of the Big Harpeth
and West Harpeth Rivers

Length
2.4 miles

Starting Point
Old Hillsboro Road (TN 46) at Old Natchez Trace Road

Ending Point
The curve in Del Rio Pike northwest of Franklin

Traffic Level
Moderate

Meeting of the Waters is named for the meeting of the
Big and West Harpeth Rivers.

This walk passes the confluence of the two largest rivers called
Harpeth—the Big Harpeth and the West Harpeth—and visits
the handsome house named for the junction, Meeting of the
Waters. It passes three other antebellum houses and travels
through the West Harpeth's rich, tree-shaded bottom.

Start this walk where the previous one ends. Walk south a
short distance on busy Old Hillsboro Road to Del Rio Pike and
turn left.

As you walk through the green pastures bordering straight,
level Del Rio Pike, you'll see the rear of Meeting of the Waters
up ahead. If you love fine, old houses and have an eye for pure
architectural styles, your heartbeat will quicken as you round the
curve and get a full view of one of the oldest and best-preserved
houses in Middle Tennessee.

Almost as soon as Williamson County was established, Thomas Hardin Perkins and his wife, the former Mary Magdalen
O'Neal, settled along the Harpeth. A Revolutionary War veteran, Thomas was the son of yet another Nicholas Perkins (see
the previous walk). Here in the wilderness, the Perkinses dupli-

cated what they remembered of their former home in Virginia, a grand, two-story, Federal-style house.

Construction started in 1800 and took eight years to complete. The bricks was fired on the property, the limestone was quarried here, and the timbers and flooring came from trees cut locally. Nails were nearly nonexistent on the frontier, so wooden pegs were used instead.

Today, Meeting of the Waters is practically unaltered from its original construction. Even some of the window glass is original. And what's more, the house has never left the Perkins family.

Bigbee Nicholas Perkins and his wife, Polly, daughter of the builders, moved to Meeting of the Waters after her parents died. Bigbee left the house to their son, Nicholas Edwin Perkins, who lived here with his wife, the former Martha Maury, granddaughter of Abram Maury, the founder of Franklin and the man for whom Maury County is named. The present owners are Ridley Wills II and his wife, Irene Jackson Wills, a descendant of Bethenia Perkins Bostic, a sister of Thomas Hardin Perkins, the home's builder. Their love of the place is apparent just from looking at it.

Where the road curves to the right just past the house, a rough private road leads down to the junction of the Big and West Harpeth Rivers. Del Rio Pike dips through the rich, often soggy bottom of the West Harpeth and crosses the river at 1 mile. The bottom is covered with flowers in spring and summer.

The road then makes a long, gentle climb and passes a large, columned house off the road to the left. Rosehill, as it is now called, was originally located on Columbia Avenue in Franklin. The frame part of the house dates to 1838 and the log part in the rear to 1825. The house was moved to this spot in 1986 and has been creatively renovated by its current owners.

Del Rio Pike crests the hill in front of Two Rivers, the second Perkins house built along the Harpeth. Like Meeting of the Waters, it takes its name from the junction of the rivers. It was built by yet another Nicholas Perkins, Nicholas Tate Perkins, cousin, brother-in-law, and neighbor of Bigbee Nicholas Perkins. Nicholas

Tate Perkins married Ann Perkins, the daughter of still another Nicholas Perkins. They completed the house in 1820. Like Meeting of the Waters, it's in the Federal style.

The house was acquired by Simeon and Amelia Shy in 1848. Their son, William M. Shy, was a Confederate officer killed in December 1864 during the Battle of Nashville. If you know your Nashville geography, you know Shy's Hill off Harding Place, named for the young colonel killed there.

Just past Two Rivers, you'll come to the first of several right-angle turns on Del Rio Pike. Bear right, walk a ways, then follow the pike as it turns left. At the next turn, you'll come to the drive leading to River Grange, another Perkins family home. Located near the Big Harpeth River, off to your left, the house is surrounded by trees that hide it most of the year.

In 1823, a Perkins kinsman, Thomas Moore, married Mary Tate Perkins, the only survivor of the 14 children born to Nicholas Tate Perkins and Ann Perkins of Two Rivers. Following the death of the Moores' first child, they returned from Arkansas to Williamson County. Nicholas Tate Perkins built this Federal-style house for his daughter in 1826. Otey Walker bought the place in 1889 and made some alterations according to the popular Victorian style.

The walk ends here, but Del Rio Pike continues on to Franklin.

OLD SMYRNA ROAD WALK

Old Smyrna Road

Highlights
Sunken road between stone fences, historic houses

Length
1 mile

Starting Point

The starting point is on Old Smyrna Road at the edge of the Carondelet subdivision. Turn onto Old Smyrna Road off Wilson Pike (TN 252) 0.9 mile south of Church Street in Brentwood.

Ending Point

Cottonport on Old Smyrna Road

Traffic Level

Moderate to heavy

Though Old Smyrna Road is in the sprawling suburb of Brentwood, the feeling here is decidedly rural. The road passes working farms presided over by some of Middle Tennessee's most historic houses. On this walk along a lovely, tree-lined lane, you'll encounter the site of Williamson County's earliest settlement.

The stories of three families—the Mayfields, the Sneeds, and the Frosts—are woven through the history of Old Smyrna Road.

James Mayfield was one of Nashville's original settlers. After he was killed by Indians, his heirs claimed his 640-acre grant on this spot. James Mayfield's son, Southerland, took a risk when he moved his family here, as the tract was located a good distance from the security of the forts and stations closer to the Cumberland River.

It proved a fatal decision. Creek Indians attacked Mayfield Station in 1788, killing Southerland, one of his sons, and another man. Another of Southerland's sons, George, was captured; he lived with the Creeks for 12 years. After the attack, Southerland Mayfield's widow moved the survivors to a safer station located closer to the river.

James Sneed and his wife, the former Bethenia Harden Perkins, brought their family here in 1798. Bethenia was the sister of Nicholas Tate Perkins and the niece of Thomas Hardin Perkins (whose houses are visited on the Meeting of the Waters Walk, pages 292–93) and the cousin of Nicholas Perkins of Montpier (visited on the Old Natchez Trace Walk, pages 289–90).

James Sneed was from an old Virginia family; the first Sneeds settled near Jamestown in 1635. James and Bethenia had 12 children, three of whom built fine houses along Old Smyrna Road. Two still stand here, and the third has been relocated to Brentwood's Crockett Park.

Captain John Frost was the son of a Tory—a colonist who sided with the British in the Revolutionary War. The elder Frost was eventually killed for his loyalties, and his family's land was confiscated. Captain John Frost and his wife, the former Rhoda Miles, came here from South Carolina around 1810 as part of a westward migration of Quakers. They bought land at the headwaters of Mill Creek and settled on the site of the long-abandoned Mayfield Station. A thriving community called Cottonport grew up around their house. Captain Frost earned his title by serving as a company commander in the War of 1812.

Old Smyrna Road didn't get its name because it's the old road to the town of Smyrna. Instead, it's named for Smyrna Church, founded in 1829 on land given by Captain Frost. The church lasted until the late 1930s, when it merged with Brentwood Methodist Church.

After the road straightens out between two moss-covered stone fences, you'll pass two of the Sneed houses, one on each side of the road.

Windy Hill, the one on the right, was built by Constantine Sneed, son of James and Bethenia Sneed. Constantine served with Andrew Jackson in the War of 1812. He married Susannah Perkins Hardeman in 1825, the same year Windy Hill was completed. The house is unusual in that it's not in the typical "glorified pioneer" style, which features a central passage. Instead, it has entrances into two rooms on the first floor.

Foxview, across the road, was built by Alexander Ewing Sneed, the youngest of James and Bethenia's 12 children. The house was constructed shortly after Alexander married Elizabeth Guthrie in 1834.

Brentvale, once the third Sneed home along Old Smyrna Road, has been moved to Crockett Park. William Temple Sneed and his wife, the former Elizabeth Guinn Crichlow, built the log

Windy Hill, one of several historic Sneed family houses

house in 1830. Their son, Dr. William Joseph Sneed, helped establish Nashville's Meharry Medical College and taught there for many years.

Just past Windy Hill, you'll see the Sneed family cemetery on the right. Then you'll come to the original Sneed house, the one James and Bethenia built in 1798. This log structure covered with siding may be the oldest house in Williamson County.

Continue along Old Smyrna Road past a modern mansion on the left and the beautiful, new stone fence that goes with it. The road dips and curves among big cedars before reaching Cottonport at 1 mile. This is the house John and Rhoda Miles Frost built in 1810. The portico is probably a later addition. During the years when the community of Cottonport existed here, the post office was located in the Frosts' house. When the railroad came through in the 1850s, the town of Brentwood was developed, and Cottonport faded away. This house is the only remnant of it.

The walk ends here, but if you like, you can continue on Old Smyrna Road 1 mile to Edmondson Pike. It's a nice walk, mostly through woods, but it offers no more historic houses.

ZION WALK

Old Zion Road

Highlights
1849 Zion Church, historic houses

Length
2.2 miles

Starting Point
The starting point is at the intersection of Old Zion Road
and Trotwood Avenue (TN 243) between Columbia and
Mount Pleasant. This intersection is 2.1 miles from the junction
of Trotwood Avenue and Cayce Lane in Columbia.

Ending Point
Old Zion Road at Zion Road

Traffic Level
Moderate

Some of the Volunteer State's most prosperous farms await you on this walk through the historic community of Zion, one of Middle Tennessee's more intriguing early settlements.

Historian John Trotwood More called this area "the Dimple of the Universe," in recognition of its fertile soil and stunning natural beauty. The deep, well-watered soil is high in organic matter, rich in phosphate, and free of rocks and stones. It was inevitable that settlers would flock here after Indian treaties in 1805 and 1806 made it legal. In those days, most of the land was held in three large tracts, one owned by Gideon Pillow, one by William Polk, and one by the heirs of Revolutionary War hero Nathanael Greene. Greene had been awarded a 25,000-acre grant

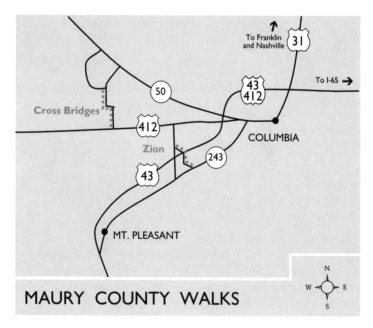

MAURY COUNTY WALKS

Zion Church, one of Tennessee's most important historic churches

for his war service, but he died in 1786 before ever coming to Tennessee to see it.

Around the same time the treaties legalized settlement, a group of Scots-Irish Presbyterians was looking for a place to relocate. These Presbyterians had lived in the Williamsburg District of South Carolina since the 1730s, but conflicts with newer, less devout arrivals from Northern Ireland and the desire for richer land prompted a move west. They were in search of a single tract large enough to relocate as many of their number as cared to move. The first group came to Tennessee in 1805, rented farms near Franklin, and started looking for land.

The newcomers found what they wanted in General Greene's grant. They bought 5,120 acres from his heirs in 1807, divided the land among themselves, and moved here. Additional settlers followed, among them the Reverend James White Stephenson, who would lead the Presbyterians until 1831. The settlers called their community Zion. It remained a distinct, separate settlement until the Civil War ended the plantation economy upon which it was based. This walk is wholly within the boundaries of the Zion settlement.

While you're in the area, you may also want to see places associated with the other two original landowners. Both Gideon Pillow and William Polk divided their land among their sons, who built fabulous plantation houses, most of which are still standing. Of particular note are Clifton Place, the home of Gideon Pillow, Jr., which you passed if you drove out from Columbia, and Rattle and Snap, the home of George Washington Polk, located farther toward Mount Pleasant.

Just after starting the walk, you'll pass an interesting white frame house on the right. It's set beneath a row of tall cedars planted in the 19th century. The original 1850s log house on this site burned and was replaced with the present house in 1889; the original kitchen was incorporated into the new home.

Where Old Zion Road makes the first of several sharp turns, a drive leads to Pine Hill, a large brick house that's clearly visible only when there's no foliage. This Federal-style house with a Greek Revival portico was built in 1839 by Anthony Gholshon for Agnes and Samuel Henry Armstrong. The Armstrongs had come to the area on the migration from South Carolina when they were children.

Its substantial number of well-preserved antebellum buildings is one of Maury County's major draws, particularly during the pilgrimages held each spring and fall. If you spend any time here, you'll quickly learn that many of the houses, churches, and commercial buildings of that era were constructed by either Anthony Gholshon or Nathan Vaught. Vaught built Clifton Place for Gideon Pillow, Jr.

Past the Pine Hill drive, Old Zion Road follows a row of pine trees before making a sharp right turn. It then heads due north and crosses a railroad. Construction of the line linking Columbia to Florence, Alabama, on the Tennessee River started in 1879. The line later became a branch of the Louisville & Nashville Railroad.

Past the railroad, walk across US 43. Be careful—it's a high-speed road.

As Old Zion Road continues through the rolling bluegrass, you'll encounter another beautiful house on your left. One look at the huge trees in its substantial front lawn and you'll know why it's called Tree Haven. The Tennessee Historical Commission describes Tree Haven as "one of Maury County's most graceful and interesting vernacular houses." This irregularly shaped home embodies elements of both the Italianate and Queen Anne styles, popular in the mid- to late 1800s. The original part of the house, though, is much older. It dates to 1812 and is believed to have been the home of pioneer minister James White Stephenson.

The road climbs gently, crests a rise, and makes a slight curve to the left. Here, you'll pass a log house on the right. It dates to 1808, making it one of Zion's oldest.

Where the road makes another sharp turn, you'll pass the drive leading to the Frierson house, another of Zion's earliest homes. William James Frierson was in the second wave of Zion pioneers, who arrived near Franklin in April 1806. When the group left South Carolina, it divided into two parties. One party pushed hard, even traveling on Sundays, a practice frowned upon by this strict society. The other party rested and prayed on Sundays. In the end, the two groups arrived from their six-week journey just one hour apart.

From the Frierson house, undulating Old Zion Road heads due west to intersect Zion Road. Walk diagonally across Zion Road to Zion Church.

This church was central to the life of the solemn Presbyterians. Before they built their first dwelling, they constructed a log meeting house. They then completed a more permanent church in 1810. With immigrants continually arriving at Zion, it wasn't long before the congregation outgrew the church. Construction of the current building started in 1846 and lasted until 1849.

This often-studied, often-admired building incorporates the ideas of some Pennsylvanians of German origin—Pennsylvania Dutch—who joined the community. The church remains much as it was at the time of its completion. The only significant alterations are the Tiffany stained-glass windows, the pulpit, and the pipe organ, all of which were added in the late 1800s.

One interesting feature of the church's design is the placement of the doors. They are located on either side of the pulpit, so worshipers arriving late would have to endure the embarrassment of facing the whole congregation. Inside the church, you can see the chair, the Bible, and the Psalter of James White Stephenson, as well as a copy of the 1807 deed from General Greene's heirs.

The subordination of the individual to the community was the essence of Zion society. The church exercised incredible control over its members. The governing body, or session, conducted disciplinary proceedings for such offenses as missing church, using profane language, and being intoxicated. One married couple was summoned before the session on a charge of "living unhappily together." Ordinary crimes such as theft and assault were tried before the session, too, regardless of whether the accused had already been tried in civil court. The most common punishment was a public admonition or rebuke.

Slave ownership existed in this Christian community just as it did throughout the South. Indeed, Zion's entire economy was based on slavery. Yet at the same time, slaves were admitted into full church membership. They were subject to the same discipline as their owners and were brought before the session for the same types of offenses. On at least one occasion, a slave owner was tried on a charge of mistreating a slave. The races continued to worship together even after emancipation. At one point, black membership outnumbered white. But the former slaves eventually came to want their own church and organized the Canaan congregation, which still meets nearby.

You can end your visit to Zion Church with a tour of its cemetery, where more than 1,500 people are buried. Among the dead are 15 Revolutionary War soldiers, three soldiers from the War of 1812, and 108 Confederate soldiers. The cemetery also contains a monument to the slaves of the early Zion settlers.

CROSS BRIDGES WALK

Cross Bridges Road

Highlights
Historic houses, wooded hills, bluegrass pastures

Length
2.3 miles

Starting Point
The starting point is at Cross Bridges Baptist Church.
To get there, take Hampshire Pike (US 412) west from
Columbia to the Cross Bridges community. Just short of the
bridge over Big Bigby Creek, turn right (north) onto Cross
Bridges Road and drive 0.3 mile to the church.

Ending Point
Cross Bridges Road at Jimmy Gray Robinson Road

Traffic Level
Light

The prettiest landscapes in Middle Tennessee are to be found
where two physiographic regions meet. You'll encounter such a
place on this walk. Here, the bright bluegrass pastures of the
Central Basin sweep up to the green hills of Western Highland
Rim outliers—broken hills severed from the highlands proper by
the Duck River and its tributaries. And if the beautiful countryside isn't enough, three well-preserved antebellum mansions await
you.

The Websters were to this part of Maury County what the
Pillows and Polks were to the section between Columbia and
Mount Pleasant. They owned most of the land and were the most
prominent family. Jonathan Webster was a Revolutionary War

veteran from Georgia who came here in 1807. By 1810, he built the fine Federal-style house located to the right of Hampshire Pike 0.8 mile west of the Cross Bridges Road junction. Webster gave land to his sons, each of whom built his own fine house. You'll visit two of them on this walk.

The community that grew up around here was called Webster's Mill, after the family business on Big Bigby Creek. There were four toll bridges at Webster's Mill. Travelers on Hampshire Pike often referred to "crossing the bridges." Before long, the name stuck.

After a short climb from the church, Cross Bridges Road levels off near several attractive farmhouses. Where the road makes a climb over a cedar-covered rise, a beautiful panorama of rich pastures in the valley of Big Bigby Creek spreads in front of you.

You'll soon walk along a white fence on the left and come to Liberty Hall. This beautifully preserved plantation house surrounded by tall trees has the look of many of Middle Tennessee's antebellum homes. It's a Federal-style house with a Greek Revival portico. Its brick walls are 14 inches thick.

George Pope Webster hired noted builder Anthony Gholshon to construct the house. Gholshon's slave laborers completed it in 1844, the year Webster's friend and fellow Maury County resident James K. Polk successfully ran for president of the United States.

Past Liberty Hall, Cross Bridges Road makes a short, steep descent to intersect Morel Road. The immaculate farm at the intersection is called Lipscomb Place, after its original owner, Major George Lipscomb, a veteran of Andrew Jackson's Seminole campaign. The oldest part of the house dates to the late 1830s. Lipscomb Place Farm has produced some famous horses over the years. One pleasing feature of the farm is the good taste evident in the construction and upkeep of its outbuildings.

Go left, staying on Cross Bridges Road, which parallels Stockard Branch as it tumbles through the moist, tree-shaded bottom. Look up the hill on your right and you'll see Vine Hill, one of the region's most beautifully situated houses. It's claimed

Vine Hill sits atop a hill overlooking the Duck River valley.

that you can see parts of five counties from Vine Hill's perch. The view of the rich valleys and distant ridges is truly magnificent. You'll pass the entrance to Vine Hill after the road swings to the right, away from the creek.

James Henry Webster, another of Jonathan Webster's sons, completed the home in 1835. Vine Hill is a huge, 60-foot-square, wood frame Greek Revival house. Its cross-axial plan features two 60-by-16-foot hallways. The home has two columned porticoes, one facing east and the other south.

Vine Hill was the first house in these parts to have built-in closets. Houses were taxed according to the number of rooms they had. Since closets were considered rooms, they were not included in early plantation houses. But James Webster, who had landholdings in Arkansas, Mississippi, and Middle Tennessee, was wealthy enough to build the closets and pay the taxes.

Another first for Vine Hill was the use of mules on the plantation. Indeed, thanks to Vine Hill, Columbia became known as the mule-trading capital of the world before World War II. Mule Day is still a major event in Columbia.

Vine Hill passed from the Webster family around 1900 and was abandoned by the late 1950s. In 1963, Mrs. Charles Deere Wiman, the great-granddaughter of James Webster, bought it. Wife of the heir to the John Deere tractor fortune, she used her considerable resources to completely restore the place. Mrs. Wiman later donated the estate to the Maury County Historical Society, which used Vine Hill as its headquarters from 1971 to 1993. At that point, Mr. and Mrs. Randolph Scott Jackson—Maury County natives then living in Houston—bought Vine Hill with the intent to make it their residence.

The road passes an old stone fence, then climbs over a hill covered with cedars before reaching Jimmy Gray Robinson Road, where the walk ends. If you want to continue, follow Jimmy Gray Robinson Road as it strikes out for the beautiful valley of the Duck River.

STATION CAMP WALK

Lower Station Camp Creek Road

Highlights
Scenic stream, bluegrass pastures

Length
2.8 miles

Starting Point
The starting point is the junction of Lower Station Camp Creek Road and Long Hollow Pike (TN 174) between Goodlettsville and Gallatin. You can also reach this intersection by turning north onto Lower Station Camp Creek Road off US 31E between Hendersonville and Gallatin.

Ending Point

The railroad underpass on Station Camp Creek Road
north of US 31E between Hendersonville and Gallatin

Traffic Level

Moderate to heavy

A walk along Station Camp Creek is a walk through some of
Middle Tennessee's earliest history. Even though suburban development is closing in, you can still enjoy the tranquil beauty
of rural countryside as you follow Lower Station Camp Creek
Road between rich pastures on one side and the unspoiled stream
on the other.

Look across the creek to the two-story white frame house on
the opposite bank. As is the case with many of the region's oldest houses, the original part of this home was built of logs that
were later covered with siding. William F. and Emma Douglass
Clark lived here during the Civil War. They lost three of their
four sons in the conflict. But the history of the Clark house goes
back long before the Civil War.

All of what is now Tennessee was once part of North Carolina. In 1783, North Carolina set aside all of today's Middle Tennessee as Davidson County. Three years later, it established
Sumner County. The first meetings of the Sumner County government were held at the house of James Hamilton on Station
Camp Creek.

According to early records, when a decision was made in 1788
to construct a courthouse, "Mrs. Clark's place" on Station Camp
Creek was selected as the location. Local historians believe that
one of the log pens now hidden by siding on the Clark house is
the original 1790 Sumner County Courthouse. Gallatin, the current county seat, was not established until 1802.

Andrew Jackson was a frequent visitor to this early log courthouse, for he was the district attorney for the Mero District. In
1788, the North Carolina legislature combined today's Middle
Tennessee into one administrative district. The Cumberland set-

tlers, unhappy over their relationship with North Carolina, were flirting with the Spanish, headquartered at New Orleans. James Robertson apparently intended to flatter the Spanish governor, Don Estevan Miro, in suggesting that the new district be called the Miro District. A clerk's error changed the spelling to Mero. Today's Midstate was known as the Mero District for nearly a decade.

Lower Station Camp Creek Road is like a flower garden much of the year. Spring brings an abundance of Virginia bluebell, phlox, and purple phacelia. Summer flowers include dayflower, bouncing Bet, common chicory, and trumpet creeper.

Station Camp Creek was one of the first bodies of water in Middle Tennessee to be given a name. During colonial days, men from the fringes of white settlement came into the Cumberland wilderness to hunt. The 1772 party of long hunters included frontiersmen who were destined to play major roles in later settlement: Isaac Bledsoe, Kasper Mansker, Joseph Drake, John Montgomery.

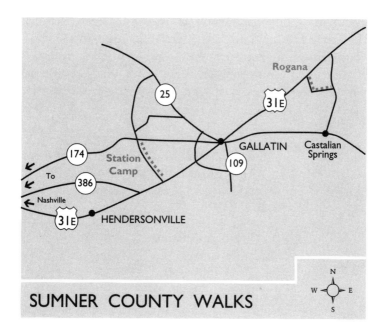

SUMNER COUNTY WALKS

They camped here along the creek. It's been called Station Camp ever since.

The walk ends where the road goes under the CSX Railroad. This historic line started as the Louisville & Nashville, one of the region's first railroads. Back in the 1840s and 1850s, corporate charters were granted by state legislatures. Louisville and Nashville, both important steamboat ports, were commercial rivals, and Tennesseans were apprehensive about a rail line between the two. An 1850 charter granted by Tennessee specified that the railroad from Louisville had to stop at the Cumberland River. In an effort to keep Nashville's commerce vibrant, the legislature provided that freight had to be hauled into Nashville on horse-drawn wagons. It was feared that Nashville would otherwise become just a way station, instead of a terminus for traffic.

Railroad fever gripped much of the nation in those days. The L & N's Louisville promoters raised funds from towns along the proposed routes that were eager to have a railroad. A lively competition arose. Gallatin outbid Springfield, so a route through the Sumner County seat was selected. Bowling Green, Kentucky, outbid rival Glasgow, which is why the line turns north at Gallatin instead of going straight toward Louisville.

Construction was slow. It wasn't until 1860 that the first train steamed between the two river towns that gave the L & N its name.

ROGANA WALK

Rogana Road

Highlights

Site of the village of Rogana, remains of an old
railroad, Bledsoe Creek

Length
2.1 miles

Starting Point
The intersection of Rogana Road and US 31E, 4.5 miles northeast of the Main Street/US 31E junction in Gallatin

Ending Point
Rogana Road at Rock Springs Road north of Castalian Springs

Traffic Level
Light

This walk will take you to the site of some of Middle Tennessee earliest settlements.

Rogana Road runs along Dry Creek before curving away to weave through open bluegrass pastures. Where the road makes a sharp left turn, take a look to the right to see the remnants of a railroad trestle over Dry Creek. You're standing near the site of the Rogana railroad depot.

Promoters had big plans when they inaugurated this railroad in the mid-1880s, naming it the Chesapeake & Nashville. Unfortunately, it only made it from Gallatin to Scottsville, Kentucky— a distance of 25 miles—before it went broke. The L & N took over the line in 1906. It continued to operate through the 1960s.

Rogana was typical of the crossroads villages that sprang up as Middle Tennessee's frontier period started winding down after 1800. Farm families had the freedom to turn their attention to something other than just surviving, and they needed places to buy goods and services and sell some of their own produce. Villages like Rogana usually had a general store, a gristmill, a blacksmith's forge, and a tavern. Some communities also had a school and a church.

After the railroad came through, Rogana became an important shipping point for livestock raised in this rich bluegrass country. But when paved highways began providing easy access to larger towns in the 1920s and 1930s, places like Rogana faded.

Rogana is now nothing more than a name on a map.

The road runs along the old railroad grade before curving downhill to cross Bledsoe Creek. The iron bridge that once carried the road rests next to the modern one. Bledsoe Creek got its name on the same 1772 long-hunter expedition that gave Station Camp, Drake, and Mansker Creeks their names. Isaac Bledsoe eventually settled near here at Bledsoe's Lick, now Bledsoe's Fort Park at Castalian Springs.

A railroad junction was once located just about where the road turns to cross the creek. This was the terminus for another ambitious late-1800s rail project, the Middle & East Tennessee Central Railway. It was supposed to go all the way from this point to Knoxville but never made it more than a few miles to Hartsville. It, too, was absorbed into the L & N in 1906.

Bledsoe Creek's two forks meet just upstream from the bridge. The creek is too low for boating most of the year, but when the water is up in winter, the 5.3-mile stretch from here to the bridge at TN 25 makes a nice, easy canoe run.

Where the road curves left to run along the creek, look to the right up the hill to see a farmhouse dating to 1891. It was built on land that once belonged to frontiersman Hugh Rogan. Rogan's own stone cottage still stands on the hill. He called it Rogana, which is how the community got its name.

Hugh Rogan—described by one historian as an "Irishman of superlative courage and strength of will" and by another as a "man without fear, with a big kind heart"—was one of the most colorful characters on the Cumberland frontier. He and Daniel Carlin, who was married to Rogan's sister, came to America from County Donegal, Ireland, in 1775. They intended to find a place to settle, then return for their families. But the outbreak of the Revolutionary War ended travel to Ireland—then controlled by England—so they ended up in North Carolina.

In 1779, Rogan signed on as a guard for surveyors setting the boundary between North Carolina and Virginia. It was then that he made his first trip into the Cumberland wilderness. He came back in 1780 with John Donelson and his party on the harrowing 1,000-mile water voyage to start the settlement of Nashville. For his work with the surveyors, Rogan was awarded a land grant where Vanderbilt University stands today. He later exchanged it for land here in Sumner County.

When 1783 brought peace and a resumption of shipping to Ireland, Rogan set out to get his wife, Nancy, and their son, Bernard. He stopped off to visit Carlin in North Carolina. Carlin had by then abandoned Rogan's sister and started a new family in America. Fearing that Rogan would tell on him in Ireland, Carlin made up a tale. He told his brother-in-law that Nancy had believed Rogan dead and married another man. A broken-hearted Hugh Rogan trudged back over the mountains to the Cumberland settlements.

In 1796, a nephew of Nancy Rogan's turned up in Sumner County bearing a letter that carried this instruction: "Deliver to your uncle if alive and on the continent of America." She was still waiting for him. A happy Hugh Rogan made his way to Ireland and brought back Nancy and Bernard, who was by then a 22-year-old man. The Rogans later had a second son, Francis.

Just as settlers from Virginia and Maryland built houses according to what they remembered from back home, the Rogans constructed a two-room, Irish-style stone cottage with a thatched roof. It survives today, attached to the brick house son Francis Rogan built in 1825.

Plans call for the Rogans' cottage to be removed to Bledsoe's Fort Park. That park already has one pioneer home from near here, Nathaniel Parker's 1790s log house.

Bledsoe Creek soon forks. The road parallels the tree-lined, shallow East Fork along a bottom covered with wildflowers in spring and summer. Both the road and the creek straighten out, then curve before Rogana Road ends at Greenfield Lane. Anthony Bledsoe, Isaac's brother, built his own station a few miles north of Isaac's. He called it Greenfield, which is how the road got its name.

Rock Springs Road is just ahead. To the right, it leads past several handsome old houses before ending at historic Castalian Springs.

APPENDIX

Hiking Areas of Middle Tennessee

Beaman Park
c/o Metro Greenways Commission
Park Plaza at Oman Street
Nashville, TN 37201
615-862-8400

Bledsoe Creek State Park
400 Zieglers Fort Road
Gallatin, TN 37066
615-452-3706

Burgess Falls State Natural Area
Route 6, Box 380
Sparta, TN 38583
931-432-5312

Cardwell Mountain
c/o Cumberland Caverns
McMinnville, TN 37110
931-668-4396

Carter State Natural Area
(Buggytop Cave)—*See* South
Cumberland State Recreation
Area

Cedars of Lebanon State Park
328 Cedar Forest Road
Lebanon, TN 37087
615-443-2769

Cordell Hull Lake
Route 1, Box 62
Carthage, TN 37030-9710
615-735-1034

Dunbar Cave State Natural Area
401 Old Dunbar Cave Road
Clarksville, TN 37043
931-648-5526

Edgar Evins State Park
Route 1
Silver Point, TN 37852
931-858-2446

Fall Creek Falls State Park
Route 3
Pikeville, TN 37367
423-881-3297 (park headquarters)
423-881-5708 (nature center)

Fort Donelson National Battlefield
Box 434
Dover, TN 37058
931-232-5706

Grundy Forest State Natural Area
(Fiery Gizzard)—*See* South
Cumberland State Recreation
Area

Johnsonville State Historic Area
Denver, TN 37054
931-535-2789

Lady Finger Bluff Small Wild Area
c/o TVA
Norris, TN 37828
423-494-9800

Land Between the Lakes
100 Van Morgan Drive
Golden Pond, KY 42211-9001
502-924-5602

Long Hunter State Park
2910 Hobson Pike
Hermitage, TN 37076
615-885-2422

Montgomery Bell State Park
Box 39
Burns, TN 37029
615-797-9052

Mousetail Landing State Park
Route 3, Box 280B
Linden, TN 37096
901-847-0841

Natchez Trace Parkway
Route 1, NT-143
Tupelo, MS 38801
601-680-4025

Old Stone Fort State Archaeological Area
Route 7, Box 7400
Manchester, TN 37355
931-723-5073

Radnor Lake State Natural Area
1160 Otter Creek Road
Nashville, TN 37220
615-373-3467

Rock Island State Park
Rock Island, TN 38581
931-686-2471

Savage Gulf State Natural Area—
See South Cumberland State Recreation Area

Shelby Bottoms Greenway
c/o Metro Greenways Commission
Park Plaza at Oman Street
Nashville, TN 37201
615-862-8400

South Cumberland State Recreation Area
Route 1, Box 2196
Monteagle, TN 37356
931-924-2980

Standing Stone State Park
Livingston, TN 38570
931-823-6347

Stones River National Battlefield
3501 Old Nashville Highway
Murfreesboro, TN 37129-3095
615-893-9501

University of the South
Sewanee Outing Club
Sewanee, TN 37383
931-598-1286

Virgin Falls Pocket Wilderness
c/o Bowater Southern Paper
   Corporation
Calhoun, TN 37309
423-336-7301

Warner Parks
50 Vaughn Road
Nashville, TN 37221
615-370-8050

Backpacking Trails

Though most of the hikes described in this book are day-hikes, back-country camping is allowed on some of the trails. In almost all cases, camping is at designated campsites only. At most places, a permit is required. Back-country camping is permitted on selected trails at Cordell Hull Lake, Fall Creek Falls State Park, Grundy Forest State Natural Area, Land Between the Lakes, Long Hunter State Park, Montgomery Bell State Park, Mousetail Landing State Park, Savage Gulf State Natural Area, and Virgin Falls Pocket Wilderness.

Hiking Organizations

Sierra Club
The Sierra Club is an international conservation and outings organization. The Tennessee chapter's five regional groups conduct outings open to members and nonmembers alike. A complete statewide outings schedule is published in the monthly newspaper *The Tenne-Sierran*. As of this writing, the outings chair for the Middle Tennessee group is Alan Ball (615-228-1962) and the outings chair for the Upper Cumberland group is John Harwood (931-528-2301). Membership information is in *The Tenne-Sierran* and can also be obtained by writing the Sierra Club, Box 52968, Boulder, CO 80322-2968 or by calling 615-792-5306.

Tennessee Trails Association
The TTA is a statewide hiking and trail advocacy organization. Middle Tennessee chapters are located in Nashville, Clarksville, Murfreesboro, and the Upper Cumberland. Members and non-members are welcome on hikes; a complete list of TTA hikes appears in the monthly newsletter *Tennessee Trails*. As of this writing, the contact for the Nashville chapter is Libby Francis (615-889-5718), the contact for the Clarksville chapter is Wanda Cumberland (931-358-3338), the contact for the Murfreesboro chapter is Mike Harvey (615-893-9594), and the contact for the Upper Cumberland chapter is Denise Charvoz (931-738-3595). Membership information is available from TTA, Box 41446, Nashville, TN 37204. The address for the TTA web page is www.tn-trails.org.

Park Advocacy Groups

Friends of Beaman Park
1201 16th Avenue South,
Suite 201
Nashville, TN 37212

Friends of Long Hunter State Park
2910 Hobson Pike
Hermitage, TN 37076

Friends of Radnor Lake
1160 Otter Creek
Nashville, TN 37220

Friends of Rock Island State Park
82 Beach Road
Rock Island, TN 38581

Friends of Scotts Gulf (Virgin Falls)
Sparta–White County Chamber of
   Commerce
16 Brockman Way
Sparta, TN 38583

Friends of South Cumberland
   State Recreation Area
Route 1, Box 2196
Monteagle, TN 37356

Friends of Standing Stone State
   Park
1674 Standing Stone Highway
Hilham, TN 38568

Friends of Stones River National
   Battlefield
Box 4092
Murfreesboro, TN 37133-4092

Friends of Warner Parks
50 Vaughn Road
Nashville, TN 37221

Land Between the Lakes Association
100 Van Morgan Drive
Golden Pond, KY 42211-9001

Natchez Trace Trail Conference
Box 1236
Jackson, MS 39215

BIBLIOGRAPHY

Ambrose, Stephen E. *Undaunted Courage: Meriwether Lewis, Thomas Jefferson, and the Opening of the American West.* New York: Simon & Schuster, 1996.

Brady, Kathy. "Lovely Ladyfinger Beckons." *Tennessee Conservationist* 60 (September/October 1994): 6.

Brandt, Robert. *Touring the Middle Tennessee Backroads.* Winston-Salem, NC: John F. Blair, Publisher, 1995.

———. "Why There Are Deer in Nashville." *Sierra Club Bulletin* 62 (September 1977): 6–7.

Braun, E. Lucy. *Deciduous Forests of Eastern North America.* Philadelphia: Blankiston Company, 1950.

Caplenor, Donald. "The Vegetation of the Gorges of the Fall Creek Falls State Park in Tennessee." *Journal of the Tennessee Academy of Science* 40 (January 1965): 27–39.

Carlton, Mike, and John Netherton. *Tennessee Wonders: A Pictorial Guide to the Parks.* Nashville: Rutledge Hill Press, 1994.

Coffey, Clarence. "River Otters: Environmental Barometers." *Tennessee Wildlife* 16 (November/December 1992): 21–24.

Coggins, Allen R. "The Early History of Tennessee's State Parks, 1919–1956." *Tennessee Historical Quarterly* 43 (1984): 295–315.

Coleman, Bevley R. *A History of State Parks in Tennessee.* Nashville: Tennessee Department of Conservation, 1967. This was originally a 1963 master's thesis at George Peabody College for Teachers.

Cooling, Benjamin Franklin. "Forts Henry and Donelson: Union Victory on the Twin Rivers." *Blue and Gray* 9 (February 1992): 10–20, 45–53.

Cornwell, Ilene J. "Devon Farm: Harpeth Landmark." *Tennessee Historical Quarterly* 34 (1975): 113–29.

Crutchfield, James A. *The Harpeth River: A Biography.* 1972. Reprint, Johnson City, TN: Overmountain Press, 1994.

———. *The Natchez Trace: A Pictorial History.* Nashville: Rutledge Hill Press, 1985.

———. *A River through Time: Man's Emergence and Early Settlement along the Cumberland River.* Franklin, TN: Cool Springs Press, 1995. This was originally published in 1976 as *Early Times in the Cumberland Valley.*

Davis, Louise Littleton. *Historic Travelers' Rest*. Nashville: Travelers' Rest, 1976.

Denny, Norman R. "The Devil's Navy." *Civil War Times Illustrated* 35 (August 1996): 25–30.

Durham, Walter T. *The Great Leap Westward: A History of Sumner County, Tennessee, from Its Beginnings to 1805*. Gallatin, TN: Sumner County Library Board, 1969.

Durham, Walter T., John F. Creasy, and James W. Thomas. *A Celebration of Houses Built before 1900 in Sumner County, Tennessee*. Gallatin, TN: Sumner County Historical Society, 1995.

Egerton, John. Introduction to *Radnor Lake: Nashville's Walden*, by John Netherton. Nashville: Third National Bank, 1984.

Ford, Bob, and Bob Hatcher. "A Tennessee Sampler of Neotropical Migrants." *Tennessee Wildlife* 16 (March/April 1993): 8–12.

Hamel, Paul. *Tennessee Wildlife Viewing Guide*. Helena, MT: Falcon Press, 1993.

Hankins, Caneta Skelley. "Hugh Rogan of Counties Donegal and Sumner: Irish Acculturation in Frontier Tennessee." *Tennessee Historical Quarterly* 54 (1995): 306–23.

Hedgepath, Randy. *South Cumberland State Recreation Area Hiker's Guide*. Monteagle, TN: Monty Wanamaker Studio, 1986.

Hemmerly, Thomas E. *Wildflowers of the Central South*. Nashville: Vanderbilt University Press, 1990.

Johnson, Leland. *The Parks of Nashville: A History of the Board of Parks and Recreation*. Nashville: Metropolitan Nashville and

Davidson County Board of Parks and Recreation, 1986.

Klein, Maury. *History of the Louisville & Nashville Railroad.* New York: Macmillan, 1972.

Luther, Edward T. *Our Restless Earth: The Geologic Regions of Tennessee.* Knoxville: University of Tennessee Press, 1977.

Manning, Russ. *The Historic Cumberland Plateau: An Explorer's Guide.* Knoxville: University of Tennessee Press, 1993.

Manning, Russ, and Sondra Jamieson. *Tennessee's South Cumberland.* Norris, TN: Mountain Laurel Place, 1990.

Matthews, Larry E. *Cumberland Caverns.* Huntsville, AL: National Speleological Society, 1989.

McDade, Arthur. "The Strange Case of Meriwether Lewis." *Tennessee Conservationist* 56 (September/October 1990): 2–4.

Miller, Robert A. *The Geologic History of Tennessee.* Nashville: Tennessee Department of Conservation, 1974.

Moore, Harry L. *A Geologic Trip across Tennessee by Interstate 40.* Knoxville: University of Tennessee Press, 1994.

Plumb, Gregory. *Waterfalls of Tennessee.* Johnson City, TN: Overmountain Press, 1996.

Reeves, Reggie, and Paul Somers. "Cedar Glades of Middle Tennessee." *Tennessee Conservationist* 57 (May/June 1991): 11–14.

Richardson, James, and Dorothy Richardson. "Mousetail Landing State Park." *Tennessee Conservationist* 60 (September/October 1994): 4–6.

Robinson, John C. *An Annotated Checklist of the Birds of Tennessee*. Knoxville: University of Tennessee Press, 1990.

Rozema, Vicki. *Footsteps of the Cherokees: A Guide to the Eastern Homelands of the Cherokee Nation*. Winston-Salem, NC: John F. Blair, Publisher, 1995.

Simbeck, Rob. "Tennessee Marvels." *Tennessee Conservationist* 61 (January/February 1995): 18–22.

Smith, Arlo I. *A Guide to Wildflowers of the Mid-South*. Memphis: Memphis State University Press, 1979.

Spearman, Charles M. "The Battle of Stones River: Tragic New Year's Eve in Tennessee." *Blue and Gray* 6 (February 1989): 8–28, 36–45.

Weiler, Patsy. "The CCC: Roosevelt's Tree Army." *Tennessee Conservationist* 56 (May/June 1990): 2–5.

West, Carroll Van. *Tennessee's Historic Landscapes: A Traveler's Guide*. Knoxville: University of Tennessee Press, 1995.

INDEX

Buggytop Trail, 263-66
Burgess Falls, 195-98
Burgess Falls State Natural Area, xvii, 195-98
Burgess, Tom, 195
Burns Branch, 116-18
Buzzard Bluff, 214

Carlton, Mike, 26
Cane Creek, 228, 230, 232, 236-37
Cane Creek Cascades, 227, 232, 235
Cane Creek Falls, 227, 232-33, 235-37
Caney Fork River, xviii, 13, 181, 199-208, 215, 219, 221-25
Cardwell Mountain, 209-16
Cardwell Mountain Trail, 210-14
Carter, Harry Lee, 263
Carter State Natural Area, 263-66
Cave Spring Rockhouse, 254, 262
Cedar Forest Trail, 49-50
Cedars of Lebanon State Park, xvi, 41-50, 230
Center for Field Biology, Austin Peay State University, 141
Center Hill Lake, 181-86, 198-99, 206
Central Basin, xvi, xviii-xxi, xxii, 3, 31-32, 41, 47, 54, 79, 111-12, 116, 175, 183-84, 204, 305
Cheek, Leslie, 9
Cheekwood, see Tennessee Botanical Gardens and Fine Arts Center
Chickamauga Path, 200-201, 211-13

Chimney Rocks, 255, 262
Civilian Conservation Corps, 104-5, 250-51, 261, 271, 276
Clark, Emma Douglass, 310
Clark, William F., 310
Clement, Frank, 98
Collins River, xviii, 199-205, 214-16, 239, 241
Collins River Trail (Cardwell Mountain), 214-16
Collins River Trail (Rock Island), 202-5
Coon Creek, 234
Coon Creek Falls, 227, 235, 238
Cooper Mountain Trail, 191-92
Cordell Hull Lake, 79-85
Cordell Hull Wildlife Management Area, 83-84
Corps of Engineers (U.S. Army), 51, 80, 84, 137, 140, 181, 202, 207
Cottonport, 297
Cragfont, 76, 284
Creech Hollow Lake, 99, 106
Criley, Walter, 24
Cross Bridges Road, 305-8
Cross Bridges Walk, 305-8
Crow Creek, 263-65
Cumberland Caverns, 209-13
Cumberland Plateau, xvii, xviii, xix, xxi, xxii, 149, 187, 197, 199, 209, 219-21, 235, 236-38, 245
Cumberland Presbyterian church, 102
Cumberland River, xviii, 35-40, 71, 79-85, 117-18, 129-38
Cunningham, John, 205